SEEING THROUGH

CRYING AND ATTACHMENT

JUDITH KAY NELSON

Routledge
Taylor & Francis Group

NEW YORK AND HOVE

Published in 2005 by
Brunner-Routledge
Taylor & Francis Group
270 Madison Avenue
New York, NY 10016

Published in Great Britain by
Brunner-Routledge
Taylor & Francis Group
27 Church Road
Hove, East Sussex BN3 2FA

© 2005 by Taylor & Francis Group, LLC
Brunner-Routledge is an imprint of Taylor & Francis Group

Printed in the United States of America on acid-free paper
10 9 8 7 6 5 4 3 2 1

International Standard Book Number-10: 0-415-94967-X (Hardcover) 0-415-94968-8 (Softcover)
International Standard Book Number-13: 978-0-415-94967-5 (Hardcover) 978-0-415-94967-5 (Softcover)
Library of Congress Card Number 2004019951

Library of Congress Cataloging-in-Publication Data

Nelson, Judith Kay, 1941-
    Seeing through tears : crying and attachment / Judith Kay Nelson.
        p. cm.
    Includes bibliographical references and index.
    ISBN 0-415-94967-X -- 0-415-94968-8 (pbk.)
    1. Crying. I. Title.

BF575.C88N45 2005
152.4--dc22
                                                                        2004019951

Taylor & Francis Group
is the Academic Division of T&F Informa plc.

Visit the Taylor & Francis Web site at
http://www.taylorandfrancis.com

and the Brunner-Web site at
http://www.routledgementalhealth.com

For

Lori Jean,

Lisa Ingrid, and Cynthia Lynn

Contents

Acknowledgments

When I first began to study crying, I did not foresee that my work would continue for decades. Neither did my family, friends, and colleagues. We have all been challenged by the process at one time or another, but I have never lacked for enthusiastic supporters and generous caregivers. I would like to thank each of them for their faith and patience.

For help with writing, I thank Russell Nelson, Cynthia Nelson, Lori Pesavento, Gregory Bellow, Kimn Nielson, Jane Anne Staw, Valerie Andrews, Saul Rosenberg, Maureen Adams, and Victoria Shoemaker. I thank Annette Krammer for help with the art work.

I thank George Zimmar, Dana Bliss, and Prudy Taylor Board of Routledge for applying their creative insight and professional diligence to the realization of this book. Their support and enthusiasm has been invaluable.

For being friends and companions in the writing process, I thank the women's group who inspired me from the beginning: Margo Arcanin, Margaret Ballou, Barbara Miller, Judy Morhar, Donna Rosenheim, Susan Sandler, and Ruth Sands; the "Ds," who always understood and fed me well; Laura Thomas and Irwin Keller, who helped with some of the more esoteric research; Lucy and Danny Markarian, who are the best at being good neighbors; Donal and Brenda Brown, who know reading and writing from the inside out; Ana Kowalkowska for the poetry; and Opal Nations and Ellen Humm, hiking partners and music lovers who make me laugh about crying.

For helping me to think this through and see this through, I thank my dear friends and colleagues Lise and Neal Blumenfeld, Cynthia O'Connell, Mary Ahern, Gareth Hill, Verniece Thompson, Chester Villalba, Norman Sohn, Patricia Damery, Markus and Désirée Binder, Merle Davis, Matilda Stewart, Randa Diamond, Margaret Pranger, Judith Day, Doris Pick, Sudie Pollack, Pat Sable, Allan and Judy Schore, and Sally, Mark, Gabriel, and Rebecca Perkins.

To all my patients, thank you for being part of this process and for being willing to share so much.

To my family, thank you for making it all possible: Lori Jean Pesavento, Lisa Ingrid Nelson, Greta Christina, Cynthia Lynn Nelson, Russell Nelson, Marcia, Craig, Corrie, and Dirk Hoogstra, Kenneth and Lucille Baker (my father and mother), and all of the extended Payne and Baker families.

I am forever indebted and forever attached to each one of you.

Introduction

I have been curious about crying since childhood, but I did not start consciously asking questions about tears until I began practice as a psychotherapist in the late 1960s. One of my first patients had an unusual way of crying. She would burst into tears in mid-sentence and continue crying hard for half a minute or more. Then she would compose herself just as abruptly and continue speaking as if nothing had happened. I could only guess that her crying was linked to buried feelings so threatening that she could not face them or acknowledge the source of her tears.

Intrigued and puzzled by this experience, I began to look for articles on crying in the psychological literature. To my surprise, I was unable to find a single reference on crying, even though I worked at Case Western Reserve University Hospital and had access to their complete library system. Crying at that time was not even listed as a topic in *Psychological Abstracts* (it was added in 1972). I found long lists of titles on laughter, smiling, and the meaning of jokes, wit, and humor, but absolutely nothing about crying. Certainly none of my professors or clinical supervisors had directly addressed crying during graduate school or my internships.

I wondered why this was so. Did a cultural aversion to crying keep scholars from writing about it? Was crying so woven into the fabric of the therapeutic process that it could not be translated into spoken language? Was the role of crying so obvious that it was not considered worthy of study, or was it subsumed under discussions of sadness or depression rather than being considered as a separate phenomenon?

A women's consciousness-raising group that I began attending in the early 1970s revived my interest in crying. The subject came up spontaneously one evening when we were talking about women and emotion. It quickly became clear that crying was a topic that touched all of us deeply—personally and in our closest relationships. The discussion that night raised so many questions that I went home and wrote them down. What, I noted, are the differences between male and female crying, and what accounts for them? Why do pregnant women cry? Does crying mean a person is irrational and does it interfere with thinking and talking? How do actors and actresses cry on cue? Is it truly "all right" for women to cry? What is the physiology of crying? I wondered if a researcher could do for crying what Masters and Johnson had done in their studies of sexual behavior—wire up subjects in a laboratory and test all of the physiological changes that a crier's body would show.

A few years later when it was time to select a topic for my doctoral dissertation, crying was the obvious choice. I wanted to find out how often adults cry and how they feel about it. However, I would first need to develop a theory so that I would know what to look for and how to make sense of any findings. I knew from my earlier frustrated search that I would need to construct a body of literature out of disparate bits and pieces buried in all kinds of professional and clinical articles, including anthropology, philosophy, and religion. Crying in fiction, memoirs, and poems would also be relevant. I could gather data about crying by visiting art museums, watching movies and television shows, and talking to family, colleagues, patients, and friends. I wanted to know everything that anyone had written or thought about crying to help me in constructing a theory. In the days before computer searches did this job electronically, it was a daunting prospect, but one that excited me.

My fellow doctoral students teased me about turning in a tear-stained dissertation and we all laughed. It never occurred to me then that I might be struggling with any painful personal issues. I heard that suggestion in a comment from one friend who said, "Judith, you are the only person I know who could intellectualize this topic." However, I smiled and took this as a compliment about being such an intrepid thinking type that I would not hesitate to research this delicate emotional topic. Not until much later did I find myself confronting issues and struggles that I never imagined at the beginning.

From the first, however, I did diligently probe my own psyche, trying to uncover the source of my drive to understand what is going on beneath the surface of tears. My first revelation came as I recalled the crying habits of my mother and her family. My grandmother, my mother, and her sisters and brothers were almost always cheerful and happy, with one glaring exception: they cried without fail whenever it was time to say good-bye. Mother cried every July when I went to camp. She cried all the way from Detroit to Chicago when she delivered me for my freshman year at college, and every time I returned to school after a vacation.

The "Payne" family, I decided, was aptly named for dragging out their sorrowful farewells. Their reactions even cast a shadow over good times. Once, at the start of a family reunion, my grandmother began to cry. When we asked her why, she said that it was because she dreaded the moment when everyone would have to go.

When my uncles came home for family visits, my Aunt Pauline said their departures were "grieved like a funeral." Uncle Grady would get so emotional that the whole family conspired to protect him for fear he would have a heart attack. They allowed him to slip away in the predawn hours without a word to catch the train back to Texas. At the end of one visit, he actually did have a heart attack and spent a month recovering upstairs at our house.

Aunt Pauline traced these crying dramas to a link between death and departures forged in their childhood by their paternal grandmother. After each visit, their Grandma Payne, who apparently took every ailment of aging to be a sign of "the end," would hug all seven children to her, sobbing because this was to be the "final farewell." She would die and never see them again.

My clinical work and these family crying traits brought crying to my attention, but the reason I have studied it for so long goes much deeper. I wanted to understand the meaning of tears in the same way that I want to understand the meaning of life. I had a deep intuitive sense that the two were related. The act of shedding tears has as much depth, symbolism, and meaning as a poem or a dream and as much magic and mystery as sex. Crying, too, touches all the themes that bind us together in the totality of human experience. Crying, quite simply, has soul. That soul is not what first aroused my curiosity, but it is what has kept it alive for so long.

During the same decade in which I began my research, attachment theory first gained prominence. In his ground breaking three-volume work, *Attachment and Loss*, British psychoanalyst John Bowlby made the courageous, though tiny, leap from findings about animal imprinting and bonding to a theory explaining the dynamics of human attachment. Crying, along with sucking, clinging, and smiling, was on the lists of attachment behaviors identified by both Bowlby and by animal researchers.

These behaviors are part of our evolutionary survival kit for initiating and supporting infant–parent as well as adult–adult bonding. Attachment theorists and researchers identify crying as one of the triggers and indicators of the attachment bond. For them, crying sheds light on attachment. I reversed the process, using attachment theory and research to illuminate the function and meaning of crying.

Using attachment theory, I was finally able to get a clear picture of the relationship between crying and the formation of human connections, and the grief that is activated when those connections are threatened or broken by death or separation. I could define the role of crying in infancy, childhood, and adulthood. I could categorize different types of crying and inhibited crying (the absence of tears at times when they would be expected or appropriate). Because attachment is by definition a two-way, two-person process, I also came to see that crying is an interpersonal rather than strictly individual behavior: crying and caregiving go hand-in-hand. A view of crying as attachment behavior also served to integrate the historical, socio-cultural, artistic, and even the spiritual meaning of crying. The theoretical framework of attachment is big enough to embrace the universals underlying the psychological particulars of crying.

As I was developing a theory of crying throughout the life cycle, I was treating patients, raising children, teaching students, and presenting to colleagues. In these arenas, I was testing the applicability of the theory, working out its clinical implications, and refining the ideas and the language with which to express it. This book is rooted in that dialectic of thought and action, of theory and practice.

Seeing Through Tears is divided into four parts:

- Part I lays the foundation of an attachment theory of crying and caregiving. This theoretical discussion provides the background necessary for reflecting on and understanding experiences, social values, and unconscious assumptions related to crying and caregiving.
- Part II applies the theory in Part I to the clinical assessment of crying or inhibited crying and to the assessment of caregiving and care-receiving. When is crying (or inhibited crying) healthy and when is it dysfunctional? When is it a healing process and when is it a symptom? When does it elicit caregiving and when does it push people away? How does the physiological aspect of shedding tears have an impact on diagnostic understanding?
- Part III applies the theory to crying as it occurs within the therapeutic relationship. "Crying in the Clinical Hour" focuses on crying from the standpoint of the patient, what it says about the state of past and present attachment dynamics, and about the nature and

state of the therapeutic bond. It offers guidance in knowing how, when, or whether to respond to crying or its conspicuous absence. "How Therapists Deal with Crying and Caregiving (Including Their Own)" is directed to the therapist's side of the crying/caregiving equation. This chapter emphasizes the importance of the therapist's experiences with, and feelings about, crying and caregiving, and suggests ways to recognize and deal with personal struggles related to each.

- Part IV, "Attachment and Caregiving: Beyond the Personal," bridges the psychological, social, and physical aspects of crying and its symbolic, spiritual, and aesthetic dimensions, and shows how attachment theory integrates all of these facets.

PART I
A Theory of Crying

CHAPTER 1

There Is More to Crying Than Meets the Eye

Andrea, a nurse at a local hospital, called me one day because she was concerned about Sharon, a patient whom she had been unable to console after a chemotherapy treatment. Andrea had tried repeatedly to reassure her, saying that crying was understandable and even healthy under the circumstances, but her words had no effect. Sharon was increasingly desperate—almost angry—because she could not stop crying. She just kept insisting that "having cancer is bad enough—crying only makes it worse! I *have* to stop." Expressing her fear and grief in tears clearly was not helping.

Knowing of my long-standing interest in crying, Andrea asked if I could help. I saw Sharon that same afternoon and at first I, too, tried to reassure her that crying might help to bring comfort as she faced this life-threatening illness. As a way to help her accept it more, I even suggested that the medications she had been given might be physiologically inducing some of her tears. However, as with Andrea, Sharon was unmoved by my efforts. All she wanted to do was to stop crying.

I asked then if she could tell me why she was so vehemently opposed to shedding tears. *Not* crying, she said, was a lifelong credo learned in childhood from her mother, whom she described as an "iron lady" with a serious drinking problem. Her mother would tolerate no "baby" behavior, no weakness and no neediness of any kind. At the first sight of a trembling lip or tearing eye, she would rage: "My mother died when I was 5, my father when I was 8 and I never cried, not once. What could you possibly have to cry about?"

I knew then that something much deeper than being taught to value self-control was at stake. Sharon obeyed her mother's teachings not just to get approval; she did it in a desperate attempt to get some mothering. Her only hope of receiving nurturance—and what she received in that department was slim indeed—came from being strong enough not to disturb her mother's hidden fragility. Sharon had to be like a mother, strong and caring, to her own mother to get what little emotional sustenance she could.

For Sharon, crying meant attack and banishment rather than connection and care. Her need for comfort at the hospital was the very thing that made her hate crying. In her experience, it brought the opposite of what she needed: isolation instead of connection. She could not bear to cry because it would make her feel more alone. Her only means of connection to her loved ones was through taking care of them. She had no hope that anyone would take care of her. She had to gain control so that she could return to the security of her responsibilities for family and work. Being there for others substituted for having others be there for her—it was her only source of sustenance.

Sharon was dealing with the tremendous stress of her illness and treatment. After hearing her history, I could see that she needed her coping mechanisms back as quickly as possible. This was no time to add to her pain and stress by focusing on her monumental sense of being alone and vulnerable. Understanding the horrible anguish crying created for her, I changed my tactic. Instead of trying to help her accept crying, I shared every technique I knew to get crying to stop: inhaling, eating, diverting her thoughts, renting comedies—anything that would alter the physical and mental stimuli for shedding tears.

My nurse friend's attempts to reassure Sharon were based on the commonly held idea about the universal benefits of crying: "letting go" of emotions is good and "bottling them up" is harmful. This idea originated in early Freudian theory, which held that suppressing or repressing emotions—"damming them up" was a frequent metaphor—could lead to symptoms like anxiety, depression, or unexplained physical ailments. In *Studies on Hysteria*, Breuer and Freud (1893/1955) referred to tears as "involuntary reflexes" that discharge affect so that "a large part of the affect disappears." Using the German term "*sich austoben*," which means to "cry oneself out," they indicated that feelings build up and crying helps them dissipate.

In early psychoanalytic theory, emotions were seen as quantitative, capable of building up to a certain level of pressure and needing then to be released or discharged in order to prevent psychic damage. In contemporary psychoanalytic theory, emotions are no longer seen as quantitative but rather as ever changing, interactive, and communicative. However, the earlier view of crying has persisted in informing popular psychology and clinical practice. Magazine advice columns proclaim messages such as "Go ahead, cry yourself a river—it's good for you," or "Cry now, you'll smile later." In clinical literature, crying is generally treated as a necessary and important component of a successful therapy process. The words "the patient cried" are often used in clinical articles to imply that a good thing has happened and the therapy is moving forward, as if this were self-evident from that comment and no further analysis required. Culturally and clinically, crying has been oversimplified and misunderstood.

The "crying-is-good-for-you" credo has also been used in an attempt to promote social change by encouraging emotional expression. In the 1960s, young people first began to challenge the ideal of emotional control and encouraged each other to "let it all hang out" and "tell it like it is." Educators and social activists questioned the value judgments that labeled crying as "weak" and female and waged a campaign to make it more acceptable. The classic children's record in the 1970s, "Free to Be You and Me," included the song "It's All Right to Cry" performed by stereotype-defying football player Rosie Grier. Therapists, in keeping with these trends, have emphasized the positive benefits of crying as a way to help it gain greater acceptance for men and women. A psychologist, for example, gave this advice: "You should take advantage of a crying session. Get it all out. You'll feel wonderful afterwards."

Has there been any change? On the surface it would appear so. Most people, if questioned, will agree that crying is a "good" thing. Ask them, however, if they feel all right about crying in front of other people, or even by themselves, and a different picture emerges. Many people, men as well as women, remain conflicted about, confused by, and vaguely ashamed of their crying.

Leslie made the women's consciousness-raising group laugh when she said, "My husband thinks crying during an argument is inappropriate; he thinks pounding on the wall is more appropriate." Ruthie was serious when she said that she was never comfortable crying at her work managing a construction firm: "I have to argue rationally in the business world. If I feel close to tears, I walk out and come back when I am composed enough to continue." Jane was clearly opposed to any crying—hers and everyone else's: "Crying is like diarrhea," she said, "because you can't control it." A man I know told me that he cries easily in conversation at parties or meetings but he does not like it because people get overly concerned and think something terrible is wrong in his life.

A number of women also disagree with the often-quoted maxim that crying is "all right for women." Barbara told the group she found that idea ridiculously off-base:

> They say boys are taught not to cry. Okay, but so are girls! Women are supposed to be strong and not show that they feel pain, like you are not supposed to cry during labor or when someone dies. Everyone thinks they should be like Jackie Kennedy and keep it together so they can comfort everyone else.

Many people, female and male, feel uncomfortable when they cry and many more struggle with how to respond when they are in the presence of someone else's tears.

Putting a positive spin on crying has not succeeded in undoing the ambivalence about it because we have been addressing the wrong issue. The problem is not with emotional control; it is with emotional closeness. Crying is above all a relationship behavior, a way to help us get close and not simply a vehicle for emotional expression or release. We do not cry because we need to get *rid* of pain, but because we need connection with our caregivers—literal, internal, fantasized, or symbolic—in order to accept and heal from our pain and grief. Crying is not about what we let *out* but about whom we let *in*.

Beginning in infancy, the reason that we cry is to beckon our caregivers and to keep them close and nurturing. Crying disturbs others for a reason: so that they will know to come and help us. In fact, crying not only alerts caregivers to our need for them, but also unsettles them to the point that they feel viscerally compelled to respond, even if it is inconvenient or annoying and even though they sometimes ignore the message. Crying, along with clinging, sucking, and smiling, is one of the inborn attachment behaviors that help keep infant caregivers in close proximity. With many repetitions over time, the infant–caregiver exchanges evoked by these behaviors that stimulate closeness and regulate arousal help to establish and maintain the attachment bond.

Throughout our lives, crying is one of the primary ways in which we ask for, and know when to give, love and care. At a small family gathering recently, sitting on the bed at the Holiday Inn, I began crying when my grown daughters asked me to tell them more about the reasons why I separated from their father 17 years earlier. As I spoke, my sister moved closer to me on the bed and my niece got up from the floor and came over to hug me. No matter how much crying I do, I doubt that the sadness of the divorce will ever go away. I hope it does not because the tears and the sadness are a reminder that I still feel connected to those family years long ago. Not the crying itself, but rather the comfort and care that I receive from my loved ones, has enabled me to heal and move forward in my life.

Theories of Crying Based on Emotional Expression and Discharge

A view of crying as emotional expression is inadequate when it comes to formulating a comprehensive theory of crying throughout the life span. The first problem emerges from the fact that virtually any emotion in the human repertoire may be expressed by crying. It is impossible to classify different types of crying by compiling long lists of the emotional reasons for which people cry at various ages. The end result leads to a collection of overlapping feelings that form multiple meaningless and indistinct categories.

A second problem in formulating a theory based on emotional expression alone is that the "emotions" of infants are based on physiological states rather than cognitive ones. Their crying is therefore irreconcilable with a theory based on emotion and catharsis. The developmental line is missing between their tearless and noisy cries and those of adults who cry tearfully and silently about pains that are thought induced and only rarely physiological.

Gender differences in crying also make no sense from the standpoint of emotional expression. A need for discharge and catharsis does not explain lopsided crying-frequency statistics—women cry from two to seven times more frequently than men. Crying is a biological behavior that is part of the human condition from birth onward and a theory of crying needs to reflect that.

On a practical clinical level, too, a theory of crying as emotional discharge can lead therapists and health professionals into some brick walls, as it did with my nurse friend Andrea as she tried to reassure Sharon about crying after chemotherapy. Alvin, a therapist in one of my consultation groups, questioned his "burn-out" factor when a patient of his was sobbing and he could feel no empathy. From the standpoint of discharging emotion, he thought he should be wholeheartedly supporting her tears but that did not fit clinically for the situation. A discharge theory of crying does not help other clinicians who struggle with their own impulses to cry in a therapy session. They are left to wonder whether their crying helps by serving as a role model or is interfering with the patient's process.

Of the few clinical writers who have directly explored questions related to crying, most see crying as a release valve for pent-up feelings. Some directly assert that crying is a form of catharsis and healing in and of itself. Others see crying, or suppressed crying, as a symptom, again from the standpoint of repressed or suppressed affect in need of discharge. Clinical theorists who have alternative views see crying as a learned behavior, a form of nonverbal communication or a call of distress.

Some of the early psychoanalytic writers looked at crying as a symptom of castration fear or penis envy. Phyllis Greenacre (1945a, 1945b) wrote several articles comparing urination and weeping, which she related to various manifestations of penis envy. Her early work focused on literal tears shed in a psychoanalytic session rather than on the larger meaning of crying behavior. Twenty years later, Greenacre (1965) wrote another article reflecting some of the changes in psychoanalytic theory. In that article she looked at the association between weeping and loss and anticipated a relational view of crying as attachment behavior triggered by separation.

Another psychoanalyst, Lars Löfgren (1965), described adult crying as equivalent to the tantrum crying of infants and children. He thought of crying as affording adults a safe, acceptable way to express aggression that could be harmful to the individual or a relationship if it came out directly. Ambivalence, as well as aggression, might be purified of "negative feelings" if it came out in the form of tears.

Two decades later, Wood and Wood (1984) discussed tearfulness from the standpoint of layers of consciousness. Instead of looking only at the current trigger for crying, they assumed a link between present and past. Adult crying, they wrote, represents "a variety of stages of development, times and places" at varying levels of consciousness (p. 132). They also viewed crying primarily as emotional expression and, along with Löfgren, saw it as regressive and utilizing "primitive, infantile and early childhood pathways of expression" (p. 132).

Cathartic therapies are those that actively encourage the expression of emotion. Crying is often a centerpiece of the theory and the therapeutic experience. Some of the more well-known cathartic therapies (bioenergetic, Reichian, gestalt, and primal) suggest that crying in and of itself can bring relief from psychological suffering and symptoms.

Thomas Scheff (1979) advocated cathartic therapy in the 1970s, the decade when it was most prominent and visible. He suggested that the therapist should actively encourage crying. He advised therapists to assist noncriers by helping them to establish "optimal distance" from their painful stimuli. The therapist would encourage patients who were too cut off emotionally to embrace emotional triggers. For those whose losses or traumas were too overwhelming, the therapist should help them to get greater distance from the pain.

As an example of helping a person who needed to move closer to his feelings, Scheff wrote about a man who could get only as far as a slight lump in the throat by saying to himself the phrase "I hurt a little bit." Scheff suggested that he repeat the phrase over and over until he began to cry. At first it was tense and painful "like the dry heaves." After 15 or 20 minutes, however, his tears did begin to flow and in the end he cried almost daily for a year. On the other hand, a man whose father had attacked him with a knife was unable to cry until Scheff helped him to get more distance from his pain. To accomplish this, Scheff asked whether he could recall any good times with his father. The patient smiled, recounted a memory, and then burst into tears.

In his book, *Affect, Imagery, Consciousness: The Negative Affects* Silvan Tomkins (1963) focused on the centrality of crying as an expression of emotional distress. He analyzed a wide range of childhood transgressions that may lead to punishments or harsh interferences and thus to crying. If a child is curious about a breakable vase, for example, or overly exuberant or getting in the way while playing or trying to help, the parent's reprimanding response may cause the child to cry. Such negative childhood associations between distress and crying, he suggested, explain how crying in adulthood can be triggered by any "affect or group of affects" or even by "no affect" (p. 52).[1]

Cry-inducing distress, he wrote, might also stem from behavior such as being passive or active, bold or cautious, friendly or reserved, or by external events such as separations, war, illnesses, and all manner of personal misfortunes. His conclusion that crying could represent distress over any affect or combination of affects, behaviors or situations clearly illustrates the problem with trying to understand crying from the standpoint of emotional expression. The question, "Why is that person crying?" keeps branching out to infinity. Even trying to find a common link in "distress" leaves out experiences of crying that transcend personal distress and instead express love, awe, joy, and union or those in which distress is mixed with these positive emotions.

Cognitive theories hold that affect is determined by the beliefs that a person uses to structure his or her world based on past experience. Emotional reactions, including crying, that are inappropriate or excessive signal dysfunctional thought patterns or cognitions. Cognitive therapists Beck, Rush, Shaw, and Emory (1979) are among the few writers who discuss how to handle crying clinically. They believe that patients' crying should be handled according to the meaning that it conveys. Some people might benefit from encouragement to cry, they suggest, especially if they are in need of some self-sympathy. On the other hand, they say, therapists should be on the alert not simply to give blanket encouragement for crying because they might deliver the message that the patient is *expected* to cry.

For patients who cry too much, they suggest a diversion such as focusing on an object in the room or setting a time limit on the amount of crying in a session. This approach to crying is individualized rather than the same for everyone. Each patient's crying is linked to specific ideas, beliefs, and attitudes and the therapist responds in that context.

Behaviorists start from the standpoint that crying is an aversive behavior and that infants are "taught" to cry because caregivers respond to them when they cry. Their advice to parents was to resist their babies' cries so as not to "reward" or "reinforce" the crying, which would "teach" the baby to cry more. However, attachment research has shown that babies to whom someone does not respond promptly and consistently actually cry more, rendering that advice obsolete. Babies whose crying is not responded to do learn from the experience, but unfortunately what they learn is that no one is reliably there for them as a caregiver, a hallmark of insecure attachments.

The view of crying as communication has been recently and thoroughly written about by Jeffrey Kottler in *The Language of Tears* (1996). He holds that crying is a "language system" that "transcends words" (p. 49). Crying, he writes, has "its own special rules of grammar and its own unique vocabulary" (p. 49). He says that, "to understand the meaning of this behavior, it makes sense that first you would have to identify accurately just which emotion is being spoken for" (p. 83). In concert with those who see crying as strictly an emotional expression, he looks to understand it based on the particular emotions communicated. He acknowledges (Kottler, 2001) the complexities in trying to develop a comprehensive theory of crying when it is necessary to factor in mixed emotions, body biochemistry, socialization, situational precipitants, "gender scripts," reactions of others, unconscious attitudes, and moment-to-moment changes in affects.

Theoretical, social, and clinical issues are left unresolved regardless of whether crying is seen as a symptom, learned behavior, release valve for pent-up feeling, nonverbal communication, or call of distress. Why, for example, in response to any one of the emotions or combinations thereof, do adults cry? Why not shout or spit or stomp our feet? What is the significance of the fact that crying is one of the very few emotional expressions—along with sexual excitement and orgasm—that is to a large degree "involuntary"?

Ordinarily, when expressing feelings, we are able to trace a conscious path from thoughts, communications, events, or associations to the emotional expression. That is sometimes possible with crying but often tears appear unexpectedly without conscious forethought. It is also generally

possible to interrupt the chain from stimulus to response consciously at any point along the way. A strong desire to scream or hit or kick, unlike the lump in the throat and shedding tears, may be consciously controlled. Adults are capable of fighting back and resisting tears or of inviting and embracing them, but tears have a life of their own. They come unbidden or, conversely, elude us even though all the requisite emotions are present along with a strong desire to weep. As a spontaneous behavior operating outside exclusive conscious control, crying is of a different order than other expressions of emotion, verbal as well as nonverbal.

A theory of crying must also account for its physicality. Crying can never be approached dualistically: mind and body are always one in the act of shedding emotional tears. At the very least, crying involves five body systems: respiratory, cardiovascular, nervous, musculoskeletal, and endocrine. Furthermore, a comprehensive theory of crying also needs to consider the possible impact of physiological gender differences that might account for the imbalance in male and female crying frequency since both genders are given overt and covert social messages to discourage crying.

Reading about emotions and crying cross-culturally reveals another intriguing finding that must be encompassed by a theory of crying. Cultural differences are not to be found in the emotions (Ekman, 1969, 1971), but in the rules that each culture has for displaying the various emotions. Universal display rules would be a most unlikely occurrence. However, the abundant anthropological literature on funerals and death rituals, much studied because they are public and observable, shows otherwise (Habenstein & Lamers, 1963). There are no cultures in which crying and death are not associated and no tribe in which crying at the death of a close loved one is unknown or never occurs. As predicted, however, display rules for who should and should not cry at funerals vary tremendously from one group to another. Some encourage (or allow) it in all close family members and friends, but others only in either males or females. Some groups decree that it must happen only at the moment of death but others on specified days or anniversaries. Still others relegate it to paid professional mourners.

Some cultures expressly forbid crying at the death of a close loved one because it is an affront to a supreme being, because it will hinder the journey of the departed in the next world, or because it may bring danger to the living. Amazingly, however, even when crying is expressly forbidden based on the firm belief that it will bring death to the crier, some among the bereaved are still unable to suppress their tears (Kracke, 1981, 1988). In spite of vast cultural differences and expectations, crying at the time of the death of a close loved one is known in every culture in the world. A theory

of crying must be broad and deep enough to encompass the universality of infant crying and of crying at the death of a close loved one.

The context and the cognitive associations may tell us why a person is crying in the moment but still leave unanswered the bigger question: Why do human beings cry? "Look at crying as one key on a ring of keys," my colleague Cynthia O'Connell suggested when I was struggling with these questions and issues some years ago. Her comment immediately brought to mind the idea that crying is one of the behaviors that is "key" in the establishment of an attachment bond between parent and child. It is one key on a ring of keys, which also includes smiling, clinging, sucking, arms-up, calling, and following, that helps to establish and maintain human bonds. It is one of the ways we learn to feel secure, to love, and to be loved. Crying keeps parent and child close together in infancy and helps them form that invisible yet palpable bond of love. Also, crying is what human beings of all ages in all cultures do when the attachment bond is threatened or ruptured.

John Bowlby, psychoanalyst and attachment theorist, wrote three books (1969, 1973, 1980) and numerous articles that include references to crying and its relationship to attachment and loss in infancy and childhood. In discussing the development of attachment behaviors over the life span, he remarked that although they begin in infancy, they continue throughout life. They may change in form or intensity, he theorized, based on endocrine changes over the course of development. His suggestion that attachment behaviors change but do not disappear over the course of the life span inspired me to use attachment theory to link the crying of infants, children, and adults: infants cry at separation from the parent or caregiver and adults cry at permanent separation from a close loved one through death. In both instances, crying is attachment behavior.

When I began to think seriously about what it might mean to view crying as attachment behavior throughout life, I found that it could provide a solid foundation for a comprehensive theory of crying. Bringing an attachment perspective to crying explains everything from the physiology of crying to gender differences to outpourings of bereavement around the world. It also addresses social learning and individual and cultural differences. Because the attachment system is by definition a relational one, it always in some way implies or involves caregiving. The caregiving response system, triggered in others by attachment behaviors (especially crying), completes the framework. Attachment and caregiving operate as compatible, interlocking systems. Together they show crying to be an interpersonal behavior rather than a purely intrapsychic one, what

contemporary psychoanalytic theorists call a "two-person" as opposed to a "one-person" behavior.

From the standpoint of attachment theory and research paired with caregiving, crying makes sense personally, socially, physically, cross-culturally, spiritually, and psychologically. An attachment theory shows why and when crying helps and why and when it does not, when it is healthy and when it is dysfunctional, distancing, or a signal of depression. It brings a new perspective to understanding parent–infant and parent–child interactions, including the development of secure and insecure attachments, adult-to-adult closeness and distance, and the relationship between professional caregivers and their clients and patients.

CHAPTER 2

The Circle of Tears

Attachment, Loss, Crying, Caregiving, and Reattachment

At a point in his therapy when Reggie, a man in his early 40s, was starting to recognize his tendency to push people away and handle his pain alone, he received a phone call from his neighbors telling him that his beloved dog, Mitch, had been killed on the road. He called Mary, his partner, to tell her the news, but when she offered to come right home, he said that it was not necessary; he would be all right. Reggie started to cry as soon as he hung up and continued as he went out in the vineyard to dig a grave for Mitch, his companion of 10 years. He said that every time he became too overcome with tears, he "collapsed into the shovel" and stood there until he could go back to work on his digging. Reggie showed me how he hugged the shovel when he needed comfort, resting his head on the handle as if it were a shoulder.

I could not help thinking of the poor baby monkeys who were assigned to a wire mother surrogate instead of a soft cloth surrogate or a real mother in Harlow's classic study of mother–infant bonding. They, and we, can survive by making do with substandard caregiving but that deprivation has an impact on our physical and emotional development. Understanding the meaning of crying helps to explain more about the ways in which we suffer as a result.

Reggie is a man who is comfortable with crying. There was no doubt in his mind as to what was making him cry: he was desolate over the loss of Mitch. From the standpoint of expressing his grief, his crying was on the right track, but from the standpoint of comfort and healing, something was amiss. He had rejected the offer of closeness and comfort from Mary; therefore, instead of facing loss within a protected circle of connection, he faced it alone with his shovel. His grief highlighted what he had just lost—the comfort and closeness of Mitch. Now, there would be no more affectionate welcome-homes and wet kisses, no more curling up next to Mitch's warm furry body on the bed.

Stepping back from Reggie's crying as an expression of grief to examine it from the broader standpoint of attachment, the question becomes not only why Reggie is crying, but also why human beings cry. These two questions distinguish between what evolutionary psychologists call the *proximate* cause for his behavior, or what stimulates it in the moment, and its *ultimate* cause, or the adaptive purpose the behavior serves in support- ing human survival. To understand crying in this broader sense, it is necessary to begin with the function of crying from the beginning of life.

Crying as Attachment Behavior

Crying is part of a system of biologically based, inborn attachment behaviors that helps to establish and maintain the parent–child bond. Human babies cry for "proximate" reasons like being hungry, startled by a loud noise, in pain, or too cold. Behind all those immediate precipitants, however, is the "ultimate" cause: human infants cry to bring their care- givers to them and keep them there until equilibrium has been restored. "Come here, I need you" is the default message of all infant cries.

In order to survive, an infant must first and foremost have the presence of a caregiver. Soothing and nurturing ministrations require physical proximity or contact. Peter Wolff (1969) tested babies' priorities in this regard. The research design was simple: one group of crying babies were rediapered with the same wet diaper that had just been removed while a second group got dry ones. The babies in the wet-diaper group stopped crying just as the babies who got the dry ones did. Apparently, it was the need for physical contact that prompted their cries, not the physical discomfort of the diaper. It was the caregiver's touch and handling that quieted them.

Infants need a powerful come-hither signal to assure that their caregiv- ers stay close and return quickly. Human infants lack the locomotion and clinging skills of our close animal relatives, whose young have the ability to maintain proximity with their parents by clinging or following. Baby primates are able from birth to stay attached to their mothers at five points—gripping her with all four limbs while sucking on the nipple, even when their mothers are walking or running.

The primary survival reason for a behavior that discourages separations and terminates them quickly, according to attachment theorist John Bowlby, is for protection from predators. Infants in most parts of the world today are no longer vulnerable to wild animals. All infants are nonetheless still equipped with the emergency calling device that says, "Come here, I need you—now!" They use it whenever they are vulnerable, especially when they are not in physical contact with their caregivers. Human infant cries are acoustically most effective in calling over a short distance unlike, for example, the high-pitched shriek of certain tree-dwelling monkeys, which, in keeping with their habitat, are effective over long distances. Infant cries form what Peter Ostwald (Ostwald & Peltzman, 1974) called an "acoustic umbilical chord" connecting the baby to the caregiver even when they are apart.

When caregivers respond to infant cries and provide nurturing and soothing, they reduce infant arousal and distress. This helps to establish a sense of safety and security in the infant. Repeated experiences of infant crying followed by caregiving responses, especially physical contact, contribute to the establishment and maintenance of the infant–parent bond. The crying/caregiving cycle in infancy also provides the experiential and neurological base for the regulation of negative affect and arousal throughout life.

Crying is one of the primary interactive behavioral components in the establishment of attachment in infancy. Other attachment behaviors (see Figure 2.1) that trigger interaction and physical contact within the first 6 months include clinging and grasping, sucking, smiling, cooing, and babbling. Later in the first year these are joined by the arms-up signal, laughter, early speech with proximity-beckoning messages like "Ma Ma" or "up," and locomotive behaviors such as crawling or walking that enable the young toddler to stay close to the caregiving parent.

Crying is distinct from the other attachment behaviors in several ways. First, crying is initiated at *separation from* the caregiver (during the first 6 months of life) and terminated by the caregiver's presence and soothing. The other attachment behaviors—clinging, smiling, laughing, and arms-up—are initiated *in the presence of* caregivers. Babies of animal species that leave their infants alone in nests while the parents forage for food, such as rabbits or birds, only cry in the *presence* of their parents because their cries might otherwise attract predators in the neighborhood who could then descend on them before their parents return (Blurton Jones, 1972).

Crying is also the only attachment behavior that is unpleasant and aversive. The others are warm and inviting, bringing mutual pleasure and "positive affect" to the infant and the caregiver. Bowlby speculated that the smiles, coos, laughter, and clinging of their infants help caregivers deal with the inevitable frustration, and sometimes outright pain, of a crying infant. Allan Schore, who writes about the neurobiology of attachment, points to evidence that the pleasure accompanying moments of "positive affect synchrony" between infant and mother also contributes to the organization of the infant's right brain and appears to have a positive impact on the mother's brain functioning as well (Schore, 2003, p. 80).

We are "hard wired to connect," to quote Allan Schore. This idea is supported by two consistent maturational patterns of infant crying during the first year of life. The first, the diurnal pattern, refers to the frequency of infant crying over the course of a 24-hour period (Bernal, 1972; Brazelton, 1962; Rebelsky, 1972). Regardless of how much crying an individual baby does and no matter where the baby is born and raised, more crying is done in the evening. The second maturational pattern is a gradual increase in the amount of crying through the first 6 weeks of life, after which it plateaus until 12 weeks (the age when "3-month colic" also stops) and then declines sharply (Brazelton, 1962; St. James-Roberts, 1989).

This consistent pattern, however, also illustrates the interaction among infant "hard-wiring," caregiving styles, and culture because it has only been found in infants from the United States, Canada, New Zealand, Finland, and the United Kingdom whose physical contact with their caregivers is limited to 2 to 3 hours per day. In other words, it is consistent only for infants who are not in constant physical contact with a human being. In societies in which infants are continually carried and fed at intervals up to several times an hour, or in Western cultures when additional carrying is introduced (Hunziker & Barr, 1986), babies do not show this same pattern of increased crying frequency in the first 6 weeks. Infants who are literally attached to their mothers' bodies with a variety of slings, shawls, or carriers cry much less overall and show no increase in the amount of crying in the early weeks of life. They also have much less colic and reach the first-year developmental milestones sooner than the separation-challenged, comparatively high-crying babies in Western cultures, in which infants spend hours of the day separate from their caregivers' bodies in infant seats, play pens, baby strollers, cribs, and separate rooms for sleeping (Brazelton, 1969).

A number of other behavioral systems, in addition to attachment, are also part of the human repertoire. Each has its own biological core that interacts with social learning during development. Attachment behaviors work in conjunction with, and sometimes overlap, a number of other systems including the caregiving, eating, fear, exploratory, and locomotion systems. For example, the behaviors that comprise locomotion are also used by the infant to maintain proximity and seek soothing and security from their caregivers once crawling and walking begin. Locomotion becomes, in effect, an attachment behavior when used to establish and maintain proximity.

In early childhood, some attachment behaviors, such as smiling, laughing and making verbal connections, also serve to establish affiliations and friendships. Affiliative relationships (with siblings, babysitters, family friends, and neighbors) represent social connections and even closeness, but do not generally have a soothing and security-providing function. That function is exclusive to primary caregivers until adolescence. Crying children, as well as adults, continue to show preference for the presence of their attachment figures, rather than friends or acquaintances.

In late adolescence and adulthood, sexual behaviors such as gazing, hugging, and kissing also overlap with attachment behaviors. In adult romantic partnerships, the attachment, caregiving, and sexual systems interact and overlap frequently and often seamlessly.

Caregiving Behavior

The caregiving system (see Figure 2.1) is the behavioral system most intimately connected with attachment. Crying and caregiving are mutual and intersubjective from the outset. Infant attachment behaviors are meaningless in a vacuum; a real human caregiving presence is their only aim. Because it takes two to attach, it makes survival sense for a matching system of behavior to be released or evoked by the signals and approaches of attachment.

Infant crying is interactive and relational from the very beginning of life. Infant cries must alert and unsettle protectors enough to bring them close, if not to bring them running. Something must jar a busy parent into putting down the laundry basket and picking up the baby. Attachment and caregiving are reciprocal systems of behavior necessary for the establishment of the attachment bond and for survival. Wire and cloth mothers may have enabled Harlow's monkeys to survive, albeit barely, but human infants clearly need the warm body of a caregiver close and immediately available to them at all times.

Crying is the most effective elicitor of caregiving behavior. Infants may be helpless in most respects but crying gives them a power to be reckoned with. When there is trouble, crying is their clear, no-nonsense, fail-safe signal: "Come here; I need you!" The cries of infants send out little lightning bolts to parents, an electric current that crackles across distances striking at the core of their parents' physiological beings. Deeper than obligation, more physiological than responsibility, and as emotional as

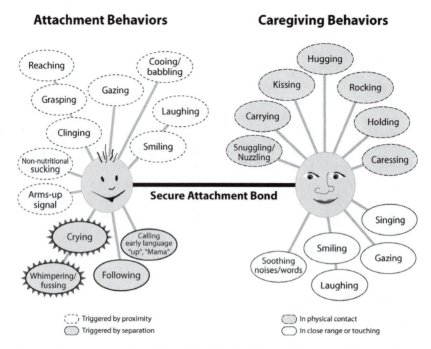

Fig. 2.1 Attachment behaviors and caregiving behaviors (infant and caregiver with secure attachment bond).

love, altruism, and empathy rolled into one, caregiving behavior is the biologically adaptive parental response to infant attachment behaviors, especially crying.

When a baby cries, the combination of tension, caring, and urgency—or, for some caregivers, irritation, frustration, or rage—that it evokes is a powerful guarantee of some kind of parental response. Parents wired to test heart rate, blood pressure, and skin responses showed physiological changes in response to infant cries (Boukydis & Burgess, 1982; Boukydis, 1985; Donovan & Balling, 1978; Donovan & Leavitt, 1985). Parents watching videos of crying infants also had marked physiological changes that they did not have when the videos were of smiling infants (Frodi, Lamb, Leavitt, & Donovan, 1978). The parents' diastolic blood pressure and heart rates increased, as did their skin conductance measures. These indicators of tension and attention are associated with autonomic arousal and an urge to take action.

Well known to all nursing mothers is the physiological response to their crying infant known as the "let-down reflex." The sound of her baby's cry is all it takes to get the milk flowing in a nursing mother. Infant crying cuts through teaching, experience, and conscious rational evaluations and goes straight to the parent's nervous system, heart, gut, and blood stream, literally.

I was in graduate school when my first daughter was born. Although I set up a card table next to her playpen to work on my papers, she was never content for more than a few minutes and, try as I might, I could not ignore her cries. I could see that she was all right, but I could not tolerate the way her cries made me feel. They twisted up my insides and jarred my brain so that I could not concentrate on my reading or research. She got her point across: holding her was more urgent than any deadline facing me at school. I would pick her up, nurse her a few minutes, dance with her, take her for a walk outside, or rock her to sleep, and then I would go back to my card table.

I did not start out thinking that human beings have a "genetic bias" toward caregiving. However, in doing this research over the years, the evidence of at least some measure of a biological substrate for caregiving has accumulated. I was first struck by a comment made by animal researchers that care of the young is too important to survival to be left "entirely to chance," which is to say social learning. Then, looking at pictures and reading about animal mothers, like the one in Jane Goodall's report of the baby chimpanzee "Flint" and his mother "Flo," underscored our biological kinship. When Flint was pulled off Flo's body by his sister, he demonstrated three attachment behaviors: the arms-up signal, a facial expression of distress that included pouting lips, and cry sounds. His mother scooped him up instantly, cuddled him and kissed him on the head, caregiving behaviors perfectly familiar to my mothering self. Another moving story, captured on video, of the youngster who fell into the gorilla enclosure at the Chicago zoo is a vivid portrayal of the link between the caregiving of humans and other primates. The gorilla Binti Jua, with her own baby on her back, picked up the unconscious child and carried him to a door where he could be reached by the zoo staff.

The data on the near-perfect ability of mothers to recognize their infants by cry alone within hours or days of birth also contribute to answering the question of whether caregiving behavior has a biological substratum (Formby, 1967; Morsbach, 1980; Morsbach & Bunting, 1979). If mothers are to care for their infants and respond to their cries, they must certainly be able to recognize them from afar in case of separation. Fathers are very good at this, too, though their scores lag somewhat behind the mothers'. (Days-old babies prefer their parents' voices to those of a stranger but they have been exposed intrauterinely to those voices for 9 months, whereas the parents are hearing the child's cry for the first time.) Again, we are like our close animal relatives in this regard: mother cows will only nurse their own calves; this is one way ranchers use to reunite them if they have been separated by rustlers (McPhee, 1993).

Another argument for the biological component of caregiving is how early it appears in securely attached children, which logically follows from early attachment/caregiving experiences. My youngest daughter, by 6 months of age, would pat *my* shoulder when I picked her up to soothe her, copying one of my primary and almost unconscious caregiving methods.

I saw a vivid example of early childhood caregiving one evening when I was looking after 18-month-old Jena, my little next-door neighbor. I had the television tuned to a dramatization of the life of Elspeth Huxley in Africa as I was looking at a picture book with Jena. A baby in the family compound in the television story was burned in a fire and began to cry pitifully in pain. Jena got up from the sofa and tried to hug the television, undeterred by the static electricity. When the baby continued to cry, she took a pillow from the sofa and pressed it up against the television screen, concern and compassion written on her every move and expression.

I have long suspected a connection between the ability of women to cry more easily and frequently than men and nature's preparation of women to nurture infants. The association between increased crying, menstruation, and childbirth in females across cultures (Davidson, 1972; Gordon, Gordon, Gordon–Hardy, Hursch, & Reed, 1986; Hargrove & Abraham, 1982; Harris, 1981) points to a link between crying and the hormones associated with the reproductive system. Perhaps women have a genetic tilt toward crying in preparation for becoming caregivers who can communicate and respond on a more physiological/biological wavelength than the cognitive one with which they typically function in adult life.

In the end, though, it is the subjective experience evoked by cries that offers the most persuasive evidence supporting the idea that caregiving has a biological component. Everyone who hears a crying infant is alerted and affected. With crying babies in restaurants and on airplanes, crying babies in supermarkets and in strollers on the street, we do not simply hear their cries, we feel them. We might feel sympathy or annoyance or frustration, we might even laugh. Feelings vary in intensity, depending on who is crying and how, and on the listener's needs and moods at the moment. However, almost certainly, people within earshot are going to be engaged at some level and not relaxed, neutral, or indifferent.

Whatever genetic bias might be operating upon exposure to infant cries may be overridden consciously. Every day, parents make moment-by-moment decisions about whether to finish chopping the vegetables or go pick up the crying baby. Many try alternative soothing mechanisms like talking or singing, which enable them to multitask. Others use earplugs or stereo headphones to block out the cry sound. Caregivers may be compelled to respond internally and physiologically, but the caregiving behaviors may be, and often are, consciously controlled or overridden.

In her book, *Death without Weeping*, anthropologist Nancy Scheper–Hughes (1992) writes about poverty-oppressed mothers in a market town in northeast Brazil who, at the time she studied them in the 1970s, would consciously decide not to give care to certain vulnerable crying infants whose survival chances they considered poor. That they seemed to do so without showing anguish, she suggested, might argue against a genetic bias toward caregiving. I strongly suspect that, instead, it shows the power of culture to determine how we care for our children. That attachment behaviors require the presence of reciprocal caregiving behaviors is made painfully obvious by the fact that the infants could not decide to override their attachment needs and eventually died. Scheper–Hughes was not able to override her own caregiving sensibilities, either. When she was unsuccessful in trying to persuade one of the mothers to care for her malnourished 1½-year-old child, Scheper–Hughes fed and cared for him for 6 months, thereby saving his life (Schoch, 1992).

The fact that infant crying arouses discomfort in parents can also lead to disastrous consequences. Infant crying is a significant factor, if not the primary factor, in 80% of infant child abuse cases. Certain parents who had insecure and unattuned attachment/caregiving experiences in infancy may be at great risk for abuse in the parenting relationship. Because their negative arousal and affect was not interactively soothed and regulated in infancy, they are unable to do so for their own infants. Their infants' crying arouses them, but they strike out to eliminate the crying rather than trying to soothe the infant.

Adult Crying as Attachment Behavior

The beckoning, attachment-building power of infant crying and the way in which it evokes caregiving responses provides a point of orientation for understanding crying throughout life. Attachment behaviors continue to play a central role in establishing and maintaining close and intimate relationships from infancy onward. Adult crying, too, is attachment behavior and, if we look at it as attachment behavior rather than as emotional discharge, it changes our understanding of its meaning and impacts the ways in which we think about it and respond to it. Instead of being a "one-person" behavior aimed at discharging negative affect, crying is a "two-person" relationship behavior, aimed at recharging and rebalancing internal equilibrium through human connection after a separation or loss.

Reggie, who cried alone as he buried his dog, provides an example for comparing the attributes of crying as an attachment behavior in infants and adults. Infants have the ability to cry in order to bring or keep their parents in proximity to them and they cry when they are separated from their caregivers. Reggie, too, cried because of a permanent separation from an attachment figure, his dog Mitch. My colleague Maureen Adams (2003), who has studied and written about the human–animal bond, would say that Reggie's relationship with Mitch was, in fact, an attachment bond. For some people, no doubt including Reggie with his history of insecure attachment, bonding with an animal is a safer, less threatening form of attachment than bonding with human beings.

Our bodies are designed to sound a cry of alarm at emergencies such as abandonment or the death of a close loved one. With such events, everything is at stake: our health and well-being and, even, it seems, our survival. The cycle that we come to expect, if we have secure enough early attachments, is separation, followed by attachment behavior (crying if the threat to security is great enough), followed by reunion. We cry when a loved one dies for the same reason that infants do: to get him or her to return. It may not literally be true that adults cannot survive without the presence of loved ones, but that is how they feel. Lovers everywhere can relate to songs and love poems filled with some variation on the theme: "If you go away I'll cry; if you leave me I will die." Crying and dying not only are convenient rhymes, but also inextricably linked in our minds with the loss of love.

In Reggie's case, the separation from Mitch was permanent; there could be no reunion. John Bowlby points out that, by far, most separations do end in reunion, especially those in infancy. A permanent separation from a loved one—including Mitch as many animal lovers fully understand—triggered Reggie's attachment behavior of crying. He cried because he wanted Mitch not to be dead, even as he was burying him.

Crying at separation from the caregiver is universal in infancy and crying at the loss of a close loved one is universal in adulthood. Infants around the world cry when left on their own and people around the world cry when a close loved one dies (Habenstein & Lamers, 1963). In cross-cultural emotion studies, regardless of where they live, their social or educational background, or their exposure to the outside world, people are able to identify and reproduce upon demand the facial expressions associated with grief and loss (Ekman, 1969, 1971, 1973). When asked to show the face of someone whose child has died, they will all make the same face; when shown pictures, they are able to recognize and identify it.

Although it is not a scientific study, I like the observation of a 5-year-old quoted in the newspaper (Caen, 1994). He was an English-speaking child and heard the voices of some children speaking Chinese in the yard next door. "How did they learn Chinese so young?" he asked his grandfather. Then one of the children fell and began crying loudly. "Well," the little boy said, "at least they cry in English" (C-1). He knew instinctively that crying transcends languages and cultures.

Bowlby pointed out that it makes good biological survival sense for closeness to be pleasurable and separation painful. In case the joys of connection are not enough to keep us bound together, whether parent to child or mate to mate, painful separations make us prefer togetherness and connection, if for no other reason than to avoid the hurt. As Bowlby indicates, the most intense reactions and affects are stirred up in the context of our attachment bonds. Many adult patients enter therapy around these very issues.

The biological substrate for adult crying behavior may be difficult to pinpoint, but something in our make-up keeps us crying in these circumstances of extreme loss throughout our lives. We physically shed tears—and not because we decide consciously to do so. Our bodies, our neurological systems, our brains, and our hormones decide for us, many times in spite of a conscious wish *not* to do so.

Adult Caregiving

Not only infant crying triggers caregiving responses; adult crying does so as well, even silent adult weeping. We notice people who are crying; we wonder about them and worry about them and about what, if anything, we should do in response. If a student is crying quietly in the back of the classroom, everyone is aware and uncomfortable. If a solitary man is crying at a bar, he will not go unnoticed and it will unsettle the patrons around him. Criers cease to be neutral, anonymous people. They stir us viscerally and we feel a need to do something such as asking what is wrong or if we can help. If we know the person, we feel an urge to hug or touch him or her or do something to resolve or remove the cause of the tears—or, on the negative side, to attack or ignore the behavior. Like parents of infants, we may not always heed or sympathize with the message that crying implies—connection and comfort—but we do understand it at a very deep level.

A friend of my daughter's, Andrea Tetrick (1996), wrote a poem about a crying stranger (not knowing anything of my theory) called "F Train." It says, in part:

> Tonight on the F train we pretend not to watch a woman cry
> all tangled hair and grief. We pretend not to watch her alone
> ...

We wonder did her parents die? Did her lover leave?
Would she be dead within the year?
...
We wonder is she crazy or are we crazy not to touch her,
not to touch her even with our eyes. (14)

Silent adult crying beckons almost as effectively as infant cry sounds, but with facial expression and tears alone. Our early experiences at being soothed and nurtured by our caregivers help us to remain attuned to others. We may also be drawn to each other's cry signals because we have a built-in response system that leads us to notice and feel a tug toward any crier, just as parents do with their children. Neurological imaging studies (some of which are now in the planning stages) of adults listening to, or seeing videos of, the cries of other adults will be able to show more about how crying adult attachment behaviors affect us.

Human beings need behaviors that move us toward each other and keep us there. Crying is one of the most powerful and essential of those behaviors. Vulnerability can strike at any age—when we lose loved ones, become ill or fatigued, for example—and crying lets other people know that has happened. Adult survival is, from an evolutionary perspective, as dependent on the care and protection of others as infant survival, even though this is hard to comprehend in this highly autonomous, self-reliant age. That is why adults need a powerful signal for connecting with others just like infants who are in need of their adult caregivers. In tribal cultures, it is easier to see that isolated individuals, even more than the young, aged, and ill, are vulnerable to threats of death if not protected by other members of the group. Adults also need the presence of someone who will come to them, respond to their pain, and give them the help that they to survive and recover.

When Reggie called Mary to tell her about his dog's death, the first thing she did was to offer to be with him. Her caregiving response was intact, but his ability to receive caregiving was not. His security was easily disturbed and difficult to soothe. His struggles ran deep but the healing process was underway in his relationship with Mary and in his therapy.

Reggie refused her offer for two other, more social reasons. Like so many people, he grew up with an overdose of independence training. Self-reliance is our strong suit; it is with intimacy and closeness that we have more difficulty. Reggie also had some particular social wounds that came from being cruelly teased by his adolescent peers for being a brilliant, geeky nerd. He was resolute in never showing his vulnerable side to anyone.

Reggie is not alone in his preference for solitary crying. This preference is ubiquitous in our culture even though it contradicts the very reason we cry: for connection. We learn to hide from each other rather than expose our need for closeness.

Even solitary crying is an attachment behavior with a caregiving message, however. If the crier has "secure enough" attachments, inner resources will permit self-soothing. Allan Schore writes that for the securely attached individual, "the representation of the attachment relationship with the primary caregiver encodes an implicit expectation that homeostatic disruptions will be set right, allowing the child to self-regulate functions that previously required the caregiver's external regulation" (Schore, 2003, p. 245).

A friend was home alone with her small children when she heard of the sudden death of her mentor and thesis advisor. So as not to upset the children, she calmly continued caring for them until her husband returned from his errands. Then she drove up into the hills and sat crying. She told her husband what had happened and allowed him to empathize with her. She chose to cry alone but did not, like Reggie, feel cut off and alone.

Crying at its core is a separation behavior that functions as an appeal for the caregiver's presence. Instead of being deactivated when out of contact, like an electric cord removed from the socket, crying is triggered by disconnection and separation. Even in infancy we do not fizzle and go passive when left alone. We cry and scream and make very clear our wish for reunion. The feelings may be more discreet in adults, but they are nonetheless active and intense.

A means for us to call for, cling to, and comfort each other throughout life, crying is like an inoculation against permanent separation and loss. Fully appreciating the depths of the need for human connections on all levels—biological, social, and psychological—places adult crying in a much larger context. It also offers a way to translate the meaning of crying behavior as a whole and to distinguish different types of crying and inhibited crying.

CHAPTER 3

Protest, Despair, and Detachment
A Classification of Crying

> Women on planes are crying because someone they love or loved
> is dead or dying. Every plane has them.... Death can do this;
> death has the power to do this.
>
> Martin Amis (1995, p. 216)

When we grieve, we sometimes cry, but when we cry, almost without exception, we grieve for some loss, however hidden or obscure it may seem in the moment. The theme of separation and symbolic death that runs through almost all adult crying eluded me when I approached crying from the standpoint of emotional discharge. Not until I began to look at crying as attachment behavior did a pattern begin to emerge.

From the standpoint of attachment, the two universally recognized moments for crying—at separation from the caregiver in infancy and at the death of a close loved one—may be seen as prototypes for almost all crying throughout life.[1] As Bowlby (1960, 1961, 1973, 1980) and others have observed, both these experiences of separation and loss result in grief reactions that occur in a sequence of predictable stages: protest, despair, and detachment (or reorganization, in an adult who successfully works through a loss). These stages of grief, triggered by rupture or loss of primary attachment bonds, then become a template for classifying types of crying and inhibited crying (Nelson, 1979, 1998, 2000) that accompany each stage.

Separation and Loss

Separations do have the power to make us cry, but not only the extreme ones such as abandonment or death. We may also weep over the separations and little deaths of everyday life. We endure separations from material possessions, money, familiar surroundings, jobs, self-esteem, health, and dreams, as well as our children, parents, friends, and lovers. We also die a little every time we undergo a major life change, for better or worse, as the old makes way for the new: children leaving for college, retirement, or even receiving an inheritance.

The theme of loss in relationship to crying becomes clearer when the definition is expanded to include not only literal major losses but also losses at all levels of severity, and those which may be threatened, imagined, or symbolic (Simos, 1979; Viorst, 1986). I wrote a poem one fall day several years ago when I was feeling discouraged. The final stanza is:

This is the time for flowers
For spring.
I shed tears like Inanna's
to resurrect her lover
from the winter of the underworld.
But then I look outside
And see by persimmon, pumpkin, frost and leaf
That I am off by two seasons.
The new has to die its way in.

The poem recorded my realization that I would have to face some grief of my own—die a little—to write this book. I could not skip the dark and dying seasons of autumn and winter if I hoped to achieve the growth spurt of spring and the summer harvest of a completed manuscript.

Some losses, such as physical health, are literal; others, such as self-esteem, are intangible. Joe, my father's neighbor, wept when the doctor told him he could no longer play tennis. His game had been a source of pride for him as the oldest playing member in his club. He lost something tangible—his ability to play the game—but that was not what made him weep. The loss he felt most keenly was of his pride and the positive regard of his younger fellow players. They were sympathetic, but what he craved was admiration.

Some losses may be merely threatened or implied. Perhaps a boyfriend's off-hand comment that he is sick and tired of listening to complaints from his girlfriend about his race car is not a conscious threat, but when she cries she is letting him know that she experiences it as one. Perhaps her self-esteem is threatened as well, if she sees herself as an ideal, caring partner but hears herself described instead as nagging and unsupportive.

Symbolic or imagined losses may also trigger tears. I once made up a story about leaving a diamond wedding band I inherited from my mother in a restaurant ladies' room as a vignette to illustrate solitary crying. Losing the ring, I said, was bad enough, but because of its symbolic connection to my mother, the sense of pain and loss was multiplied. To describe the inner experience that the solitary crier has of the absent caregiver, I summoned up a memory of my mother's reassuring voice: "It is only an object; you remember the day Daddy gave it to me and how it looked on my finger and that is what is important."

I did, in fact, inherit my mother's ring, but it is hiding safely in a jewelry box under my sweaters. By the time I finished writing the paragraph, however I was crying anyway, just from imagining how I would feel if I lost the ring, and perhaps even more over the fantasy of my mother's comfort, missing in real life since her death in 1988. An editor friend who was reading this piece returned it with "me too" written next to the place in the text where I confessed that I had cried. My fantasy made us both cry, a phenomenon familiar to those who cry over fictional losses in books and movies. Gertrude Stein in her inimitable style put it this way: "I liked to cry not in real life but in books in real life there was nothing much to cry about but in books oh dear me, it was wonderful there was so much to cry about" (as cited in Stendhal, 1994, p. 1).

So-called "tears of joy" may also contain expressions of loss, although the losses are often somewhat more difficult to recognize. Tears shed over an acceptance letter to medical school or at the return of a lost child acknowledge the opposite side of the experience—the feared or averted loss or the ones experienced on the way to victory or success. Perhaps this is the crier's third attempt to get into medical school and the tears of joy also recall earlier feelings of fear and hopelessness. Certainly, when a lost child comes home, the parents can easily feel the agony of all the other possible, now averted, outcomes, along with their joy. The tears shed by just-crowned Miss Americas or by gold medalists at the Olympics may include the dread or threat of defeat in the moment of victory. The winners cry in celebration, but they can also identify with the losses of the other less-fortunate contestants, or recall earlier losses and the sacrifices they experienced in the years it took to achieve this success.

Ubiquitous crying at weddings is also about loss as much as it is about celebrating the new union. Weddings represent a major life change and, although there may be many exciting gains—romance, security, a new spouse, and new in-laws, much is lost and left behind as well. When my sister went to see the comedy, *Father of the Bride*, she was amazed to hear the audience all around her crying audibly. They were no doubt identifying with the losses associated with weddings—a child leaving home and passing from the carefree days of youth to the serious responsibilities of grown-up family life—and perhaps recollecting a few bittersweet memories of their own.

The extensive international Adult Cry Inventory, developed by Ad Vingerhoets (2001) of the Netherlands and administered to 3,906 subjects from 30 countries (Scheirs & Sijtsma, 2001), contains nine categories of reported causes of crying. Three categories (loss, conflict, personal inadequacy) directly relate to loss as broadly defined and account for 59% of the reported causes of crying. Four of the remaining categories, "physical state, psychological state, combination of causes, and other" are in all likelihood largely related to various kinds of losses as well. This group represents another 18% of the reported causes of crying. The two remaining categories, "witnessing suffering and witnessing positive events" (24%) might also include an element of vicarious personal loss, or perhaps a layer of loss beneath the joy.

Grief Reactions

Bereaved Infants

We do not typically think of infants as having grief reactions, but that is exactly how Bowlby (1960) characterized the traumatically abandoned infants in his article "Grief and Mourning in Infancy and Early Childhood." Bowlby, Anna Freud, and D.W. and Claire Winnicott, along with other psychoanalysts practicing in Britain during World War II, studied very young children sent to rural nurseries for safekeeping during the London blitz. Bowlby (1960) observed that the first response of any young child over the age of 6 months recently left by his or her mother was to "cry loudly, shake his cot, throw himself about, and look eagerly towards any sight or sound which might prove to be his missing mother" (p. 15). This type of crying was clearly directed at getting his or her mother back soon. Bowlby called this a "protest" reaction because this intense crying clearly represented resistance to the separation with the aim of bringing about a reunion.

Eventually, if their mothers did not reappear, the infants began to despair. They no longer cried loudly and impatiently. Instead there would only be an occasional despairing wail. The youngsters appeared resigned to their terrifying plight. They looked and sounded miserable, helpless, and defeated. Bowlby fittingly labeled this type of response "despair."

If not reunited with their parents and lacking a consistent substitute caregiver, the infants finally withdrew into silent detachment, sometimes called "anaclitic depression," "hospitalitis," or "failure to thrive," which could be life threatening to them. Some of the infants stopped crying and appeared to make a superficial adjustment, accepting food and care from a series of caregivers. Others, however, stopped growing and some eventually died because they became too detached from human connection. Human survival, in the early months and years of life, depends on more than food and protection from the elements. It is as if physical nourishment will not "take" without the social nourishment of a bond with at least one primary caregiver.

When I did child welfare work as a Peace Corps volunteer in Nigeria, I was called by neighbors to check on a 9-month-old girl whose parents had left her with relatives while they went to study in England. I had not been there to hear her initial cries of protest when they left her and I did not hear those angry, demanding cries wither away into occasional wails of dejection and despair as she began to give up hope. By the time I saw her, she was silent and detached. I can still see her as we found her lying on a baby blanket in the middle of a double bed. She was silent, still, and gruesomely thin—no bigger than a 3-month-old. My Nigerian social work colleague, Dinatu, sat on the back of my motor scooter with the tiny, almost lifeless bundle cradled in her arms as we rushed her to the pediatric ward at Kano City Hospital. We sent an urgent message to her parents abroad but it was too late to save her life.

That tiny baby girl is an enduring picture of loss in my mind. She lost her parents, her security, her health, and, ultimately, her life. Her crying was the only weapon she had to fight the life-threatening separation from her parents over which she had no control. Sadly, her crying did not bring them back.

Later, when Bowlby (1961) studied the reactions of older children and adults to the loss of a close loved one, he discovered that the same three reactions—protest, despair, and, in certain instances, detachment—also occurred consistently. He concluded that "though it might affront his sense of reality were he to be aware of its origin and function, when he weeps the bereaved adult is responding to loss as a child does to the temporary absence of his mother" (p. 333).

Bereaved Adults

In the early stages of a loss by death, bereaved adults, like infants, also protest a separation. Often this takes place when the news first comes (the telephone call or the policeman at the door) and the bereaved loved ones are desperate to reject it. They shriek or scream or shake their heads, refusing to take in the words. They want a reunion. They want the news undone, the separation ended, the reality changed back to the way it was before, in the same way in which infants want their mothers to return.

A San Francisco taxi driver, Brad Newsham (2000), writes a column about his work experiences. In the early morning hours on one of his shifts, he was called to a restaurant by the owner, who then helped a sobbing man into the cab. From the back seat, the man called out to Newsham in an anguished voice, "My mother, she's dead!" When Newsham looked back, he saw the man sitting with his arms "folded in an X across his chest, fingers spread wide, clutching his shoulders as though to keep his quaking body from flying apart. 'I want my mother back!' he bawled" (p. D8).

Protest makes sense in the immediate aftermath of a sudden loss by death. No matter what our age, we want our dad, mom, sister, brother, husband, or wife to be alive and with us, not dead and gone. These powerful, often loud, anguished sobs make those around feel a painful degree of empathy because the provocation is so clear and the reaction so understandable. We can imagine being there only too well. Cab driver Newsham wrote that his thoughts went to the loss of his own father 10 years previously and to himself he said, "Aw, man, don't get *me* crying. I gotta drive." We understand the desperation to undo such news and go back to the untroubled moments before it came.

At this stage, people resist comfort from others; they want action. Comfort implies a loss and they are not ready to accept that yet. In a scene in the film *Steel Magnolias*, the bereaved mother, normally a mild-mannered, soft-spoken woman (played by Sally Field), erupts in tearful protest at the grave of her adult daughter, her face and words unambiguously angry. She is surrounded by close female friends, one of whom (played by Olympia Dukakis) pushes the other one (Shirley MacLaine) in front of the raging mother and says, "Hit her! This is your chance!" There was no question of putting an arm around the grieving mother and offering her solace when she was so overwrought by anger at her daughter's death. Instead, her friends empathized with the anger and supported her protest, albeit with a touch of humor that eventually melted the protest to a sad smile.

Compare these angry tears of protest at the time of death to the despair of an old fisherman in a Jamaica Kincaid (1990) story whose partner had been swept overboard. The young woman who narrates the story says, "He was so pitiful my heart broke just looking at him" and when he started to cry, "... it was such a sorrowful sound I did not know a man could sound like that" (p. 32).

Here we see another reaction to a loss by death: despair. This reaction to grief has an altogether different feel from that of protest, which aims at avoiding or undoing a separation or loss. Tears of sadness and despair emerge when we face the inevitability or reality of our loss. The fisherman, like the despairing babies left behind by their caregivers, had given up hope and accepted the reality of his situation. The loss could not be undone; his companion was not coming back. No fight was left because no hope was left. In adults, we call this weeping. The tension of protest is gone. Sadness and resignation, which we perhaps mistakenly call acceptance and should instead call surrender, take its place.

Crying in despair is a powerfully evocative type of weeping that will melt the hearts of all but the most detached caregivers. As Kincaid's character put it in the story, "I wanted to say something to him, something that would be comforting and at the same time take his mind away from his sorrow, if only for a moment" (p. 32). This kind of grief is eventually healing because it helps us to stay connected with the one whom we have lost while at the same time connecting us with the other people around us who are still available. Going through despair with a sense of connection is what will ultimately lead to the stage of grief that Bowlby calls "reorganization," when the bereaved person is able to find energy for new pursuits and new attachments.

Some adults also respond to grief with tearless detachment, analogous to that final life-threatening response in some infants. It is the condition expressed by the English poet Samuel Taylor Coleridge in "Dejection: An Ode":

> A grief without a pang, void, dark, and drear,
> A stifled, drowsy, unimpassioned grief,
> Which finds no natural outlet, no relief,
> In word or sigh or tear—

(as cited in Bernbaum, 1948, p. 178, 11. 21–24)

Those who react to a significant loss with dry-eyed detachment shut down altogether and withdraw. They cut off their expression of feeling, which is "stifled, drowsy, unimpassioned," and the possibility of any comfort or consolation from other people; the grief is truly "void, dark, and drear." Such a reaction can stall the grieving process and signal a deep depression. For adults it may be a form of symbolic death if the person becomes so cut off that he or she is barely living. Life may literally be threatened if detachment leads, as it sometimes does, to thoughts of suicide.

In the weeks that followed his wife's death, Hank was profoundly sad but did not cry. He told everyone he wanted to remember Wilma in the happy times. His daughters knew that he was not one to cry so they did not press him. As the months went by, however, Hank began to get increasingly depressed. He sat in his recliner chair with the television on but did not seem to care about baseball or the news, his favorite shows. His daughters left meals for him, but would find them still in the freezer when they came back. Most worrisome, Hank withdrew and stopped talking with them. He would answer their questions but when they tried to hug him hello and goodbye, he was rigid and seemed to reject all contact and comfort. Hank was clearly in a detached, tearless depression—a silent, unreachable, and potentially life-threatening state of grief. At that point, his daughters realized that their father was in need of medical help and took him to see his physician.

A Classification of Crying and Inhibited Crying

When less dramatic or less significant losses trigger grief, we may also cry in protest, weep with despair, or go into a dry-eyed state of detachment. We cry in protest to fight acknowledging or accepting a separation or loss or, failing that, to try to hang onto, recover, or fix whatever or whoever is gone, broken, or out of sight. We cry in despair when we realize we cannot do any of these things. We surrender, give up hope, and recognize, sadly, the reality of our loss. Alternatively, we may be dry eyed and feel depressed and alone, seeing no way to restore hope or find other goals, friends, loved ones, or values to replace what has been lost. Each different type of crying (and inhibited crying) has its own unique context and presentation, communicates a particular emotional message, and evokes a different kind of caregiving response from others.

Protest Crying

Things were troubled in the household of Dr. Juvenal Urbino and his wife Fermina Daza, a married couple in the novel *Love in the Time of Cholera* by Gabriel–García Márquez (1988). As Dr. Urbino grieved for the lover whom he had just renounced, he said just enough to his wife that she was able to put all the pieces together. In bed that night, she began to sob with "abundant salty tears that ran down her cheeks and burned her nightdress and inflamed her life ..." (p. 250). The bitter tears that "burned her nightdress" did not bring Fermina Daza any relief from her pain; rather they "inflamed" it more. Nor did her tears elicit any gesture of comfort from her husband. Dr. Urbino could feel, without being told, that these were tears of protest and rage; he "did not dare to console her, knowing that it would have been like consoling a tiger run through by a spear ..." (pp. 249–250).

Because the clear purpose of protest crying is to avoid or undo the loss, the anguish, like Fermina Daza's, has an angry quality, a bitter refusal to surrender to the loss. All the crier's energy goes into re-establishing the threatened connection and fighting any indication that the loss is irrevocable or permanent.

Everyday tears shed in angry protest over a real, symbolic, or threatened loss are a call for action. Angry tears of protest resist the boss's critical remarks and hold them at bay, demanding in their own nonverbal way that this injustice must not continue. Angry crying protests a boyfriend's teasing about his former girlfriend's sex appeal, striking out against the threat to the security of the current relationship and demanding that he stop his banter. A mother's protest cries pressure a cocky teenage son to withdraw his threat to take her car and drive off in a rage.

Tears of protest over everyday losses are what give crying its bad name. They have a hostile and demanding edge. They are the tears that get labeled manipulative because they are designed to evoke action rather than comfort. Protest criers feel the pain of their anger and resistance deeply and they want everyone around them to know about it and do something immediately to make it go away.

Protest crying often breeds resentment and makes friends and family retreat instead of triggering their compassion. Who can feel compassion when he or she is attacked? Who can feel like reaching out to comfort when he or she feels pressured to give in? Protest crying is responsible for most of the interpersonal difficulties experienced with crying. With its bitter, critical, and sometimes accusatory edge, protest crying often pushes people away. They may feel resentful toward the crier or critical of what feels like a ploy to gain attention or control. Often these tears convey anger or blame and are especially difficult because the implicit message to a potential caregiver is: "You are making me cry, so stop what you are doing and do what I want so that I will quit crying."

Jessie started crying when Charles told her he was going to a motorcycle race on their anniversary. "You never think of me and you obviously don't care about our relationship!" she said. Charles got angry instantly and stalked out of the room. The last thing he felt like doing was comforting Jessie because she was blaming him and expecting her tears to change his mind. Jessie's crying was sincere because she did feel pain at Charles' sense of priorities; however, mixing her anger in with tears only made matters worse. Charles left sooner than he had planned and stayed away longer.

Sometimes, however, protest crying works. Charles could have given in because the emotional weight of Jessie's argument was convincing or he could have acquiesced just to avoid dealing with her blame and his guilt. Protest crying in situations like this may be effective at undoing a loss, but at the price of honest communication and intimacy. The resentment and bad feelings, in the end, may represent a loss for both sides. Charles was in a bind. What he felt most like doing was ignoring Jessie's pleas, but when he did that he had to contend with the guilt that dampened his enjoyment of the motorcycle outing. If Jessie had gotten her way, would she have felt better or worse? The only outcome that would have helped her would have been for Charles to reverse his decision convincingly and reassure her that he would far rather spend the day celebrating with her—an unlikely occurrence after the provocation of her protest tears.

Once speech has been mastered, protest is best accomplished with words, even if they are angry or demanding. If Jessie had been able to express her dismay and hurt feelings directly rather than resorting to tears, Charles would have been forced to deal with the issue head on instead of feeling accused and manipulated by her tears. Protest crying, with its demand for caretaking through action, leaves a trail of messy, confusing, and potentially damaging consequences for crier and loved one.

Sad Crying of Despair

Facing a loss means we realize that we cannot turn back time; it does no good to hope that things will turn out differently. We feel desolate and broken; a cold physical pain soaks into every muscle, bone, and fiber of our body. Then a wave of grief overtakes us and we weep tears of a different kind. When we cry in despair over everyday losses, we acknowledge that no happy ending, reunion, or reconciliation is possible. Our pleas of protest have not worked and our efforts have failed; the loss cannot be avoided.

For many months, Beth got extremely angry every time Walt got drunk after work. When he came home slurring his words and reeking of alcohol, she would burst into tears of protest. "How can you do this? You look awful and smell worse! I don't want the kids ever to see you like this." Eventually, however, she realized that Walt had a real problem with alcohol. She stopped being angry and accusatory and became frightened and sad. For several days after her realization she cried, but her feelings and her crying were different. Her protests, anger, and accusations were gone as she faced the real loss implicit in Walt's alcoholism.

In this phase of grief, sad cries of despair are like those of the abandoned infant who has given up on the mother's return. These are tears most often shed in silence. The body slumps over in the universally recognized posture of despair. The crier's face is frequently buried in a pillow, hidden behind the hands, or covered with his or her arms or handkerchief. With these cries, we retreat and face our losses. We take them on rather than resisting them or pushing them away. Someone or something is gone and not coming back. This kind of crying can take us to the other side of loss, back to love and connection. This type of crying can heal and bring us peace and make it possible to hope again. Gradually, we can re-establish a symbolic and internal connection with whomever or whatever has been lost and we find ways to reconfigure our lives, relationships, and goals.

Filmmaker Spike Lee (1991) describes how angry tears of protest and then sad tears of despair followed a failed 1984 movie he made that lost a lot of money and caused him to lose credibility and confidence.

> One day, soon after the ship be sunk, I sat in a bathtub, filled with water, and cried—cried like a baby.... I must have sat in that tub and cried for an hour. I was wrinkled as a raisin when I got out. I rehashed in my mind what happened, what I did wrong. I was a nice guy; why did this f—ed up s— have to happen to me? In retrospect, it happened to me for a reason; it made me stronger and more determined. This experience was my turning point.

In that one long crying experience, Lee moved from protest crying, "Why did this f—ed up s— have to happen to me?" to grieving for the fact that it had happened, but "for a reason" (p. 26). He started with protest but, thankfully for him, did not end up there. Acknowledging the painful presence or permanence of a loss is a necessary part of the healing, reconstituting process.

It is the sad, acknowledging cries of despair that help us get to what Bowlby called "reorganization." Spike Lee called this resolution phase his "turning point," and we know from the steady successes he enjoyed in the years after that tearful experience in the bathtub that he was indeed able to reorganize and move ahead after that initial failure. If he had remained stuck in the protest phase, he might still be waiting to be acknowledged for his genius, rather than moving ahead to refocus his energies and demonstrate his creative gifts.

Unlike protest crying, sad crying in despair touches the hearts of strangers, friends, and loved ones. This kind of crying is so raw and heartfelt that other people cannot help but sympathize and want to reach out with compassion and comfort. I once began to cry after being dropped off at Los Angeles International Airport. I stopped in the women's restroom on my way to the gate, still in tears. I was exhausted from two nights with little sleep but my tears were brought on by more than fatigue or the sadness of this particular farewell. Rather, it was that the entire trip, which was now coming to a close, signaled the end of an era for me, then a young married woman in my 30s. In a concrete-walled restroom filled with harried travelers, three different women felt so concerned about me that they ignored the impersonal surroundings and reached out to comfort me. Without a word spoken, my crying dissolved the barriers between us.

Sad crying of despair does melt hearts and many potential caregivers respond as these three women did. However, crying in despair can sometimes cause discomfort. The ways in which adults and older children respond to each other's sad crying is greatly affected, if not determined, by their early attachment experiences. Some people have difficulty being open to their own pain and loss and find it equally difficult to respond positively to the grief and despair of others.

Social roles and social awkwardness often interfere with empathic caregiving responses as well, especially in independence-biased cultures such as our own. When Ted went into his boss's office to explain that the reason for his recent absences and poor performance was that he was going through a difficult breakup, he began to cry. His boss, immediately uncomfortable, stammered quickly "I'll leave you alone here for a few minutes" and left Ted sitting there, embarrassed, trying hastily to compose himself. The come-hither message of crying in despair is an intimate one that can easily overburden social relationships in more formal, detached settings. Ted's boss told a colleague he thought Ted needed to contain his emotions more at work. His colleague disagreed and said that he was the one who needed to take an employee-relations seminar so that he could learn to be a little more understanding of his supervisees' feelings.

Individuals often shy away from their roles as comforter, listener, or consoler by changing the subject, resorting to platitudes or false reassurances, or rushing to try to "fix" whatever has been lost or threatened. Instead of bringing the needed comfort, crying in these instances brings separation and distance. It is not surprising that many people prefer to cry in solitude to avoid discomfort—their own and that of those around them.

Inhibited Crying: Detached Type

When people do not cry at all during times of extreme loss, it is difficult to figure out exactly what is going on because tearlessness can signal a variety of different responses. Tearlessness is problematic for people who are withdrawn and detached at the time of a significant loss. Other noncriers, however, are open to their feelings of sadness and loss and find healing ways to express them without tears.

Max and his fellow emergency medics spent an evening talking about an infant they were unable to save from a burning car on the freeway. Most of them cried and some felt Max was too stoic. He told them he felt no urge to cry, but he did speak clearly about his frustration as they went over their unsuccessful efforts to save the child. He connected his feelings about losing this little boy with his concern for his own sons. He wanted to get home as soon as possible and hold his boys in his arms. A few days later, Max told his coworkers that he had an idea that might help all of them get through their grief. They could raise money for a playground and name it after the baby. Max never shed a tear but he was able nonetheless to go from protest to despair and, finally, to healing.

To do this, noncriers must be able to recognize and acknowledge their loss, pain, and sadness. They must also accept words or gestures of comfort so that they do not get emotionally cut off from those who care about them. Writing a sad poem, singing a sad song, or asking a lover for a comforting hug can help a noncrier get through the grieving process with a deepened sense of closeness to friends and loved ones.

We need to be concerned, however, for the noncrier who is emotionally frozen and unable to reach out to others. Such a reaction can stall the grieving process and signal deep depression. Unlike infants' withdrawal and detachment when they are not attached to a nurturing caregiver, adult detachment is hard to diagnose, particularly if there has not been an obvious loss. Even then, it is possible to miss the cues before they become severe.

Crying is so close to the core of our deepest and earliest wounds that feelings about it may trigger great pain and anxiety. Sharon, the cancer patient mentioned earlier, is a good example of a person whose defenses and vulnerabilities are best respected rather than forcing her grief into the open at a time of loss. Support may be given verbally or care may be offered, as I did with Sharon, by suggesting ways in which she might distract herself from her grief and find comfort in her daily routines and relationships. Concern that tearless withdrawal is really clinical depression will suggest a different course of action—a professional evaluation and possibly medication—rather than merely encouraging tears.

CHAPTER **4**

Crying at the Source
The First 12 Months

As a therapist, immersing myself in trying to understand infant crying has been of the utmost importance clinically. It has meant that I have a window not only into the roots of my adult patients' crying behavior, but also into their early caregiving and care-receiving experiences. As I observe crying, caregiving, and care-receiving within the context of the therapeutic relationship and in narrative reports from patients' lives, I can feel (as well as think) my way into a sense of whether their attachments are secure or insecure. This in turn suggests the kinds of early parenting they may have received. Instead of relying on a linear, piecemeal unfolding of data, I find instead a gestalt of early experience that lingers in the attachment sphere of the adult and finds its way directly into the here and now of the clinical hour.

Paralleling the patient's attachment issues and strengths are those of the therapist. The attachment and caregiving systems of therapist and patient intertwine, encompassing the present and the past, conscious and unconscious, of both partners in the therapeutic dialogue. In order to function effectively, therapists must have a deep understanding of their caregiving, care-receiving, crying, and attachment styles. Although personal psychotherapy is crucial for reaching this level of self-awareness, reading about infant crying and parental caregiving also provides a framework for self-understanding. With that, the therapist is ready to apply himself or herself to the ongoing task of simultaneously participating in and observing the therapeutic relationship in general and crying in particular.

The Meaning of Infant Crying

Human infants know viscerally that they must link up with a caregiving adult or they will die. For such small, weak, and helpless creatures, they are not at all demure about going after what they need. Moment by moment they register safety or danger from within their own bodies or in their environment and then act accordingly—peaceful if secure, crying if threatened. The cries are distress calls to caregivers conveying in no uncertain terms, "Come here; I need you."

Within a few weeks after birth, babies begin to monitor carefully the presence or absence of people around them, treating absence of the caregiver as the threat to safety that it is. The classic study of infant crying by Bell and Ainsworth (1972) found that during the first 3 months, almost three-quarters of the babies' cries began when the mother was out of physical proximity or physical contact.

Even at 5 to 6 weeks of age, infants clearly register the comings and goings of caregivers and on many occasions—perhaps more than caregivers realize—start to cry at the leave-takings and stop crying when the caregiver reappears. One researcher (Wolff, 1969) slowly circled around contented 1- to 2-month-olds who were on the floor in an infant seat that limited their visibility to what was directly in front of them. When the researcher walked behind them out of view, the infants began to fuss and cry. When the person reappeared, the crying stopped. If the sequence was repeated too many times—three or more—the baby's distress would not abate even when the person was in view. Separations, especially repeated separations, stress infants and trigger the crying that is the part of their attachment system from birth designed to ensure that caregivers come back and stay with them until security is restored.

I recently reviewed a research video that showed a split-screen, synchronized father–infant interaction. They were engaged in face-to-face play with smiling and funny nonverbal exchanges until the moment at which the researchers told the father to avert his face. Almost instantly, the infant looked deflated, bewildered, and upset. As the seconds ticked by, the baby became increasingly distraught, looking all around and then focusing in on both hands, trying to self-soothe. The father continued to sit in the same place but the fact that his child could not see his face was sufficient to cause this obvious separation distress. Crying was averted when the father finally was allowed to re-engage.

Baby crying, like crying throughout life, is not simply a generic distress signal. No matter the source of the distress, infant crying is first and foremost a plea for the caregiver's presence. Physical proximity or contact is an obvious prerequisite for nurturance and soothing. Even if crying is initiated while the infant is in direct physical contact with the caregiver, the message is still a plea for some assistance. Crying means it is not all right to go away now because the caregiver is needed to restore equilibrium and security. By crying, babies make their need for the caregiver's presence painfully obvious, although parents in their zeal to get at the secondary distress, such as wet diapers or teething pain, may overlook the obvious one. The generic message, "I need *you*," precedes the particular message, "I need a dry diaper, pacifier, or another blanket."

Infant Cries and Caregivers' Responses: A Cross-Cultural View

In Western cultures, baby cries are often treated as a particularly frustrating form of nonverbal communication, which is to be decoded as quickly and efficiently as possible. In other cultures, infant crying is treated differently. During my tenure as a Peace Corps volunteer in Nigeria, I noticed that infants there almost never cried. No matter what the mothers were doing—pounding yams, selling headcloths at the market, or bouncing along in the crowded lorries—their infants accompanied them, securely tied on their backs with a long cloth tie. At any sign of infant tension—waking up, squirming, making noises, or the slightest whimper—the mothers deftly swung the little ones around in front and proceeded to nurse them, rarely skipping a beat in their activity.

I was impressed by the absence of crying and interpreted it as a sign of the mothers being extraordinarily attuned to their infants' needs and less concerned about getting their babies to conform to schedules. Later I learned that in some Nigerian tribes crying is thought to be a signal from spirit children calling the newborn to come out of this world back to them. Rather than being seen as a survival behavior, crying is viewed as threatening the infant with death. Apparently the line of reasoning that infant crying is dangerous to the infant occurs in a number of cultures around the world: Hindu mothers in India, the Kagwahiv of Brazil, a Trobriand Island tribe, to name some mentioned in the anthropological literature. Public health nurses who tried to convince Bedouin mothers that some infant crying is all right were met with firm resistance: "We Bedouin can't let an infant cry."

Infant crying would have been considered "dangerous" in what Bowlby and others called an "environment of evolutionary adaptiveness" (the environment to which human survival mechanisms are adapted) because it not only alerts caregivers but also tips off predators—human and otherwise—that a vulnerable unattended infant is nearby. Margaret Mead suggested that extremely responsive nurturing may also help increase survival in groups with high risk of infant mortality. In the study mentioned earlier, Nancy Scheper-Hughes (1992) found that the opposite may also be true: high infant mortality may interfere with maternal responsiveness as mothers learn to distance themselves and withhold caregiving from an infant whose survival they consider unlikely.

Infants around the world share common needs at birth; however, a multiplicity of caregiving styles is represented in different cultures. Caregiving practices fall into two major groups: those in which mothers carry their infants continually, sleep with them at night, and feed them several times an hour; and those who carry their infants sporadically, put them in separate beds and rooms from birth, and feed them at spaced intervals.

The southwest African Zung/Twasi who nurse infants as often as twice an hour for from 30 seconds to 10 minutes (Konner, 1972) are in the former group. Typically, mothers who carry their nursing infants attached to their bodies at all times during the day also sleep with them at night. This is the case in Uganda where, as Mary Ainsworth (1967) noted, mothers would feed their babies up to five times per night without seeming to give it a second thought.

Caregivers may presume that infant crying represents an emergency such as pain or illness when the primary infant stressor of being alone is eliminated by constant carrying and lesser stresses, such as being hungry or thirsty, are removed by frequent nursing. Parental caregiving responses then can immediately move into an urgent mode. Caregivers do not first need to rule out the everyday separations and physical stressors that have an impact on infants who are fed only every few hours and carried only 1 to 2 hours per day.

The Causes of Infant Cries

I have been interested to note the changes in discussions of infant crying in parenting manuals and magazines over the years. Until recently, virtually all of the attention has been focused on causes that are immediate and literal manifestations of primarily physical distress. Every list includes the basic six, all of which are physiological: hunger, pain, temperature (too cold or hot), wet diaper, fatigue, and lack of clothing. The more expanded though still physiologically based lists also mention colic, transitions from sleep to wakefulness (and vice versa), milk or formula sensitivities, illness, loss of support (falling), swallowing air, passing urine or feces, thirst, and noxious stimuli such as bitter tastes and loud noises.

The items that comprise what might be called "emotional" causes require a lot of empathic guesswork and the list, when there is one, is considerably shorter: overstimulation (baby stress), fear, boredom, loneliness, frustration, protest, and wanting attention. If we look closely at this last group, we see hints of the underlying reason for crying from an attachment viewpoint in the categories of "loneliness" and "wanting attention," and perhaps in some of the others such as boredom or frustration as well.

All of the causes on these lists must, of course, be derived by adults working backward from what makes the baby stop crying—what attachment theorists call the "terminators" of crying. Of course, it is easier to determine that food stops crying than to know when "giving attention" works. In fact, "giving attention" is a part of all behaviors that terminate crying, as is the presence of the caregiver.

By far the most consistent cause of crying in infants—in some studies it has been the largest category—is listed variously as crying for "no reason" or for "unknown reasons" or simply "none of the above." By omitting the infant's need for parental proximity and holding, this kind of list is ambiguous for parents and supports a climate of misattunement to infants that was reinforced by the social milieu until the 1970s, when attachment theory began to have an impact on parenting advice.

Infant Cries and Caregivers' Responses: The Social View

Infants cannot "unlearn" attachment behavior and survive, but parental caregiving behavior, even if it does have some biological, hormonal basis, is regularly affected by culture, experience, and conscious decision. By the time adults become parents, they have experienced, learned, read, and observed much. They have also formed opinions, even "philosophies," of child rearing.

In a study, Peter Wolff (1969) found that when 3-week-old infants began to cry with a low pitch and intensity, many mothers identified those cries as "faking." These mothers were not necessarily insensitive but rather informed by a culture in which physiological distress was validated and babies were forgiven for this kind of crying because they could not yet voice their needs in words. Crying for attention, however, was considered faking (or a nuisance or manipulation) instead of an expression of that most basic of human needs: contact and connection. This view unfortunately persists even in the present: I heard from a new mother recently that her pediatrician told her that her 3-month-old baby was "manipulating" her by crying when put down to sleep. Hunger, pain, wet diapers, chilly or hot temperatures, loud noises, and bright lights are considered legitimate, but not the need for human contact—a touch, a voice, or a cuddle.

A former patient, Eleanor, was diligently reviewing her parenting behavior at a time in therapy when she was struggling to understand possible antecedents for a badly deteriorated relationship with her grown daughter.

Within the first few days of bringing her home from the hospital, she recalled deciding that little Betty should not be allowed to cry for "no reason." Consequently, when her daughter began to cry even though she was freshly diapered and fed, in a comfortable position, and at a comfortable temperature with no errant diaper pins or other apparent problems, Eleanor clamped her hand over Betty's mouth and said sharply, "Stop it!"

The visual image vivid in Eleanor's mind after more than 20 years was of Betty's eyes bulging open with a look of shock and fear. Before she was 1 week old, Betty had, according to Eleanor, stopped "crying for no reason." Eleanor added with tinges of regret, "Of course, no one told me that sometimes babies just need to cry." No one had told her that babies always have a reason for crying and that the reason is to have their parents pick them up, hold them, and then try to figure out what *else* is needed if the crying persists.

Bell and Ainsworth (1972) found that parents varied widely in responding to infant cries—from instantly to quickly, slowly, or not at all. The most responsive mother (during the infant's first 3 months) ignored 4% of her infant's cries and the least responsive ignored 97%. At 9 to 12 months, the median for ignoring had declined to 37% while the top ignoring score was down to 63%. The group of parents who tended to ignore their infant's cries and the group of those who responded more promptly stayed consistent over the first year, however. This was the landmark study that found that infants whose cries were ignored early on cried more than those whose cries were responded to promptly. This study refuted the then-popular advice to parents that said not to pick up a crying child for fear of spoiling, and behavioral theory, which said that picking up a crying child would teach them to cry more.

Thanks to Ainsworth's (and other attachment researchers') findings, child-care manuals since the late 1970s and early 1980s uniformly encourage parents to respond promptly to all cries of infants under 6 months of age. A current Internet advice column for parents by Anne Beal (2004), a pediatric instructor at Harvard Medical School, says that baby crying may mean, "I want to be held," even though it is fourth on the list of causes after hunger, wet diaper, and too cold or hot. She adds, "Babies need a lot of cuddling…. After being fed, burped, and changed, many babies simply want to be held. You may wonder if you'll 'spoil' your child by holding her so much, but during the first few months of life there's no such thing."

On the other hand, I was dismayed to see an advertisement for an electronic baby crying decoder, also on the Internet. The only categories the device claims to be able to discern are: hunger, boredom, discomfort, sleepiness, and stress. For the $200 that parents would need to spend on this gadget, I would wish for some acknowledgement that babies sometimes need their mom or dad *period*, not just to have a specific problem fixed.

I love watching young mothers and fathers where I live in Berkeley, California. These days they all seem to keep their young infants snuggled close to their bodies in a variety of slings, mostly attached to the front of the body rather than the back like the mothers I remember from Nigeria. Books and parenting classes, I learn from my patients who are young mothers, stress the importance of as much physical contact as possible, including what is sometimes referred to as "cosleeping." I also hear, however, that mothers who follow these precepts with zeal are often criticized by older family members and other young parents who adhere to the more usual traditions associated with early independence training. The specter of "spoiling" has not left the realm of parenting lore and folk wisdom. I also hear sad stories from young parents who decide to try one of the complicated formulas for letting infants cry through their resistance to sleeping. Many of them report sitting on the floor outside their child's door crying themselves.

The Neurobiology of Attachment

In the last decade, new discoveries relating to the neurobiology of attachment provide visible evidence in PET scans and fMRIs of the importance of early attachment/caregiving experiences on the brain development of infants. Perhaps these data will at long last put to rest the residual concerns about overgratifying infants under the age of 6 months, which is a critical period in neurological development that has an impact on the ability to attach and to regulate affect throughout life. As Allan Schore (2003) writes: "… the postnatal growth of the brain is essentially influenced by events at the interpersonal and intrapersonal levels, attachment experiences, face-to-face transactions between caregiver and infant …." These in turn "directly influence the imprinting, the circuit wiring of this system" (p. 14).

The impact of exchanges between infant and caregiver in moments of positive affect has been shown in study after study.

> Dynamically fluctuating moment-to-moment state-sharing represents an organized dialog occurring within milliseconds, and acts as an interactive matrix in which both partners match states and then simultaneously adjust their social attention, stimulation, and accelerating arousal in response to the partner's signals. In this mutually synchronized attunement of emotionally driven facial expression, prosodic vocalization, and kinesic behaviors, the

dyad coconstructs a mutual regulatory system of arousal ... (Schore, 2003, p. 96).

Although Schore is here referring to attunement and regulation of *positive* arousal—the smiles, coos, and gazes exchanged by caregiver and infant—the same process occurs in relationship to crying. The caregiver must meet and match the negative arousal with attuned facial expressions, vocalizations, and touch within milliseconds in order to soothe the infant effectively. Such exchanges consistently given over time lead to the development of a secure attachment bond and, according to these new findings, enable the individual to regulate negative affect throughout life, whether interactively in relationships with others or by secure self-regulation.

According to Schore (1994), "the language of mother and infant consists of signals produced by the autonomic, involuntary nervous system in both partners" (p. 105). Two studies have looked at the fMRIs of breastfeeding mothers (Lorberbaum et al., 2002) and nonbreastfeeding mothers, fathers, and nonparents (Seifritz et al., 2003) as they listened to an audiotape of an infant crying. In the case of the breastfeeding mothers, changes shown in areas of the brain were hypothesized to be related to maternal behavior. In the second study (Seifritz et al., 2003) comparing mothers, fathers, and nonparents, "both sex- and experience-dependent modulation of brain response to infant vocalizations" (p. 1367) were found.

Crying, which represents arousal in the infant, creates matching arousal in the caregiver. The caregiver's neurological input is necessary for soothing infant *and* caregiver; their two systems of arousal and soothing are interconnected. What I have been referring to as the "visceral" and the "subjective" responses of caregivers to crying infants is now demonstrably literal. With the emerging findings regarding the neurobiology of attachment, the developmental line between infant crying and crying throughout life (and caregiving throughout life as well) also becomes increasingly clear.

The Frequency of Infant Crying

Parents, as well as child-care professionals, teachers, and child therapists, would benefit from some normative data about the frequency of crying in infancy. Parents in particular have a very small sample—one, if it is their first child and they are not experienced with infants—from which to draw conclusions. As a consequence, some parents overlook excessive crying while others over-react to normal amounts. Studies of the amount of infant crying show averages ranging from 96 to 135 minutes per day.

On behalf of parents dealing with a single baby, it is important to note that these statistical averages represent a wide range of individual scores, from a few minutes a day to hours.

The preceding figures come from studies based on parental reports when minutes may feel like hours. A small study using a sound-activated tape recorder came up with more modest though still impressive figures during the 24-hour periods during which they recorded every other week. At 6 to 7 weeks (the age when crying peaks in cultures in which infants are not carried continually) the average amount of crying was 34 minutes a day; the range for individual infants spread from 7 to 77 minutes (Rebelsky, 1972).

The cry frequency curve—along with the diurnal pattern (over the course of a day) of increased infant crying in the evening—is the second maturational constant found throughout all the research on Western infants. From birth through the first 6 weeks, there is a consistent increase in crying. At that point, it levels off and remains at that plateau until 12 weeks of age. This typical 3-month cry frequency curve, as was mentioned earlier, seems to disappear in studies in which additional infant carrying is introduced. In one study (Hunziker & Barr, 1986), baseline crying data were collected for a study group and a control group of infants and parents. Then parents in the study group were instructed to carry their infants in their arms or a carrier at least 3 hours a day above and beyond that required by feeding and bathing. All the infants began with a similar crying frequency—from 1.7 to 1.8 hours a day—but the babies in the extra-carrying group showed an atypical downward curve in frequency over the first 12 weeks. Their crying decreased to 1 hour per day by week 12. The supplemental carrying group also fussed less in the early evening.

Individual Differences in Attachment Behavior

Caregivers differ in how promptly and effectively they respond to infant cries. Infants also differ in their thresholds for the activation of attachment behavior. Some infants cry at every loud noise; others simply become alert and get a little serious. Some infants cry a lot and some relatively little. Speaking from personal experience, some also cry more loudly than others (my loud-crying infant is now a rock singer and my less loud-crying infant is a nurse practitioner); acoustic studies show that volume is primarily related to size: the greater the weight, the louder the baby. Decibel measures of infant crying show averages in the 80s, but the individual range goes from 80 to 120 dB. Adult speech by comparison is 72 dB, adult screams are in the 90s, and rock music can get up to about 130 dB (Gustafson & Green, 1994; Ostwald, 1973; Wasz–Höckert, Lind,

Vuorenkoski, Partanen, & Valanne, 1968), which explains why my daughter Cynthia sometimes wears earplugs at her own concerts.

Neurologically at-risk infants have cry sounds that are more disturbing than their counterparts. In fact, in the days before CT scans and other modern diagnostic techniques, an impressive body of research on the acoustics of infant cries existed (Lester & Boukydis, 1985; Wasz–Höckert et al., 1968). It focused on two distinct questions: whether infant cries could be discriminated in terms of cause (hunger, pain, or birth cries) and whether they could be distinguished diagnostically in the case of infectious diseases, physical anomalies, or central nervous system disorders.

Acoustical research using sound spectrograph data first determined that every infant has a distinct "cry-print," which accounts, in part, for the finding that mothers are able to identify their own infants by cry alone almost immediately after birth (Gustafson & Green, 1994). Distinguishing pain cries from hunger cries, and the birth cry is also possible acoustically, but because of other variables (such as crying due to separation), it was not easy for adult subjects to distinguish between types of cry. The one exception was the pain cry, which, because of its sharp, loud features, imparts an urgent message. Infants with certain physiological disorders, do however, have acoustically different cries that, when recognized, could alert parents and physicians to their difficulties (Wasz–Höckert, Michelsson, & Lind, 1985).

Infants also vary in how easy they are to soothe once crying begins. At one end of the continuum are those able to self-soothe on some occasions or who calm to the sound of the mother's voice alone. Other infants, however, consistently require holding and rocking to terminate their crying. These individual differences from birth raise the question of temperamental differences in crying that may stem from genetic predispositions.

The relationship among temperament, attachment behavior, and caregiving is an important one for understanding crying in infancy and throughout life. The maternal/paternal/infant fit is, of course, affected by the infant's propensity to arousal. In turn, the infant's soothability has a severe impact on the parents. There are, of course, many unanswered questions about the source of temperamental differences.[1] However, the primary fact to keep in mind clinically is that there are differences among how much, how long, how easily, and how often infants cry, as well as how readily and successfully they can be soothed. This information is important in advising parents and in treating adults who manifest or report attachment/caregiving difficulties.

The cries of infants who have been abused or neglected have been noted to be high-pitched, irritating, or excessive. It is, of course, impossible to determine causation here: do abuse and neglect alter the cry or do highly aversive cries increase the risk of abuse? One supposes that either situation (or both) could occur because low birthweight and premature babies are over-represented in the population of failure-to-thrive and abused infants.

Lester and Zeskind (1979), who studied the abnormal cry sounds of "at risk" infants (some with physical problems), believe that the acoustical properties of their cries carry a greater sense of urgency and need. They theorize that "difficult" cries are there for a good survival reason: the baby needs more help. Optimally, these more demanding cry sounds bring about increased or qualitatively different interventions by the parents that enhance the infant's chances of recovery.

I met with the family of Jason, a young boy born with a severe neurological condition. As they recalled the stresses of his first year they remembered that back then Jason had only two states: asleep and crying. For a solid year, they were exposed to his crying almost constantly during their own waking hours and during some of the night as well. All of the family remembered the stress well, but the love and compassion they expressed for their son and little brother was moving. The two brothers closest to Jason in age expressed heartfelt wishes that he could again come home to live because they missed him so much and wanted to play with him and help take care of him. Jason's crying day after day was a constant and familiar aspect of their preschool years, but instead of leading to resentment and rejection, it deepened their empathy for their little brother.

Infant Crying and Child Abuse

Excessive crying is the reason cited by 80% of parents who batter a child of less than 1 year (Weston, 1968). Of 1400 parents surveyed in Britain and Australia, 1 in 10 had hit or shaken the baby violently or gripped it too tightly because of unsoothable crying (Kitzinger, 1989). A similar New Zealand survey of mothers' feelings about infant crying found that 80% of the women felt like "bashing" their babies. When asked, "What did baby do to make you feel like this?" the answer was "cry" (Kirkland, Deane, & Brennan, 1983). A *Washington Post* (Addenda, 1994) article noted that manslaughter charges had been brought against a woman who used an electric stun gun to silence a baby because "he cried throughout the night" (p. A-18).

Abusive caregivers, rather than attuning and soothing, intensify their infant's negative arousal. If, for example, a mother expresses loud frustration at a crying infant, the negative affect escalates. Beebe (as cited in Schore, 2003) observed: "Each one escalates the ante, as the infant builds to a frantic distress, may scream, and, in this example, finally throws up. In an escalating overarousal pattern, even after extreme distress signals from the infant, such as ninety-degree head aversion, arching away … or screaming, the mother keeps going" (p. 282).

One study (Frodi & Lamb, 1980) looked at a small sample of abusing and nonabusing mothers who were shown a 6-minute video of an infant (not their own). During the first and last 2-minute segments, the infant was quiet and alert. In the middle segment, the infant was crying (adjusted to 70 dB on the tape) or smiling. The two groups were monitored for heart rate, skin conductance, and blood pressure at the beginning and end of each segment. After the video, they were given a checklist of positive and negative mood adjectives to rate their feelings and attitudes during the smiling and crying segments.

Abusive mothers were more annoyed by and less sympathetic toward the crying infant and that was true for the smiling baby as well. The abusing mothers also showed physical signs of heightened tension in response to crying and to smiling infants, whereas the nonabusing mothers showed physical tension only when viewing the crying child.

Because of their wounded attachments and early caretaking experiences, abusing parents lose or lack the empathic response to the child's distress and become overwhelmed. Their distress outweighs the infant's. The feeling is that the crying must stop because it upsets them, rather than because the baby is upset. Other parents have an initial empathic response to their child's cries but may also eventually reach a point at which empathy for the baby turns into their own pain and suffering (Frodi, 1985). To a certain extent, all parents can relate to that feeling. I know I remember crying a few times when I was weary and frustrated at being unable to soothe one of my daughters. In those moments, my attachment behavior was activated by the unrelenting demands of theirs. It is a time when one is especially grateful for a support system and the presence of alternate caregivers.

Parents who become abusive in response to infant cries share certain psychological characteristics. They may assign age-inappropriate motivations, even to newborns, such as declaring that the baby has a terrible temper or is crying to get his or her own way. The infant may also be imbued with adult-like power and judgment so that the parents describe feeling rejected by the crying infant, or criticized or accused of incompetence. I once saw a mother tell her 14-month-old son that she was going to the store. When he screamed, "No," she shot back at him with the words, "Don't sass me back." She saw his normal protest at separation as a willful negation of her stated intention.

Psychoanalyst M.N. Searl (1963) wrote that parents experience a "boomerang" effect because their infants' cries stimulate deep memories of their own cries and, by implication, the responses that they did or did not receive from caregivers. The met and unmet attachment needs of the parents' infancy come alive again in the unsoothable cries of their infants. If parents were abused by their caregivers, they may then be overwhelmed by their own distress, anger, and frustration and strike out at the infant when she or he cries.

One woman I saw in long-term psychotherapy recalled that the crying of her infant son many years before had disturbed her "to the core." Her first thought when he began to cry was to take him back to the hospital and the second was to throw him out the window—fantasies she resisted by holding him tightly against her body.

She also was plagued by images of someone violently shaking a crying baby. She could recall her father's cruelty and intolerance for her crying throughout childhood and we speculated that his reactions to her crying in infancy had been equally harsh and possibly even violent. When she shared this theory with her brother, he said that he had not made the connection with their childhood treatment, but confided that he had manhandled his crying baby son on several occasions; on many other occasions, he had left the house because he could not stand his son's crying and feared becoming abusive.

The Development of Crying in the First Year

According to John Bowlby (1969), the development of attachment behavior is "slow and complex" with a lot of individual variation. Even accounting for individual variation, however, he writes that in most mammalian species the shifts in attachment behavior "exhibited from one phase of the life cycle to the next occur in a remarkably regular and predictable way despite variations in the environment" (p. 144).

During the first year of life, crying changes dramatically, not only in frequency and timing, but also in what causes it and what makes it stop. In fact, what works to soothe at one stage may actually cause crying at another stage. For the first 3 months, a baby will behave toward any caring person in the same way: looking, grasping, reaching, smiling, and babbling. When babies that age are crying, hearing any voice, seeing any face, or being picked up by any person will soothe them, although they do recognize and prefer the mother's smell, voice, and touch. Crying, like smiling, is initially indiscriminate; the signals are sent to any warm body in the vicinity. Peter Wolff (1969) filmed the first-time meeting between a

5½-month-old and his grandmother. She took over the feeding from the mother as soon as she came into the house and the infant boy ate, smiled, and played as happily with the totally unfamiliar grandmother as he had earlier with his own mother.

By age 6 months, however, infants know and greatly prefer their familiar caregivers. They can track the caregiver's movements by sight and sound and they direct their cries as well as their smiles to those familiar few. After 6 months, crying may only be relieved by the sound, sight, or touch of that specific person. Unfamiliar people, instead of being potential soothers, may actually trigger crying. Not all infants cry when a stranger approaches (23% in one study), but most become alert and show curiosity or fear.

By the time an infant can crawl (about 34 weeks), indiscriminate responses to other people have ended and caution occurs with strangers. This makes sense from a survival standpoint because crawling is the first physical opportunity the infant has to depart from the caregiver's presence on his or her own. Crawling also enables infants to go after a departing caregiver. When given "floor freedom" (Kitzinger, 1989) in one study, 49% of the infants crawled after their departing mothers. Only 22.5% of them cried when she walked away, though another 14.8% cried when they caught up to her, usually appealing to be picked up as well.

What I found especially interesting and upsetting was that when the self-locomoting infants in this same study approached their mother and gave the arms-up signal to appeal for pick-up, close to half of them were ignored or rejected—even though the caregivers knew that they were being observed. At a lecture, infant researcher Daniel Stern showed a video in which a single pick-up appeal was overlooked by the mother. It was a sad and poignant sight to see the baby on the floor lifting her little arms up toward her mother and being ignored. Yet this is apparently what happens a great deal of the time in the experience of many infants.

Another change in crying patterns occurs in the second half of the first year: instead of crying more when they are alone as they do in the early months of life, infants at that age cry more when their caregiver is near. (Slightly older children will even postpone crying after a fall until they have returned to their mother's presence.) Crying in late infancy and childhood is thus specifically directed to the caregiver. It may be that, from an evolutionary survival standpoint, it makes more sense for self-locomoting children to cry in proximity to the caregiver because by then they are able to wander away on their own and cries might alert predators.

Parents, of course, must make some developmental changes of their own during their child's first year. Immediately postpartum, many mothers are also crying more easily (apparently due to drastic hormonal changes),

which may help to facilitate the brain-to-brain connection between mother and infant. By 3 to 5 months after birth, crying decreases for mother and baby. Attunement, rhythms, and schedules begin to stabilize. Mutually reading cues is easier and soothing techniques are more reliable.

Once a child is crawling and walking, communication with the caregiver is more visual than tactile (Schore, 1994). The primary way in which the infant monitors safety and danger is through the mother's face. Her tone of voice and words also serve to communicate across a distance to prevent undue arousal or to soothe if the infant steers off course or begins to get overwhelmed.

After the child is self-locomoting, caregiving has a new dimension because the infant must be protected from harm. If removed from a particularly inviting houseplant or brightly colored detergent box, the infant may begin to cry. This is a new experience for parents accustomed to soothing all cries, not causing them. It is similarly a shocking change for the infant accustomed to attuned responses when he gets excited about a special toy or shiny object. When he checks Mom's face expectantly, he finds instead of shared pleasure and excitement a dark expression combining perhaps fear, anger, or disgust and barked words such as "Don't touch Mommy's plant" or "No! No! Give me that nasty old soap box." These new developments necessitate a drastic transition for infants and their caregivers. This is the developmental milestone that marks the onset of shame.

Secure and Insecure Attachment

Working from John Bowlby's theories about separation and attachment behavior, Margaret Ainsworth (Ainsworth, Blehar, Waters, & Wall, 1978) devised a brilliant research design (much replicated in the intervening years by researchers in many parts of the world) called "The Strange Situation." Its purpose is to measure the presence and quality of the attachment bond based on the reaction of 12-month-olds in a laboratory setting to two separations and two reunions, and the introduction of a stranger with and without the parent present. The idea is to stress the infants sufficiently to activate the attachment system but not enough to traumatize them. To do this, parents and infants are introduced to a playroom where they are exposed to seven 3-minute segments alternating separations, reunions, and the introduction of a stranger.

The infant's behavior during the entire transaction is important. Mild crying during the separations or when left alone with the stranger is considered a sign of attachment because it means that the baby misses the mother. By no means do all of the infants cry (even the securely attached ones), so crying is not used to measure quality of attachment. Rather, the focus is on the baby's reactions at reunion. Reunion behavior turns out to be the key variable in determining whether the attachment bond is secure or insecure.

Ainsworth and her colleagues classified infant attachment bonds as belonging to one of three groups: secure, insecure avoidant, and insecure ambivalent/resistant. Main and Solomon (1990) later identified another type of insecure attachment, which they called disorganized/disoriented:

- Secure infants were noted to show signs of missing the parent during the separations but did not become unduly upset. At reunion they would smile, vocalize, and gesture and, if upset, seek physical contact and be soothed easily and quickly.
- The avoidant group showed little reaction to separation. They did not protest by crying. At reunion, the infants looked away from or even avoided the parent. If picked up, they stiffened or pulled away and often showed more interest in the toys than in the parent.
- The ambivalent/resistant group was the most upset by the separations and at reunion would alternate between seeking and rejecting contact. They could not be comforted or soothed by the parent even if they were picked up.
- The disorganized/disoriented group showed just that: at separations, they showed interrupted movements or frozen behavior. At reunion they might show active fear of the parent, confusion, or disorientation.[2] One disorganized infant, for example, described by Main and Solomon (as cited in Schore, 2003) "hunched her upper body and shoulders at hearing her mother's call, then broke into extravagant laugh-like screeches with an excited forward movement. Her braying laughter became a cry and distress-face without a new intake of breath as the infant hunched forward. Then suddenly she became silent, blank, and dazed" (p. 250).

The attachment/caregiving experiences of secure and insecure caregiver–infant dyads are very different. The mothers of secure infants are open to the child who seeks proximity at reunion and respond appropriately and promptly to emotional expressions. They demonstrate to the child that they are available and accessible if the child is stressed or crying. They also help to keep the child's arousal from stress within a moderate range and successfully attune when shame-inducing misattunements arise from socialization. They facilitate successful interactive repair before shame and stress can overwhelm the infant.

Mothers of insecure ambivalent/resistant infants actually seem to amplify their infant's affective arousal and crying rather than sensitively and appropriately helping to reduce the stimulation. They are inconsistent in permitting the infant access at reunion; sometimes they will scoop up the child with exaggerated comfort and at other times reject or dismiss the baby. The insecure, avoidant mothers, on the other hand, show consistently low levels of affective response to their infants. They withdraw or are distant or reluctant to engage the infant, whether crying or smiling, and may discourage or even block access in response to proximity-seeking behavior. Mothers of disorganized/disoriented infants tend toward disorganization or disorientation. They may be hostile or abusive with crying infants or they may show fear or confusion.

Babies as Teachers

Understanding infant crying is a case of letting ourselves remember and letting babies teach us. Their most important lesson is that crying is more about relationship than it is about distress. Attachment and caregiving are complementary partnership behaviors. The responses to early cry signals—how prompt, how kind, how attuned to infant needs rather than parental needs, how close, how warm, how gentle, how successful, how consistent—color our experiences of intimacy throughout life. These caregiving responses also color our feelings about crying and our ability to soothe and be soothed.

Infants also teach us that we are more likely to cry when we are vulnerable due to illness, fatigue, repeated stress, trauma, or isolation, because then we most need connection to feel secure and loved. Sometimes we need it just to survive. Infants help to remind us that crying always involves our bodies as well as our minds. Infants teach us to respect individual differences while at the same time appreciating the commonality of who we are at birth. We have cultural and family differences but all infants share with each other and with adults the need for human connection. We also share in the unfolding of crying development during the early years of our lives, moving on parallel tracks as our hormones and nervous systems, as well as our cognitive abilities, grow and mature.

Infants also help us to realize the importance of our social values and their influence on our most basic physical and emotional needs. We tilt heavily toward independence in this culture rather than toward community. The values and views of our cultures influence how we interpret and respond to our infants' needs. Infants teach us great respect for the way in which we are born and how we learn to survive and thrive.

Through responses to their crying behavior, infants learn about caregiving and connection at the deepest level of the psyche and, as research now shows, in the deepest levels of the brain structure. Children, however, learn about crying and not crying as social behavior and begin to internalize the attitudes of those around them. With increased cognitive development and observational skills, crying becomes a conscious behavior, something that children do and about which they have feelings.

When therapists see adults, they see people who have established attachment styles, whether secure or insecure. A deep understanding of how these styles manifest in infancy and what the typical caregiver's role represents in relation to each style gives the therapist a more precise way to understand the dynamics of people in all their close relationships, including the therapeutic relationship. Are they secure and confident that others will be there for them and with them? Do they demonstrate insecurity by being worried, anxious, clingy, and weepy on the one hand and difficult to comfort and soothe on the other? Are they detached, well defended against any neediness, and resistant to empathy, sympathy, or comfort? Do they present as "all over the map" in terms of intimate relationships: abusing or being abused, fearful, intimidated, aggressive or dominating, or passive and victimized?

Based on the way in which adult patients present their relationship issues, we can theorize about what happened in early childhood. This may help us to withstand the frustrations and challenges that present in the therapeutic relationship. More importantly, it will help us to empathize more and be better prepared in knowing where to look in helping the patient come to better self-understanding, self-regulation, and close connections with others.

CHAPTER 5

Crying Is for Broken Legs and Lost Friends
Crying in Childhood

Graham, age 8, said, "You should cry when you are sad enough. If you are not sad enough, you should just think about nice things. I think about nice things and about other things and it goes away." He admits that he cries sometimes at school:

> I try to hold it in all the time, but I just can't so I let it out. My friends start teasing me and say that I am a crybaby. I usually try to hold it in or go in the bathroom and shut the door, then finish crying. If I can't, then I just cry in the middle of everybody. Even in the movie *Rocky*, when he got punched in the nose, he started crying! It doesn't matter, because I know crying is just normal and people do it to try and feel better. It gets you to feel kind of normal again (Kavanaugh, 1978, p. 206).

Crying in childhood bridges the wordless crying of infancy and the conscious understanding of crying in adulthood. The attachment system continues to be the core of crying, but attachment behaviors are increasingly affected by social learning. In addition to direct experiences of caregiving, children learn about crying by example and instruction and by overt and covert messages from adults, peers, books, songs, movies, and the media. At an early age, like Graham, they begin to draw conclusions about what is acceptable crying behavior—by whom, where, when, and how much.

Another 8-year-old describes a more problematic experience around crying when roughhousing with his father:

> I think that I shouldn't cry in front of my father. Sometimes me and my father box. He gets me down and he starts punching me, and then when I start crying, he says, "Stop those crocodile tears," and keeps on punching me. He thinks I'm really not crying. That's why when he finds out, he just says something like, "Sorry." That is all. It doesn't make me feel better, it just gives me a kind of tingle inside—a hurt tingle. (Kavanaugh, 1978, p. 208)

Confusing lessons such as this one leave a child vulnerable. The message about crying gets equally garbled. Is it all right to cry if you are really hurt or is that considered faking or unacceptable for some other reason?

Crying behavior changes over the course of childhood. By age 2, some children attempt to hold back their tears and by age 7, many are able to succeed. With language development, children are able to call for help as well as cry for it and to describe their feelings in words even though they are crying. Later in childhood, silent weeping takes the place of noisy crying. Facial expressions and tears carry a message that, in earlier developmental stages, was primarily audible. Empathy and sympathy also develop progressively as children with good enough caregiving experiences make kind and soothing gestures toward infants, siblings, friends, strangers, pets, and even parents.

In early childhood, crying gradually comes to be triggered by separations that are not only literal but that may also be intangible, imagined, threatened, or symbolic. The "losses" of childhood may not impress adults, but to children they are very real: a candy bar, a place in line, staying behind with a baby-sitter, not being invited to a playmate's birthday party, or a missed trip to the playground. These experiences represent the kinds of losses that trigger crying throughout life.

Types of Crying in Childhood

When faced with losses, children, like many adults, are first inclined to cry in protest because they quite naturally wish to avoid or undo the loss. They want "No, you may not have a cookie" changed to "Yes" or they want bedtime to be a half hour later. Because young children are still so vulnerable and dependent and have not mastered the words to express their distress directly, a great deal of their crying is in protest. They use the same high-intensity crying that worked so effectively to get their parents to come to them in infancy whenever they are told "no" to an ice cream cone, to one more cartoon, or when the girl next door steals their roller skate. They quite naturally cry as they always have, to get their parents to respond to their perceived needs.

Unfortunately for them, protest crying now engenders far less sympathy and far more irritation than they experienced in infancy. Designed to provoke caregivers into giving the desired response, protest crying now merely provokes them. The child experiences a double blow. First, "no" is the reply to a pleasure-seeking request, and it is experienced as a shame-engendering, negative misattunement. This is followed, in many instances, by a second level of misattunement: parental annoyance because the child cries. An additional blow to the child may come if attachment behavior is met with banishment, as in, "Go to your room until you stop crying." The behavior designed to bring their caregivers to them results instead in their being sent away. In some instances, parents are so provoked by the crying that they punish the child or threaten to do so if the crying does not stop, further confusing and shaming the child.

In infancy, high-intensity protest crying serves a biological as well as a social purpose: infants must have their caregiver's presence in order to survive. Using survival behavior for a missed snack annoys and frustrates caregivers rather than bringing about their "presence" in the form of granting the child's request. On the positive side, when handled well, protest crying provides an opportunity for interactive repair and for teaching the child how to regulate affect by cognitive reasoning, delaying gratification, or expressing protest in words. Only if the child's protest makes a logical point, like ownership of the roller skate or needing to watch a particular TV show for history homework, should children's protest cries be successful in undoing the loss. Infants do not get "spoiled" by too ready a response from parents, but young children do. One mother said she knew she had gone too far when she found herself trying to tape a pretzel back together because her daughter cried when it broke (Saber & Mazlish, 1980).

Sad crying, on the other hand, seldom (and optimally never) results in anything but sympathy and soothing. Crying is a different matter when the child realizes the kitty is never coming back or the new toy has been run over by the lawn mower. Then the child's tears make parents feel sympathetic and make them want to comfort. These are not the cries that get a child reprimanded or sent to his room. These are the ones that bring immediate hugs and sympathy—helping to maintain attachment security, achieve interactive repair, and master affect regulation.

Sad, little-kid crying is hard to take for a different reason, however, because it can tear a parent's heart out. Some parents feel the pain of their children's losses so deeply that they may try to short-circuit the expression of grief, ostensibly for the child's sake, but often just as much for their own. A mother once called child therapist Selma Fraiberg (1959) to ask how to handle the sudden death of her son's hamster. "Why don't you tell him that his hamster died?" Fraiberg suggested. "Died!" the mother exclaimed, "What I want to know is how I can break the news gently to him and spare him the pain of this whole experience." Fraiberg's comment was, "We need to respect a child's right to experience a loss fully and deeply. This means, too, that we do not bury the dead pet and rush to the pet store for a replacement ..." (pp. 273–274). Parents may be tempted to distract a sad child or prematurely divert his attention to something new. Children, however, benefit from a gentle, sympathetic response to their losses; this is how they learn affect regulation. It is also how they learn about appropriate grief and the human connections that enable them to weather losses and go on to new attachments.

It would seem that children have an intuitive sense of the attachment meaning of crying and thus sometimes recognize what adults might miss: that crying in despair may lie behind protest crying. In her study of children's reactions to picture books, Ellen Handler Spitz (1999) draws attention to this phenomenon in her discussion of a scene from the children's book *Madeline*. Madeline is in the hospital and her schoolmates have just returned from a visit to her. They are all arranged in their dormitory beds that night and they all begin crying to their housemother, "Boohoo,/we want to have our appendix out, too!" (as cited in Spitz, 1999, p. 20). The message the author intended is clear: the children are envious of the special attention and gifts that Madeline has received because of her illness. Spitz writes that, nonetheless,

> viritually every three- or four-year-old child to whom I have read the book, when asked why the little girls are crying ... invariably tells me, not that the other girls are longing for Madeline's gifts and toys, but that they are crying *because they miss their friend, Madeline*. This despite the fact that they know the story well and fully comprehend the force of the intended interpretation (p. 20).

Causes of Crying in Childhood

After infancy, the neat lists for causes of crying disappear from parenting manuals. Perhaps this is because parents can simply ask children what is wrong, or it may be because the triggers for crying are no longer simple and direct ones that lend themselves to compact lists. An infant cries in hunger, but a 4-year-old may cry because he is offered an apple instead of a cookie. An infant cries spontaneously from the pain of an injection, while a 6-year-old may fall off a bicycle and skin her knee but not begin crying until after she is safely at home with her mother.

The best way to understand the causes for children's crying is to put ourselves in their places and look at the world through their eyes. Losses and fears of losses come in all guises at all ages, but the losses feared by children often ambush adults, even those consciously trying to stay tuned in to their child's emotional state. All of my age-appropriate explanations of her impending sibling's birth when Lisa Ingrid was 2 seemed to be going well. Then one day I found her in her little rocking chair crying. "What is the matter, honey?" I asked. "I don't want my Mommy to break open," she replied. None of my explanations about the "special place where the baby comes out" had convinced her that something as big as a baby could get out of her mother's body without causing harm.

Children are concrete and literal and yet live in a marvelous world in which anything can happen. Daniel, a 6-year-old, cried because he was terrified of changing planes on his first trip to "Yurp." It turned out, on exploration by his parents, that he thought the change would need to be accomplished in mid-air (Fraiberg, 1959). It is a challenge to return to the world of childhood and help children achieve cognitive and emotional understanding. To do so, we must remember well and listen carefully. Crying is a friendly guide in the process, signaling us that the child is in need of adult comfort as well as help putting the causes for tears into words.

My favorite study of why children cry—the most complete I have seen—was done in the 1940s at the University of California (Landreth, 1940). I am assuming children have not changed that much, although it would be interesting to know whether they have. In the meantime, I also like this study because the researchers recorded the whole range of crying behavior—tears, screaming, sobbing, whimpering, whining, and squealing—for 8 weeks during free play at nursery school. In addition, parents of these 2½- to 5-year-olds kept a diary during the same 8 weeks. They recorded their child's physical condition, daily routine, and special activities, along with all instances of crying, their duration and triggers, and how the parents handled each episode. Combining these findings with the more recent ones where they are available, I have put together a list of the general causes of crying in childhood, all of which relate to losses of one kind or another.

Conflicts With Other Children

In the University of California study, conflicts with other children led the list of causes for crying at school. Hitting, refusal to share toys, and taunting words are familiar conflicts on any playground and they often result in somebody's tears. In the study, sibling conflicts occasionally resulted in tears at home but not with anything like the frequency of peer conflicts at school.

Another interesting study (Howes & Eldredge, 1985) compared the responses to aggression in preschoolers who had been abused and those who had not. The children who had *not* been abused responded to aggression from other children by crying. Abused children met aggression with aggression. Although it is difficult to know for certain, this atypical response to hostility may be linked to the disorganized/disoriented attachment style that, in turn, is also associated with infant and child abuse.

Conflicts With Adults

Conflicts with adults in the Landreth (1940) study accounted for more than half of the crying while children were at home. Establishing routines—eating, brushing teeth, washing hair, and the runaway champion, bedtime and sleep—along with adult reprimands and discipline (including spanking in the 1940s) were the sources of most conflicts that ended in tears.

Because night waking is such a big problem for parents, there is an extensive literature on its management, most of it focused on unlearning behavior by gradually withholding the parent's caregiving responses that behaviorists believe reinforce crying behavior. Some night waking, however, is not learned behavior, but rather symptomatic of anxiety. Video-tapes of night wakings of 2- to 5-year-olds whose mothers were expecting a baby found that, prior to the mother's hospitalization for delivery, night crying was almost nonexistent (Field & Reite, 1984). While their mothers were in the hospital, night crying increased significantly. During the month afterward, the children's crying diminished but was still more frequent than prior to the separation.

Children, like most adults, experience sleep disturbances during periods of great stress. Night crying is a signal for parents to address the fear or confusion that is the source of the crying by giving explanations and reassurance, rather than simply trying to eliminate the crying behavior. Even very young children may respond to soothing words and simple explanations of the triggers for their anxiety and crying: "It was lonely when

Mommy was away at the hospital but I am home now, and I will stay right here with you."

A child analyst (Novick, 1986) wrote of treating a young child—just 16 months old—for crying inconsolably up to an hour at night. The parents had no idea that she was still stressed by an ear surgery 3 months earlier, and it did not occur to them to explain and reassure a child so young. Once the analyst and the parents working together went over and over the distressing event, providing explanations and reassurance using techniques of play therapy, the child quickly began to sleep through the night again.

Manipulative Crying

I surveyed a group of parents about the causes of their preschoolers' crying. All but one parent checked the box that said their child cried when not getting his or her own way. In a separate question, I asked if their children used crying to *get* their own way. Half said yes and half said no. There is an important distinction here. All children are apt to cry when denied something they want. They are protesting a loss of the desired item. The question is whether children are protesting or deliberately making themselves cry in order to sway the outcome. Children may indeed learn that a few tears go a long way in overcoming adult obstacles to their wishes. However, suggesting that children can decide consciously to cry and that they do so is a far different matter.

Only a small percentage of adults, about 10% of women and 5% of men, are able to cry at will (Frey & Langseth, 1985). The figures may be a little higher for children, but only if they are already stressed, not starting from a calm state. Former child-actor Ricky Schroder said he could cry on cue just by thinking about something sad. Jeff Allan-Lee, who now teaches child actors, said that when he was on stage as a child he merely pretended to be crying or laughing or screaming. I have heard horror stories of child actors being told lies about the deaths of pets, friends, or even parents to get them to shed the necessary tears.

It would be fair to say that children may be "taught" to cry whenever they shed tears and thus get their way. Rewarding crying with a changed mind even on an inconsistent basis could reinforce the behavior and cause it to recur under similar circumstances. I asked my oldest daughter to recall the times when she produced some of her classic gigantic rolling teardrops out of slowly clouding eyes in response to not getting a jaw-breaker from the candy machine (she once referred to this as "kid tricks"). She said she must have been feeling genuinely bad to cry, but that she was not unaware of the effect. I certainly was not immune to the effect either and on occasion would cough up the coin in question, thus "teaching" her to cry the next time.

Stress

Illness, fatigue, and hunger can bring tears over things that might not normally bring about crying when the child is relaxed and calm. Children at nursery school (Landreth, 1940), for example, cried more at the end of the session than in the earlier hours. At home, the crying peak was between 4 and 8 p.m.—the same as for infants and adults. Stimulation from movies and television, pediatrician T. Berry Brazelton (1989) points out, may also stress children to the point of tears. "The cost to him is easily seen as he disintegrates at the end of a program—screaming, whimpering and 'raw' after a period of such intense involvement" (p. 161).

Children also react to the stress of change—moves, vacations, new teachers or schools—with additional crying. Of course, the common element in all change is separation and loss of the routine and the familiar, as well as of people to whom a child may be attached. A group of 15-month-olds and another of 2-year-olds were "graduating" to a new class at the preschool they attended full time (Field, Vega-Lahr, & Jagadish, 1984b). They would be going to a new room with new teachers and some new classmates. A month prior to graduation, crying before naptime averaged a little more than a minute. One week prior it climbed to more than 4 minutes, and a week after the change it increased still more. A month later, crying before naps was back down to just 1 minute.

Causes of Crying in Older Children

School-aged children cry less often, less loudly, and less openly than when they were younger. Crying over physical pain decreases, but crying over separations and losses increases: hurt feelings, ended relationships, fear, loss, anger, conflict, teasing, rejection, discipline, or reprimand. Tears over the early struggles with sleep, eating, and baths are replaced by more advanced conflicts over table manners or clothing and, in adolescence, telephone calls, homework, and curfew hours.

Older children also cry more when they are stressed and going through life changes. A friend whose son was just starting junior high school told me that her son had not cried all summer but cried daily during the first month of school. By high school, changes may be sought and welcomed as signs of independence. I certainly did not cry when I went to camp (I cried when I left it, however) or when I left for college (my Mother did and so did I when my own children went away). The things my daughters cried about during high school were mostly serious losses, like breaking up with a boyfriend, losing a close friend in a car accident, and, in the case of my younger daughter, graduation from her closely knit, creatively challenging boarding school.

Crying about losses and loves beyond a child's immediate experience, such as at a sad movie or story, appears in one study for the first time in children at age 8. Cynthia, my younger daughter was about that age the first time she cried over a fictional animal's plight during a television program in which Snoopy had to go to the hospital. One of my outstanding memories of crying in childhood was the day that we were reading *Lassie Come Home* aloud in fifth grade. I remember dreading my turn for fear I would not be able to complete my assigned section without crying. I do not recall actually doing that, so I must have somehow managed to maintain control.

Frequency of Crying in Childhood

Baseline data about crying frequency are essential for parents, teachers, and medical professionals who must evaluate whether a particular child's crying is excessive or lacking. I would also stress that when such an evaluation is done, it is important to bear in mind that the amount of crying and the circumstances that elicit it are, in fact, pointing to the quality of the underlying attachment bond, whether it is secure or insecure. Crying is a barometer of the problem—not, in most instances, the problem.

To no one's surprise, the few studies of crying frequency in children (Hastrup, Kraemer, & Bornstein, 1985; Gesell & Ames, 1946; Gesell, Ilg, & Ames, 1956) show that the incidence of crying declines with advancing age. For example, 1- and 2-year-olds cry a mean of 12 to 15 times a week; between the ages of 4 and 5, frequency drops noticeably. This corresponds to the age when almost all preschoolers have stopped crying at separations from their caregivers. This is the age at which attachment behavior at routine separations is naturally beginning to wane. A study in London (Blurton Jones & Leach, 1972) found that more than half of the 2-year-olds cried on being left by parents at a playgroup, compared to just 12% who were nearing the age of 3. By age 4, no children cried at separation.

Even among long-term enrollees in a day care program, crying at separation is related more to age level than to experience with leave-takings (Field et al., 1984a). I was particularly struck by the finding that children whose parents duck out without saying good-bye are *more* likely to cry, even at the younger ages. I may have overcorrected when I began routinely telling my daughters from birth where I was going and when I would be back. I could not see that it would hurt anything, and I like to think it was one of the factors in their secure attachment.

John Bowlby (1969) wrote of the decline in the activation of attachment behavior by age 3 or 4 that "it seems unlikely that ... experience is the sole influence. In the case of the major systems of instinctive behavior, changes of endocrine balance are well known to be of great importance" (p. 261). By age 4, a child has adequate verbal skills, a booming voice, and reliable locomotion. It is no longer necessary for caregivers to take the primary responsibility for coming back to the child after a separation. The child can ask or demand that the parent return, or chase after him or her. Crying is then reserved for leave-takings that unduly stress or threaten the child. By age 6, the mean crying frequency is down to seven times a week, although it is good to keep in mind the wide range of individual differences. By age 11, the mean crying frequency drops to only 2.5 to 3.5 times weekly.

There are no gender differences in frequency of crying by children under 12. Crying frequency decreases for both genders during adolescence, although the decline is sharper for males than females beginning at age 13. Girls cry once or twice a week, while the boys' mean declines to less than once in 2 weeks (Kraemer, Hastrup, Sobota, & Bornstein, 1985). The fact that gender differences in crying frequency do not appear until puberty supports Bowlby's (1969) idea that the endocrine system influences the development of attachment behavior. As he put it, "Evidence that attachment behavior continues to be rather more easily elicited in females than in males would, if confirmed, support such a conclusion" (p. 261).

Caregiving Responses to Crying in Childhood

When a child is 10 months of age, 90% of maternal behavior is positive play and caregiving. When dealing with infants in the 13- to 17-month-old range, however, mothers express a prohibition on the average of every 9 minutes (Schore, 2003). The shame that results from "conflicts with adults," interfering with the child's explorations and positive affect, disrupts the attachment bond and the child begins to cry in protest. Because the child is still too young to be able to return to a sense of well-being and security alone, the caregiver's help is needed to repair the ruptured bond.

Interactive repair requires that the mother initiate a transition from shame and protest back to positive affect. A reparative transaction might begin with a parent removing a dangerous object from the child's hands followed by tears of protest. The mother then might say something like, "Yes, honey, that is such a pretty red soap box, but it is all icky inside and Mommy's afraid it might make you sick. Let's go find your red ball instead. Where did we put that red ball?"

"Deliberate" misattunement by the caregiver leads to shame and protest crying in the child, followed by interactive repair initiated by the parent.

Under ideal circumstances, this sequence is an example of what Heinz Kohut called "optimal frustration" (Kohut, 1971). The infant is challenged by the frustration, but in a way that is manageable with help from the attachment figure (or "selfobject," Kohut's term for the parental caregiver). These repeated frustrations and repairs within the context of the secure attachment bond eventually enable the infant to learn to auto-regulate and self-soothe. Frustration that is not optimal but overwhelming, or interactive repair that is incomplete or inadequate, has an impact not only on the child's ability to regulate affect but also, ultimately, on the degree of security in the attachment bond.

Parents have access to very little advice in knowing how to respond to the crying of children. As a result, many misattunements take place in response to childhood crying, and many mistakes of consequence are made repeatedly. These parental glitches, over time, have a negative impact on affect regulation and affect expression in regard to crying. More importantly, they have an impact on attachment security and the ability later in life to relate comfortably and meaningfully with intimate others during times of need—either as the one who is vulnerable and crying or as the caregiver.

Caregiving and affect regulation in childhood include verbal instruction about how to understand and handle feelings. In the process of soothing, parents and other adults sometimes manage to confuse children by their words. For example, an exchange between a niece and her uncle in a children's story (Peterson, 1968) for 8- or 9-year-olds discusses crying in this way:

> Lucy began to cry. "Why Tina Small is probably my best friend, and I've never even seen her!" Uncle Pete limped over to Lucy. He patted her on the back. "You know my rule—no tears in front of your uncle." He looked hard at Mrs. Little. "For goodness sake, say something nice to her. Tell her what we're having for dessert tonight" (p. 11).

Uncle Pete used distraction (dessert) and prohibition (no tears) instead of attuning to Lucy's sense of loss.

It is necessary and helpful to instruct children about crying on occasion. Parents, both mental health professionals, told me their daughter (who was involved in dramatic productions) had developed a "stage cry" at home. They had been talking to her regularly, explaining the difference between drama and real life. Another example of parental instruction about appropriate crying was when my then 4-year-old nephew was crying over mismatched Snoopy socks. My sister advised him that "crying is for broken legs and lost friends." This gave him a framework for knowing when crying (sadness and loss) is appropriate and when words of frustration are more effective.

For many children, however, prohibitions against crying are accompanied by a threat. Anna Freud observed 3-year-old Patrick at the Hampstead nursery to which children were evacuated for protection from air raids during World War II. Patrick's mother told him to be a good boy and not cry or else she would not come back to get him.

> Patrick tried to keep his promise and was not seen crying. Instead he would nod his head whenever anyone looked at him and assure himself and anybody who cared to listen that his mother would come for him, she would put on his overcoat and would take him home with her again. Whenever a listener seemed to believe him he was satisfied, whenever anybody contradicted him, he would burst into violent tears (as cited in Bowlby, 1960, pp. 22–23).

Poor Patrick was unable to cry in grief at the loss of his mother for fear that crying would make him permanently lose his mother! How is a 3-year-old to cope with that, particularly when it is doubtful that he would even be able to control his crying or make the distinction between gone now and gone forever? The attachment behavior activated to prevent the threatened loss of his mother became a threat to losing his mother.

One classic mixed message is so common and so destructive that I feel like launching a billboard campaign to protect children from it: threatening to leave a crying child behind as a way of "regulating" affect. A particularly vivid example occurred outside my local take-and-bake pizza parlor. A 3-year-old girl asked her mother for a sugary soft drink just as they were paying for their pizza. Denied this by her mother, she felt a sense of loss and cried in protest. The mother first began to belittle the girl, saying sarcastically, "Oh, so now you are going to cry." By now, they were outside and the mother got in her truck and told the little girl, now seated howling on the sidewalk, that she was leaving. She added that she would go home and watch *The Little Mermaid* with Daddy and they would have a fine time without her there. Then she started the engine and began to back out of the parking space. The little girl was a picture of panic and confusion. She did not know whether to cry harder over this cruelly threatened loss or stop crying over the soda to prevent it. At that point, the mother stopped and the little girl climbed into the truck.

Crying is designed to bring the caregiver to the child. When that appeal for connection is met by its opposite—a threat of abandonment ("bye-bye" to a crying child will do it)—the child has nowhere to turn for soothing. Instead of affirming her sense of loss at the soft drink and teaching the child to deal with it ("I know they look good but you already had one today"), this mother, like Patrick's, exploited the child's most basic need for a secure bond with the caregiver to get her to stop crying. The child's "Come here, I need you" is answered with "I am leaving." It may "teach" a child not to cry in protest by substituting the threat of a bigger loss to replace the lesser one, but at the cost of attacking the very core of the parent–child connection. Such tactics do "work" to control crying and behavior in children, but at what price to attachment security and affect regulation?

Sending a child to his or her room "until you stop crying," or the ubiquitous "Stop crying or I'll give you something to cry about," is similarly confusing and potentially destructive. As annoying as protest crying is in childhood and as much as it grates on parents' frayed nerves and adds to their stress, it is an opportunity to help a child learn interactive repair, affect regulation, and, ultimately, auto-regulation or self-soothing.

To respond optimally, parents need some good information about childhood crying—about what crying means in general and what it means in particular. Understanding the difference between protest crying and crying in sadness and despair is particularly helpful. Parents can then clarify their own feelings on the subject so that they can consciously teach their children healthy messages about human closeness and the appropriate and healthy expression of affect.

I think children are less apt than adults to confuse protest crying and sad crying. They know the difference. Parents and other caregiving adults can help children put their protests into words and teach appropriate alternatives to crying. "I know you are crying because you are frustrated that you can't run as fast as Billy, but let's practice saying that in words so you won't get embarrassed over crying about it in front of the T-ball team." Adding a little child profanity like "rats" or "phooey" might help to give the angry words a little more punch.

Helping a child to deal with sad crying requires a combination of both comfort and explanations about the loss and the feelings it evokes. In this way, the child is soothed and taught by experience to find help in interactive repair and, eventually, how to find comfort internally. Occasionally, children also instruct parents about caregiving. A 15-year-old girl told her dad she was feeling "terrible," so he told her to make herself some chicken soup. She snapped back, "Daddy, you know it doesn't work if you make it for yourself!" (Caen, 1996, p. A-12).

Emotional regulation is as important a lesson for children as emotional expression. By their caregiving words and soothing behaviors, parents teach children to express their protest in appropriate words and to trust that sad crying is part of the healing process. Giving children faith in their ability to heal after a loss is a lifelong caregiving gift that they can always carry with them.

In responding to the crying of their children, parents come up against their own attachment issues and social values countless times in a day. Responses are loaded with messages that, over time, are not lost on a child. The University of California study in the 1940s was the only source of objective data I found about parents' responses to their child's crying. The top two on the list were ignoring and reasoning, followed by consoling, distracting, spanking, scolding, and threatening. These parents also tried humor, bribing, and arbitrating conflicts. All of these (with the exception of spanking and threatening, I hope) most 21st century parents would find familiar. Ignoring, though, is an unfortunate favorite that, if overused, could frustrate a child's genuine caregiving needs rather than merely teaching him or her that some crying is not appropriate.

While working on this chapter, I went to hear folk singer John McCutcheon perform. Strumming his guitar, he told a story about being in the kitchen one day and hearing his 9-year-old son, Peter, sobbing in the next room. Dish towel in hand, he went to the living room and found Peter in a big armchair reading. When John asked what was wrong, Peter just held up his book—it was *Where the Red Fern Grows*. Wishing to spare his son pain, John said, "You know, son, you don't have to finish reading that if you don't want to." "No," Peter said, "what I want to know is are there any more books like this?" John went over to the bookshelf, took down his own battered childhood copy of *The Yearling*—another coming-of-age-story about animals and loss—and gave it to Peter.

Childhood crying is first and foremost an appeal for a caregiving response from a loved one. The first thing John did when he heard Peter sobbing was to leave the dishes and go to him. Going quickly gave Peter a deep sense of his father's love, care, connection, and accessibility. Over time, it will also give him security, a sense of faith in human closeness, and, ultimately, the ability to care for himself and for others. He will also learn to withstand emotional pain, even when he is alone, because he has experienced the connection to loved ones and learned to be attuned and responsive to attachment appeals from other people as well.

John taught Peter another lesson about affect regulation: he could withdraw from this experience if he chose. John did not tell Peter to stop crying but supported him making his own choice. Peter was a good teacher also because he chose to stay with this book and asked for more like it. He had just discovered that a story about loss and death can do something besides simply bring pain. Crying can also reaffirm connection and hope.

Children and Bereavement

Following the 1981 Atlas Peak fire in Napa, California, a 3-year-old who survived it with his family would, according to his mother, burst into tears and say: "My house is dead, my toys are dead, my dog is dead" ("The Atlas Peak fire," 1991, p. 8). In order to help young children comprehend and grieve their losses, adults must, as this child's parents did, repeatedly discuss the facts and the finality of a permanent separation or loss. Bowlby believed that with adult assistance, children even as young as 2½ can express their grief directly. He (Bowlby, 1980) refers at length to an article by Marion Barnes, a social worker and child analyst in Cleveland who was one of my first supervisors after graduate school. She wrote about helping a father and grandmother of a 4-year-old girl whose mother had died. She supported the adults in encouraging recollections and questions to facilitate the girl's expressions of grief.

To protect themselves from the pain of their children's pain, adults often have a deep need to deny that children are affected by a loss. Thus, the children are left to deal with their feelings of confusion, anger, or sadness by distraction or fantasy. When their efforts do not succeed, the grief may have an impact on attachment security and lead to depression, physical symptoms, or behavior problems.

Elementary school children in Israel, whose playground was the target of a sniper attack resulting in the death of one of their schoolmates, were studied for their grief reactions at 6 months and 1 year after the event (Pynoos, Nader, Frederick, Gonda, & Stuber, 1987). The amount of crying was understandably greater in children who knew the victim best or who had been exposed most directly to the traumatic event. Of those who knew the victim well, 25% were crying about her death 1 year later.

The impression of the mental health team conducting the study was that most of the children had not spoken to anyone about their grief reactions. This left them confused, frightened, and disturbed by their normal grief responses. Because they were not crying in front of others or talking openly about their feelings, families and teachers assumed that they were not grieving and therefore did not offer them comfort and support.

Children of all ages can be encouraged to talk about loss. If there is no overt crying, it would be worth asking if the child is crying when no one is around. Explaining the normal and common grief reactions (crying, dreams, daydreams that the person returns, or fleeting sense of having seen him or her in a crowd) gives children the opportunity to understand what they are going through. Giving permission and even gentle encouragement to cry is also appropriate.

While I was working under Marion Barnes' supervision, my second child was born. Perhaps it was Marion's influence that helped me to recognize that my 2½-year-old was experiencing a grief reaction following the birth of her sister. Adding a family member can be a loss, too, especially for a first-born nudged out of the center of the parental circle. One day when baby Cynthia was asleep, I took Lisa Ingrid to the rocking chair and held her while I sang the refrain of the French folk song, "The Joys of Love." Instead of "My love loves me and all the wonders I see," I substituted all of the adults in Lisa Ingrid's world: "My Mommy loves me" followed by a verse for Daddy, Aunt Marcia, Uncle Craig, Grandma, and so on. By the end of the Daddy verse she was crying in grief, and she continued on and off throughout the song. After that I noticed a sense of lightness in her mood and play presumably because the song underscored the love in her life and reassured her that it had not changed. Over the next few months I would repeat the song as I held and rocked her, though she never again cried as I sang it.

Empathy in Children

Caregiving, the behavioral response set in motion by attachment appeals, appears remarkably early in children. The most common reactions of children to other children's crying are attempts to comfort, console, or give help. Very young children leave most of their peers' crying in the hands of adult caregivers, but when they do respond to each other, most do so with kindness and comfort (Howes & Farver, 1987). Slightly older preschoolers go over to the crying child and offer consolation, unless, of course, they were the ones who caused the crier's distress by hitting or refusing to share.

Modeling and personal experience of caregiving are crucial variables in response to another's distress. Apparently, consciously teaching empathy for other children also pays off in increased caregiving behavior. In fact, one study found that children whose mothers voiced their convictions about caring for other children with the most emotional intensity had the highest positive caregiving scores (Zahn-Waxler, Radke–Yarrow, & King, 1979). Older children learn to express empathy in words. A sympathetic big brother said to a younger sister who returned upset from her first day at kindergarten: "It's okay, Sophie. I cried on my first day of school, too. After a while you'll get used to it and think school is fun."

On the other hand, when children react to other children's crying with tears, fear, guilt, self-incrimination, embarrassment, nervousness, anger, or aggression, they show that they are reverting to their own distress instead of responding empathically to the crier. The child's caregiving system may be overwhelmed by the need of the other child, or he or she may be showing conflicts based on his or her attachment and caregiving experiences.

I remember a time in high school when my caregiving skills were overwhelmed by a classmate's crying. In a speech class in which we were assigned to give our autobiography, one of my classmates spoke of her father's death in a car accident, burst into tears, and ran out of the room. The male teacher sent me after her. I felt nervous, awkward, and completely out of my depth in terms of knowing how to comfort her. We were not close friends and until that moment I had not known anything about her family life. I did not know what to say in the face of such an enormous loss. Finally the bell rang and rescued both of us.

Symptomatic Crying and Inhibited Crying in Childhood

Crying in childhood is always a symptom that something is wrong. In that sense, it is a valuable way to assess a child's stress level. Excessive crying may also be symptomatic of insecure attachment, especially of the anxious-ambivalent type in which attachment behavior is easily activated and difficult to soothe. On the caregiving side of the equation, anxious-ambivalent children often show excessive caregiving behavior to the adults in their lives, or what Bowlby calls "compulsive caregiving." The child's attachment bond is inextricably linked in all instances to the well-being of the caregiver. With anxious-ambivalent attachment, however, the child may be drawn into the parental attachment system as caregiver rather than recipient in order to keep the caregiver available in as reliable a way as possible.

Excessive crying may also result when a securely attached child has been overgratified, especially in response to protest crying. When I asked my then 6-year-old niece, Corrie, if she knew any crybabies, she answered without hesitation, "Janie. She cried because her pockets were inside out." Corrie was expressing her judgment that Janie's frustration could better be handled by asking for help with her pockets.

A friend who leads team-building workshops for children told me about a sixth-grade boy who came to an outdoor ropes course with his class. He burst into tears repeatedly, with frustration because he could not manage an activity and with anger because he felt slighted by other children. His frequent crying stood out because none of the other children, 11- and 12-year-olds, cried even once. His age mates were clearly discomfited by his tears, although no one teased him. This type of behavior in a child this age could signal overgratification from caregivers, anxious-ambivalent attachment, or depression. The child could also be overburdened by stress in his life. Therapists, teachers, and parents who know the circumstances would be in the best position to evaluate and then respond therapeutically to help the child with the underlying issues.

Crying that is unusual for a particular child, either more frequent or more intense, or both can be a sign that some underlying anxiety, fear, sadness, or depression needs attention. Some losses may have an impact on a child even though they have not been verbalized or made conscious. Television news stories of murders, kidnappings, or war may, for example, trigger grief reactions and threats of loss in children. Adults must figure out what the stressors are and then explain and reassure in order to help the child understand and master the strong feelings.

A 6-year-old boy whose father was almost killed in an auto accident began to cry every morning before school more than a year after the accident. Upon investigation, his mother concluded that the trauma had been re-evoked for him by a television program about persecution of Native Americans. Identifying with the vulnerability and unpredictability of their daily lives revived his feelings about the traumatic near-loss of his father.

Some children, even quite young ones, do not cry in situations that would ordinarily produce cries. A physically abused child may learn not to cry for protective reasons. Avoidant children with insecure attachment bonds have learned, as a survival strategy, not to activate their attachment behavior of crying. In the Strange Situation tests, when 12-month-olds are stressed by being left alone briefly or left alone with a stranger, the avoidant youngsters are the ones who seldom cry, and who seldom seek the comfort of their parents after reunion. Nonresponsive caregiving may be the source of this type of inhibited crying. Emotional or physical abuse that includes harsh prohibitions against crying coupled with threats of abandonment may also cause a child to suppress even normal tears.

My friend Frances explained to me why she never cries. She said that she made a conscious decision to stop crying altogether when she was 4 years old and heard her father tell her three big brothers that boys do not cry. She was struggling with her position as the only girl and the baby of the family and did not want to risk adhering to a lesser standard than the boys. Secure attachment aside, she had other issues facing her that had an impact on the regulation of affect and served to dry up her tears permanently.

Children who are unremittingly cheerful in the face of all stimuli may be overly socialized to suppress unpleasant feelings in order to gain attachment and caregiving responses. I did not see Mindy until she was an adult; however, when I did, her constant smiling made my jaws ache. She had lost her father at the age of 5 and learned to suppress her tears of loss so as not to overburden her grieving, depressed mother. Not crying when tears would be expected may also be an indicator of more serious developmental difficulties such as cognitive deficits, autism, and pervasive developmental disorder. In these cases, however, it would appear as part of a constellation of other symptoms.

The tears we shed when we are children and the responses we receive from those around us influence not only our crying but also all of our close relationships for the rest of our lives. The social influences on crying, however, do not stop with childhood. We continue to be exposed to subtle messages about crying through popular culture, social mores, religious teachings, friends and relatives, ethnic groups, arts, and the media.

CHAPTER **6**

Crying Lessons and Caregiving Responses
The Social View

No one cries in a social vacuum. Even when we cry alone, the social judgments we have internalized, subliminally or consciously, influence our ability to cry and how we feel about it when we do. Attachment and caregiving behaviors take shape in the context of family interaction. However, families also exist in a larger social context with values that impinge upon their attitudes and behavior.

Social Attitudes Toward Crying

At the beginning of the 21st century, social mores related to crying reflect a confusing tangle of attitudes ranging from discomfort and negativity, to embracing it as a healthy outlet for emotion. On the whole, crying is ignored, minimized, trivialized, and oversimplified. It is tolerated rather than respected. A veneer of social acceptance almost universally espoused in academic and pop psychology (Cornelius, 2001) is consistently found in research on attitudes toward crying. We verbalize one set of values and internally hold another set. We verbalize one set of values and internally hold another set.

Social commentator Christopher Hitchens (1996) wrote a column after the 1996 Oscars entitled "Cheap Weeps at the Academy Awards" in which he criticized the tears shed on camera as "overdone sentimentality." He began by singling out Kirk Douglas' four sons who "brushed away manly streams from their manly cheeks" as their stroke-disabled father spoke (p. G1). Next he pointed to Tom Hanks, "eyes glistening and cheeks wet," following an appeal from wheelchair-bound Christopher Reeves. His final barb was aimed at the father of actress Mira Sorvino who broke down crying when his daughter thanked him in her speech. Hitchens wrote that "a thoughtful viewer or a good critic knows how to resist any too-obvious appeal to the hankie."

In addition to his mean-spirited snipes at these criers and their presumably human and humane responses to pain, loss, and in Sorvino's case, familial love, Hitchens masterfully articulates some of our cultural ambivalence about crying. He writes: "It's not weak to give way to tears but it's a bit weak to give way to them *every time*" (p. G7). The internal contradictions and confused values in that sentence perfectly reflect the state of social attitudes toward crying; should we or should we not? Publicly or privately? Weak or strong if we do? Well received or harshly judged? Good for us or bad for us? More or less often?

Social Attitudes Toward Caregiving

Social ambivalence about crying is only the top layer of a deeper ambivalence about intimacy and closeness. In Western societies, people are confused about the kinds of connections they desire and can tolerate and maintain, and about when, whether, and to whom to give what kind of caregiving. People struggle, not only with surrendering emotional control, but also with the surrender of self-reliance. In the presence of someone else's vulnerability and tears, some people also struggle with the caregiving responses and wonder what to do, if anything.

Crying disturbs potential caregivers so that they will respond. The uncertainty of whether or how to respond often creates another layer of disturbance. Crying is an intimate behavior directed primarily at close loved ones and friends, our "attachment figures." Even in intimate relationships, crying is not always well received. In more formal settings with acquaintances, coworkers, or strangers, displaying an intimate behavior such as crying can cause even more confusion and discomfort.

A mother wrote to the "Dear Abby" column (Van Buren, 1980) about her 16-year-old daughter tearfully waiting in the examining room where she was to undergo her first gynecological examination for a painful abdominal lump. When the doctor came in, the mother wrote, he "looked Sally in the eye, registered disgust and impatience" and abruptly cancelled the appointment. When asked why, he said, "I am not about to see a grown girl who is crying!" In this grown girl's body was a frightened child seeking comfort and reassurance from a man who was an officially-designated caregiver. Instead of offering the comfort and reassurance she needed, he criticized and rejected her.

A woman physician wrote to the *Journal of the American Medical Association* (Krauser, 1989) deploring the treatment she received from her teachers in medical school for crying over a dying 3-year-old. "To 'them,' my tears announced to the world that I was ill-equipped to be a physician, yet no one could point to one incident during which I had performed inadequately because of my 'handicap'" (p. 3612).

A group of female psychology graduate students (Hoover-Dempsey, Plas, & Wallston, 1986) asked their female professors to help them understand and deal with the phenomenon of crying on the job. Their request grew out of the realization that they were in conflict over whether they should cry or control their urge to do so. Crying in a work setting may cause discomfort and embarrassment because it implies the need for a comforting, caregiving response, even though neither party may want that. In other words, the real problem is with the attachment aspects of crying in a setting in which power rather than personal connection defines the relationship dynamics.

Part of our confusion about caregiving is created by and reflected in the concept of "codependency." Labeling caregiving responses "codependent" implies a negative judgment and, in the end, all caregiving may become tainted by association. Identification of this problematic form of caregiving as codependence has sometimes clouded our social view of the kind of healthy caregiving that contributes to closeness and intimacy and to simple human compassion and community. To avoid this problem, I prefer Bowlby's term "compulsive caregiving" instead of codependence to describe an unhealthy caregiving style that promotes dependency and enables certain maladaptive behaviors in the recipient.

Attitudes Toward Crying Throughout History

As with individual psychological symptoms, cultural ones also have deep historical roots. The reasons why we cry and the way in which we do it have not changed for countless generations—not, Bowlby says, since we were in our hunter–gatherer days. What has changed over time is the social attitude toward crying. The path taken by social values about crying through the history of Western civilization is more of a spiral than a straight line, with old attitudes re-emerging at new levels seen from different historical vantage points. We first see crying as a respected, sought-after—even divine—behavior, then as shameful and weak, followed by confusion and ambivalence over these opposing viewpoints. The origins of our crying values must be reconstructed from slim historical evidence.

Crying has no oral tradition—no one to tell its story. In fact, because crying is nonverbal, any history first must be translated into words or other symbols that will survive.

Prechristian Artifacts and Myths

As far back as the 10th millennium B.C., artifacts from Europe and the Middle East show eyes with symbols for tears around and beneath them. The tears are represented by water-like designs such as concentric circles, parallel lines, and chevrons. A seated goddess figure from about 5000 B.C. found in Turkey, the "goddess of moisture," has lines streaming from her eyes, covering her entire face (Johnson, 1988). A late sixth-millennium water jar takes the symbolism a step further: the protruding eyes on it are punctured in their centers so that water pours out when the jar is tilted.

Archeologist Marija Gimbutas (1989) concluded that these ancient tear symbols are "a metaphor for divine tears; the eyes of the goddess are the source of life-sustaining water" (p. 53). In the early cultures in which female generativity represented divine power (in the form of Mother Earth as well as literal mothers), tears were honored and respected. Female weeping was considered to be divine, creative, life-endowing, and life-sustaining—clearly beneficial. Women shedding tears, menstruating, becoming pregnant, giving fluid birth, and lactating demonstrate the ancient connection between the sacred female and life-giving moisture.

A number of goddess myths that survive from these ancient cultures emphasize the magical connection between female tears, the cycles of life, and the growing season. The Sumerian story of Inanna is one of a number of parallel myths with similar symbols and themes, and the Egyptian story of Isis and Osiris is another.

The goddess Inanna went on a mission to the underworld but was uneasy about a safe return. She instructed her servant to weep for her by the ruins while she was gone (tears as a sign of security and connection). If she did not return within 3 days, the servant was to go weep before Father Nanna and Father Enki (protest tears aimed at undoing the threatened loss).

Inanna was indeed held captive in the underworld but, thanks to these precautions, her release was secured. However, a replacement was demanded: her husband Dumuzi. The exchange was made but Inanna was able to negotiate for the release of Dumuzi during half of each year by substituting his sister for him while he was at liberty. The tears of Inanna, along with those of Dumuzi's mother and sister, were the means for bringing him back to earth (Wolkstein & Kramer, 1983). Subsequently, Sumerian women performed weeping rituals each year to bring about Dumuzi's release, thereby ending the dormant segment of the agrarian cycle.

The themes of descent, despair, transformation, and rebirth may be seen as symbolic of personal growth. For ancient cultures, however, the myth and the ritual were literally as well as spiritually meaningful. Water, represented by female tears, was essential to maintain the body and to grow the food needed to survive.

If, as it would appear from the myths and artifacts, female tears were once highly valued for their power and generativity, and if women cry more frequently and more easily than men, what could have occurred to alter cultural attitudes toward tears? How was the view of divine, life-giving, honored female tears transformed into judging them as manipulative, trite, and weak? In his book, *The Expression of Emotions in Animals and Man,* for example, Charles Darwin (1872/1965) singled out "savages," babies, women, and the insane "even in the male sex" as having "a tendency to weep on the slightest occasions, or from no cause." Men, especially Englishmen, he said, rarely cry, "except under the pressure of the acutest grief" (p. 153).

We now live in an industrialized society in which rationality and emotional control prevail. The attachment-based values of relatedness and emotional expression are traditionally relegated to females and often to secondary status. Even though no tribal council or boardroom strategy session probably ever dealt consciously with the "problem" of tears, it would seem a simple matter to redefine their meaning culturally. If women shed them with greater ease, then what was once considered powerful could merely be relabeled, along with women and their reproductive functions, as "weak." (The same fate appears to have awaited menstruation and, perhaps, lactation.) What once was honored was now shamed.

Because crying is inborn attachment behavior designed to protect survival in infancy and social connections later in life, the denigration of crying has not entirely succeeded. Crying has not been "civilized" out of us, in spite of at least several centuries of negativity. People, particularly women whose bodies overrule social censure, continue to cry. Our infants, our bodies, and our survival as a species see to that. Although no longer recognized as powerful in a positive sense, female tears do continue to wield a certain negative power—the power to intimidate and control—that is feared and resented.

Judeo–Christian Attitudes Toward Tears

Although most of the process of defaming divine female tears is lost to the subtleties of gradual social change, one example of it remains in the Old Testament. The ancient goddess cults (Inanna in Sumeria, Isis in Egypt, and Ishtar in Babylonia) continued their rituals and practices in the same time and place as the ancient Hebrews worshiped their Jehovah. As late as the 10th century A.D., according to the notes of a traveler through Middle Eastern countries (Warner, 1976), the ancient weeping rituals were still performed at the festival for Tammuz.

The prophet Ezekiel's vision of warning and censure about practices of the Hebrews who had been in captivity in Babylon included an indictment of the women weeping for Tammuz before the gate of the Temple, a rite he referred to as an "abomination" (Ezekiel 8:14). These women were the priestesses of Ishtar weeping to bring about the resurrection of her husband Tammuz who, like the Sumerian Dumuzi, was believed to die at the end of the harvest and thus had to be resurrected by the tears of women to initiate the new growing season. According to Jewish tradition, creation, life, and the cycles of the seasons were ascribed to the all-powerful male Jehovah and tears were denied their association with generative female power. (Not all tears were condemned, however; crying in grief and penitence is mentioned frequently and favorably throughout the Old Testament.)

Tears played a curious role in the trials and executions of women accused of witchcraft in 15th century Europe. *Malleus Maleficarum* (Montague, 1486/1970), the document written as a guide for the judges who tried the women, has contradictory references to crying. On the one hand, it says, "The tears of a woman are a deception, for they may spring from true grief or they may be a snare." On the other hand, if a woman shed tears during her interrogation, it was considered a confirmation of innocence. The Dominican friars who wrote the text believed that the Devil kept witches dry-eyed so that they could not successfully repent of their sins and would thus stay bound to his service. The judge, therefore, was advised to place his hand on the head of the accused and say

> I conjure you by the bitter tears shed on the cross by our Savior the Lord Jesus Christ for the salvation of the world, and by the burning tears poured in the evening hour over His wounds by the most florious [sic] Virgin Mary, His mother, and by all the tears which have been shed here in this world by the saints and elect of God from whose eyes He has now wiped away all tears, that if you be innocent you do now shed tears, but if you be guilty that you shall by no means do so (as cited in Carmichael, 1991, p. 132).

The tear test was clear, but there was a catch: "If she be a witch she will not be able to weep: although she will assume a tearful aspect and smear her cheeks and eyes with spittle to make it appear that she is weeping; wherefore she must be closely watched by the attendants" (as cited in Carmichael, 1991, p. 132). These poor women were required to cry under pressure of their very survival; however, if they did cry, they risked being accused of faking their tears with saliva. Instead of celebrating female creativity and strength, tears shed in these circumstances underscored female oppression.

The divine power of tears may have been seriously undermined by the religious patriarchs, but sacred female tears retain a native power all their own, even in the present, as represented by the tears of the Virgin Mary. The Mater Dolorosa, known as Our Lady (Mother) of Sorrows or the weeping Madonna, has been a popular image among Christians in Italy, France, England, the Netherlands, and Spain since the end of the 11th century. I found numerous examples of weeping Madonnas from the 13th and 14th century on a recent trip to Germany and Switzerland. At the Swiss National Museum in Zurich, I saw one painting from about 1510 that showed tears streaming down the faces of all four women at the foot of the cross.

The Archbishop of Syracuse, Sicily, described Mary's tears in terms that sound remarkably parallel to those shed by followers of the goddess in ancient fertility rituals. "A woman who weeps always becomes, in the very act, a mother. And if Mary weeps beside the Cross of Jesus—I can tell you that her weeping was fertile and made her a mother" (Warner, 1976, p. 223). The power of the weeping Madonna still grips 20th-century worshipers (and members of the press). On a trip to Washington, D.C., in 1994, I visited the statue of Madonna and Child at the altar of St. Elizabeth Ann Seton Catholic Church in Lake Ridge, Virginia, which had been seen by throngs of people to weep copious tears over a 2-year period in 1992 and 1993. Skeptical reporters (and clergy) checked the statues thoroughly for gimmicks and even went so far as to touch and taste the tears.

Even though by modern standards a weeping Madonna might be considered primitive, the popular power of these tears has persisted in spite of centuries of official denial and disapproval. People are more than interested; they are magnetized by each new report. The faithful are thrilled, skeptics are titillated, and many of the clergy are embarrassed, representing all of the levels of our ambivalence toward tears.

A Cross-Cultural View of Tears

Anthropologist and musician Steven Feld (1982) lived with and studied the Kaluli tribe in New Guinea. Crying is a centerpiece of Kaluli culture. They have an aesthetic of weeping involving poetry, music, and dance, rather than a psychology of weeping. Their weeping behavior is rich and complex. They respect it so much that they encourage each other to weep or try to evoke it as a gesture of friendship. Children play together at weeping to learn the rituals. Their gender-related crying patterns also defy stereotypes: men are the ones who cry uncontrollably.

I asked Dr. Feld whether he had ever observed any negative responses or discomfort with Kaluli crying. He said that the only appropriate response to a weeper is affirming support. Saying *Heyo!*—a combination of "sorry" and "I know what you are feeling"—combined with a cluck of the tongue, tilted head, lowered gaze, and shrugged shoulders is used to indicate empathy. There is never a negative judgment and no word even suggesting that a Kaluli weeper is overdoing it emotionally. In fact, a person not behaving supportively in the presence of a weeper would risk being accused of sorcery. The connection between crying and embarrassment or shame is totally outside their comprehension (Feld, personal communication, March 24, 1992).

As with other criers around the world, most Kaluli weeping is triggered by some kind of loss—separation or death of loved ones, a house burned down, or an important possession, such as a hunting knife, lost. Immediately following a loss, the men, joined briefly by some women, react with the uncontrolled crying that I would associate with protest. In the midst of this atmosphere of pain and chaos, the women break into evocative poetic weeping (Feld calls this "wept thoughts") that typically includes references to the deceased (if the loss is a death), the kinship bond, shared experiences, and places. Several woman weep in this way simultaneously, their texts and melodies interwoven into even more powerful wept creations. The sense is of a deeply-felt expression in a spontaneous art form doing what art does best: transmuting individual feeling into one that can be shared communally.

I see Kaluli gender differences in weeping as reflective of attachment and caregiving. At the moment of loss, everyone cries in protest, but the female weeping quickly settles into a soothing, comforting, calming structure, while the men continue crying uncontrollably. There is a division of labor, with each gender providing a valid and valuable aspect of handling grief and loss.

On certain ritual occasions such as marriages, male performers dressed in elaborate bird costumes (in honor of the "crying" fruit dove) compose songs about loss for the specific purpose of inducing weeping in the audience. These rituals reinforce the social bonds within the group and between groups because neighboring tribes are often present on these occasions.

I have written about the Kaluli's cultural view of weeping in the present tense because I want to enliven its existence and because it is painful for me to think of it otherwise. In the late 1970s, when Steven Feld was doing his field work there, however, evangelical missionaries arrived to Christianize the Kaluli and made it clear to the tribe that they did not approve of their weeping rituals. Changes began to occur. When one of the converted Kaluli left with his family to attend the missionary school, he told people he did not want any ritual weeping at his departure. Another left surreptitiously so as to avoid the whole process.

In the sung, poetic weeping of the women, Feld began to hear phrases like, "We will weep secret tears for you," in reference to the negative judgments that had begun to inhibit them. On one occasion when the body of a villager who died away at a hospital was returned by the mission air ambulance, Feld joined the friends and relatives who stood in awkward silence on the airstrip as the corpse was unloaded, inhibited from their usual response by the presence of the missionaries. Dr. Feld, who by this time had learned to compose the ritual weeping songs, began one himself and was quickly joined by the gathered mourners. That occasion was recounted with great delight afterward, firmly part of the oral history of the Kaluli.

The undoing of the intricate patterns of weeping, personal connection, nature, and art that the missionaries began was finished by the intrusion of industry. When Feld revisited New Guinea in 1990, he found that oil drilling had begun 30 miles away, bringing networks of roadways and hundreds of miles of pipeline into the rain forest home of the Kaluli. Ceremonial life had stopped. People had sold or burned their bird costumes and ritual paraphernalia. Adults under the age of 25 no longer composed the wept songs. The music of and for weeping, Feld wrote in the liner notes of the compact disc, *Voices of the Rain Forest* (1991), had become "endangered music."

The destruction of this central aspect of Kaluli culture by Christianity and industrialization may parallel the fate of the weeping of our Western foremothers and fathers, whose crying values in earlier millennia appear to have closely mirrored those of Kaluli culture. It may be that the historical drama of discrediting tears has been re-enacted in the rain forest of New Guinea in the last decade.

Immersing himself in Kaluli emotional life profoundly affected Steven Feld. At one point, he composed a song that brought tears to the eyes of one of the Kaluli and then wept with him. "In that intense, momentary, witnessing experience, I felt the first emotional sensation of what it might be like to inhabit the aesthetic reality where such feelings are at the very core of being human" (Feld, 1982, p. 237).

Crying and Popular Culture in the 21st Century

In order to understand the impact of the social context on crying and caregiving, I have been collecting data from books, newspapers, magazines, film, stage, and television during the past few decades. These references to crying are in the air we breathe every day. They enter our psychic systems and our relationships in insidious ways, just as smog from automobiles affects our respiratory tracts and body chemistry even when we think we are breathing clean air. What we do about shedding tears and responding to the tears of others and what we think and feel about crying and caregiving shift in subtle ways that integrate the social context with our early attachment and caregiving experiences.

The Language of Crying

Roy Schafer (1976), a psychoanalyst writing about the language of emotion, says, "How one thinks of the emotions establishes what they will be, not to speak of the esteem in which they will be held" (p. 267). In my collection of words for and sayings about crying, derogatory, accusatory, and just plain insulting words and phrases predominate. By far the greatest number of these are slanted toward women and children. When infantile or female words are used to describe male crying, the negative judgment is all the more extreme.

The infant crying words include "fretting," "whimpering," "wailing," "bawling," "squalling," "howling," "shrieking," "screaming," "blubbering," "fussing," and, in British English, "grizzling." Even the "whah, whah" and "boo hoo" of comic strip babies are used in everyday slang. These words have a negative tinge, especially when applied to adults.

"Cry-baby" is probably the most familiar crying insult. It is used from childhood on to brand someone who is an immature whiner, with or without tears. "Sob sisters" and "sob stories" are derogatory terms that originated in the 1920s to impugn sad or sentimental news stories and the female journalists who wrote them. Anyone of either gender who tries to play on someone's sympathy for his or her own ends may be accused of having a sob story.

The scientific word for tears is "lacrimation," from the Latin *lacrima* for tear and *lacrimare*, to cry. The short list of neutral or positive terms includes the verbs to weep, to cry, and to tear. (A male patient of a colleague told his therapist as he began to cry, "You struck a tear duct there.") One can also be "moved to tears" or "shed" them without implying negative judgment. Telling someone to have a "good cry" may be the closest we come to a positive affirmation of the experience.

The word "cry" is the most generic of all terms and I have used it that way in this book. Technically, however, it means the production of tears *and* sound. It may also be used to represent sound alone, as in that was a "cry" for help. I use "cry" in this book deliberately to retain the calling element intrinsic to the understanding of crying as attachment behavior. Weeping always refers to tear production, usually in the absence of any sounds (though it does have a silent beckoning quality). Sobbing suggests greater intensity of feeling, accompanied by motor, vocal, and respiratory activity. Being "wracked with sobs" indicates the total involvement of the body. Tears "streaming down" a face or a "fit" of weeping also represent intense crying.

The euphemisms we use for crying show our lack of acceptance and, sometimes, outright hostility toward tears. We "get misty eyed," "break down," "fill up" (my mother's favorite), "well up," "choke up," "lose control," "get overcome by emotion," or "get a lump in the throat." The media are especially prone to use these euphemistic terms—especially the milder ones such as the "glistening eyes and wet cheeks" of Tom Hanks in the Christopher Hitchens piece I quoted earlier. Still euphemistic, but harsher and almost always used for and by women, are "getting hysterical," "going crazy," "getting all broken up," or "losing it."

Roy Schafer points out how passivity (and something close to victimization) is often implicated in our emotion language. We are taken over by something alien. "Dissolving in tears," "reduced to tears," "overcome by tears," "drowning in tears," and "bursting into tears," as well as "breaking down," "coming unglued," and "coming apart at the seam" illustrate his point.

Injunctions to control crying also sound harsh: "control yourself," "get a grip," "snap out of it," "pull yourself together," and "grow up." We do have more respectful phrases that describe people who are trying to control crying, such as "blinking back tears," "choking back tears," "fighting back tears," or "swallowing" tears. All told, however, our language, unlike the Kaluli language, reflects a lack of comfort and respect decidedly aimed at female crying.

Attitudes Toward Crying and Gender

A female attorney from Southern California told me a few years ago that a judge was so infuriated when one of her colleagues cried during a summation that he called in all of the female attorneys who routinely appeared before him and ordered them never to shed a tear in his courtroom. A female judge in Indianapolis who wept when she sentenced a man found guilty of a brutal rape was asked by the defendant's lawyer to recuse herself on the basis that she was overly sympathetic to the victim. He appealed the case when she refused, but the appellate court ruled that "conspicuous compassion" did not mean that the judge was biased ("Compassionate Judge," 1993).

Adult crying is consistently viewed through the lens of gender. The prescription of the lens through which we think we look—that crying is all right for girls and women but not for boys and men—is believed to affect our judgments of crying behavior profoundly. This pervasively-expressed view, however, does not in fact bring social reality into focus. When William Frey (Frey & Langseth, 1985) surveyed adults about their experiences of crying, he found the opposite case. Of the women, 35% reported receiving negative reactions from others when they cried (ranging from embarrassment, nervousness, confusion, awkwardness, and helplessness to hostility, defensiveness, and guilt,) contrasted with only 8% of the men.

Social mores relating to male crying are in flux, leaving a trail of confusing messages not unlike those confronting women. Male crying was encouraged by the women's movement's critique of male stoicism and by the general trend toward greater emotional openness, thus making the 1970s the heyday of male crying. A short story from that era, entitled "Husbands" (McGrath, 1979), is about 22 men living communally after separating from their wives. At one point, after a failed outing with their collective children, morale is very low but, as one man says,

> [We] are beginning to "get in touch with our feelings." We cry a lot now. Crying does not come naturally to us, and our initial efforts produced only dry, self-conscious whimpers. But we have worked on our technique, and now we can simper, sniffle, and sob. We can pule. We can wail. We can heave and honk and blubber.... The sound of all 22 of us carrying on this way is so strange and so moving that it makes us cry even more" (pp. 45–46).

In a 1991 story (Frost, 1991), male crying is again the subject of hilarious and rather biting satire. A young woman with a relationship history that includes several freeloading boyfriends meets a man with a different scam for getting her to take care of him. When her car runs out of gas, he bursts into tears saying, "This is a metaphor for how the patriarchy's breaking down and me with it!" (p. 30). Then he sobs to her, "Please be my feminine principle and help me become whole again." At that, she gives him her parka and hikes to the gas station.

Some nonfictional men have also found it to their benefit to shed tears. A 40-year-old surgeon said,

> I cry every time I tell a woman I want to break up. I can't help it. I always feel that I've disappointed her, that somehow I've misled

her, that I'm being a rat. But crying seems to make it easier for her to accept. I admit that I get over it as soon as she's out of sight (Smith, 1989, p. B4).

Women may not be entirely fooled by this maneuver, however, if the character in Nora Ephron's novel *Heartburn* (1983) is any indication. She writes, "It's true that men who cry are sensitive to and in touch with feelings, but the only feelings they tend to be sensitive to and in touch with are their own" (p. 88).

Many men are still conflicted over crying, however. A sheriff's deputy in San Francisco who understandably cried whenever he went to funeral services for a fellow officer felt so badly about doing it that he quit going to funerals altogether. He said no matter how he tried he could not escape from what he called his "macho" upbringing. In spite of greater social acceptance, he still felt saddled with the stereotype of stoical male behavior.

Former President Bill Clinton, on the other hand, cried easily in public and seemed comfortable with it. When he was first elected, his tearfulness was carefully documented—some columnists even compiled lists of the occasions. A short *San Francisco Examiner* article ("Clinton Puts His Heart into Farewell," 1992) seemed to talk of little else—his crying was mentioned twice in the first sentence. The journalist used the following male-friendly, nonjudgmental language: President Clinton got "choked up" and appeared "to wipe tears from his eyes." His voice was "thick with emotion" and he appeared "moved" and "misty-eyed." Then the eyewitness accounts were given: "Journalists in the front row saw a tear trickle down his cheek." In the end, Clinton's perspective was cited as he "admitted he had been worked up about leaving" his former office, adding that "it was an emotional time for me" (p. A8).

For female political leaders, different rules seem to apply. *Time* magazine (Donne, 1991) said, "In today's political climate, men may weep, but women must prove themselves made of sterner stuff" (p. 84). Representative Patricia Schroeder, who cried when she withdrew from the Presidential race in 1987, was brutally attacked in the press for it and accused of being emotionally unfit for presidential office. Even a supporter was critical in a letter to the *Los Angeles Times* (Wilson, 1987): "If, as one reporter points out, a woman must publicly announce that she will not be running for the very office that many still question her toughness for, she probably ought not to sob while telling them" (p. 7). That was tame compared to what her critics said.

Attachment and caregiving issues definitely emerge for leaders of both genders. Because they are symbolic, communal caregivers, we look to them for reassurance, security, and strength. When they show attachment behavior by crying, they may demonstrate a need to be taken care of, rather than being stalwart caregivers. To the extent that their tears demonstrate compassion and empathy (especially for male leaders), they can be humanizing and a source of connection to their constituents. Perhaps that makes a difference for female leaders as well. Margaret Thatcher shed tears at two different points in her career as prime minister. The first time she was ridiculed as being too weak to perform her duties. The second crying incident (further along in her career) softened her so-called "iron lady" image and was reviewed sympathetically.

Solitary Crying

Crying in solitude contradicts the reason we cry: for connection. Rather than show feelings and reveal the need for closeness, many people learn to hide their tears from others. Eleanor Roosevelt was taught as a child that if she had to cry she should go into the bathroom and close the door so she would not bother other people. In fact, a great deal of adult crying takes place in bathrooms. The shower has particular advantages—no one can see or hear the crier and the evidence is washed away as soon as it appears. The obvious advantage of bathroom crying, however, is that privacy is condoned there and tears may be shed in secret. Alone behind closed doors, we avoid shame or embarrassment, as well as social awkwardness or judgment. The result is that many people are inclined to choose isolation and distance in their moments of need.

Crying is designed to bring us closer together, but the discomfort, misunderstandings, and interpersonal judgments it evokes often drive us further apart instead. The fact that crying in front of other people is an issue gives us away, however. It shows that we know tears have a powerful interpersonal impact, one that, by solitary crying, we seek to avoid.

Crying and Grief Reactions

Crying is a common occurrence at funeral services. Social values generally support crying by the bereaved, although the opposite is also true: not crying at the death of a close loved one is often admired. Refraining from tears is called "bearing up," "being strong," or "doing very well under the circumstances." A friend spoke to her mother after a cousin's funeral and asked how it had gone. Her mother said, "It was good. No one broke down." A researcher surveying adults in Great Britain (Gorer, 1965) turned up frequent responses characterizing open grief as "morbid and unhealthy" and inhibited crying after a loss by death as psychologically healthy. As with so much that has to do with crying in our culture, we are confused and ambivalent about crying and bereavement.

These mixed messages can be confusing for people dealing with a loss. James Carville, one of President Clinton's campaign advisors, lost his father in 1978. One of his siblings said:

> [James] gathered us all together at the funeral home—he was the man of the family now—and said, "There will be no breaking down now. If Jackie Kennedy can do it, so can we." And the first person to arrive and say something to James, he broke into tears. Then he told us, "O.K., breaking down will be allowed" (Wills, 1992, p. 93).

As with so many other aspects of crying, hard data about crying and bereavement are scarce. One study (Glick, Weiss, & Parkes, 1974) reported that 92% of the widows studied cried when they first learned of their husbands' deaths and most continued to do so through the first year. About 66% of the widowers also cried at the time of the deaths of their wives, but less than half of them continued to cry at the end of the first year.

Forty-six percent of the widows, however, also said they felt the need to control their feelings for the sake of others. One was proud that she had maintained her composure in accordance with her husband's instructions before his death: "If anything ever happens to me," he told her, "I don't want you to go to pieces. I want you to act like Jacqueline Kennedy—you know, very brave and courageous. You've got to have class. I just don't want you screaming and hollering" (Glick et al., 1974, p. 60).

Another study (Kalish & Reynolds, 1976) looked at the mourning behavior of African–, Mexican–, Japanese–, and Euro–Americans in Los Angeles, offering a rare cross-cultural view within the United States. Three fourths of the African–, Japanese–, and Euro–Americans (but not the Mexican–Americans) said they would try very hard to control their emotions in public at a funeral, although crying in private was considered appropriate. Overall, Mexican–Americans were the most publicly expressive and Japanese–Americans the least.

Although members of the African–American community claimed they would restrain from public grief, many of the mourners cried openly at the funerals studied. Attending an African–American funeral as part of the study protocol, one of the researchers, a Japanese–American, was so touched by the displays of grief that she cried too, even though she did not know the deceased.

Another variable that impacts the appearance of crying at funerals and, perhaps even more, the conflicted feelings of mourners about crying, is religious teachings regarding the expression of grief. A Mexican–American fundamentalist minister told an interviewer (Kalish & Reynolds, 1976): "We grieve according to whether the person who died was a believer of God.... If you have hope that you'll see that person again someplace, sometime, you won't feel as bad." In traditional Latin–American Catholic practices, parents were discouraged from crying when a child died because a child in "gloria" (called an "angelito" or little angel) could offer salvation to those left behind. Tears of the mourner might then invite rejection by calling the child's soul back to this life. Anthropologist Nancy Scheper-Hughes (1992) writes that the Catholic church in Brazil now teaches that "celebrating" the death of "child angels" is wrong because it throws mothers into "moral and ideological confusion" (p. 529).

Sometimes the caregiving side of the crying equation confuses mourners. One young mother I saw for therapy a year after her husband died of a heart attack reported that when she began to cry with friends and family, they would begin to cry as well. At that point she felt obliged to stop crying and take care of them instead of receiving their comfort and support. A colleague who works with bereaved elderly people reports that their most common experience when they begin to cry with friends and family about a loss is for potential caregivers to quickly change the subject, putting the bereaved in conflict about their crying.

Rather than show our feelings and support our need for connection in public expressions of grief, we withdraw from each other. As anthropologist Steven Feld (personal communication, March 24, 1992) said to me about the Kaluli, "The thing they would find absolutely the most amazing about our culture is that we wear sunglasses at funerals to hide our tears." To them, tears are the essence of community and comfort, designed to bring people together for healing from a loss. Our social anxieties about attachment and caregiving interfere with our grieving process and, ultimately, with our healing process as well.

Perhaps some cultural anxiety and ambivalence about crying and caregiving at funerals is beginning to shift. Several years ago, I attended a memorial service at Napa High School for a much-loved high school senior who had died in a tragic water slide accident on a class trip the week before graduation. As I looked around the gymnasium, I saw people crying and people touching and hugging each other—an emergency medical technician who had treated her at the scene, the school bus drivers in their uniforms, her classmates and teachers, her parents, her best friends, her prom date, the entire school choir. Many people were crying, but no one was crying alone. We were all together in that giant cavernous space, literally and symbolically clinging together. Crying is not only a way for us to get rid of our pain; it is a way to help us do something positive about it: join together and thereby reaffirm our hope for ongoing connection in the face of loss.

CHAPTER 7

Healthy Adult Crying or Inhibited Crying, and Healthy Adult Caregiving

Healthy crying and healthy caregiving go hand in hand with secure attachment. Because of the interlocking nature of the attachment and caregiving systems, securely attached individuals are confident that when they cry a caregiver will be there, in person or in spirit. Securely attached people are also best able to respond with empathy and attuned caregiving to attachment messages from other people. Whether adults cry or do not cry, their type of crying and their feelings about it reveal much more than their ability to express, or defend against, affect. Because crying is an attachment behavior throughout life, it carries an attachment valence: secure or insecure. Careful observation of people who inhibit crying when it would be expected or appropriate can also provide clues as to attachment security.

An assessment of adult caregiving styles that takes into account the giving and the receiving of care is equally revealing. Ease in responding to the crying of other people, coupled with the expectation that comfort is available and effective when one is personally in need, represents what might be called "secure caregiving," the mirror image of secure attachment. It makes sense that securely attached individuals would have the easiest time with seeking and accepting caregiving and with making positive, reparative use of it. They are able to use interpersonal caregiving connections to repair and soothe the so-called "negative affect" underlying their tears or, alternatively, to use their internal resources to soothe and comfort themselves.

Securely attached people who do not cry when it would be expected or appropriate may nonetheless be able to use others to whom they are closely attached—or themselves—to heal their grief. To heal from grief and vulnerability without tears when an external caregiver is not present requires the experience of an available and accessible internal caregiver, a hallmark of secure attachment.

The illustration in Figure 7.1 shows examples of behaviors from both attachment and caregiving systems and their interlocking nature. Caregiving and attachment coexist in mutual adult relationships, although in certain pairs, and at various times in any pair, caregiving may tilt more heavily to one side or the other. In healthy, secure pairs, the attachment bond is a constant, even in times of conflict or extreme dependence.

Adult Attachment Styles

For research purposes, Hazan and Shaver (1987) translated Ainsworth's infant attachment styles into adult terms for their study of attachment and romantic love. Since then numerous researchers have incorporated their descriptions into other studies. The Hazan and Shaver shorthand version of designating attachment styles relies on a few brief questions to

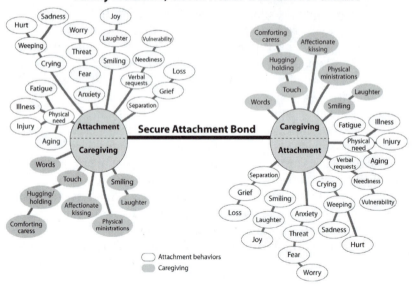

Fig. 7.1 Reciprocal attachment/caregiving behaviors between adult family members, close friends, and romantic partners.

participants about their expectations and beliefs about close relationships. The terms that Hazan and Shaver use to classify adult attachment styles are the same as those used for infants and children: secure, anxious-ambivalent, and avoidant.

By contrast, the more thorough Adult Attachment Interview pioneered by Mary Main involves a long personal interview and uses unique, although related, language to categorize adult attachment styles. For purposes of clinical assessment, when the administration of a full Adult Attachment Interview is not practical, possible, or clinically indicated, I have amplified Hazan and Schaver's descriptions of adult attachment styles to include crying and the caregiving behavior that it evokes (Nelson, 2000). The parallel adult attachment categories used by Main and others (Hesse, 1999) are noted in parentheses after the name of each style described.

Secure Attachment Style (Secure-Autonomous)

An adult with a secure style of attachment is confident in the reliability and availability of attachment figures, able to activate attachment behavior (crying) when vulnerable, and capable of intimacy (including being comfortable with the soothing, caregiving behavior evoked in others by his or her crying or evoked internally by the crying of others).

Anxious-Ambivalent or Resistant Attachment Style (Preoccupied)

Individuals with the anxious-ambivalent style are unable to trust in the availability of attachment figures. They demonstrate a desperate desire for connection along with a strong fear of rejection. They are likely to hyperactivate the attachment system (crying) during times of distress and to cling to their attachment figures, showing an anxious, even demanding, need for caregiving and soothing coupled with great difficulty in being soothed. They are prone to compulsive caregiving to others as a way of containing their anxiety and securing the presence and caregiving responses of the attachment object.

Avoidant Style (Dismissing)

A person with an avoidant style is unable to trust in the reliability of attachment figures and defensively attempts to deactivate the attachment system (crying) during times of vulnerability and distress. He or she is typically seen as emotionally distant and compulsively self-reliant and tends to be intolerant of caregiving from others and uncomfortable with giving care to others who cry.

Hazan and Shaver's original research did not include the fourth category of attachment style, "disorganized-disoriented," which was later discovered and described by attachment researchers Main and Solomon (1990). I have attempted to transcribe that style of attachment and caregiving for purposes of clinical conceptualization and comparison.

Disorganized-Disoriented Attachment Style (Unresolved-Disorganized)

Individuals who display this adult attachment style demonstrate chaotic, confused relationships with attachment figures, unpredictably mixing approach and avoidance. Attachment behavior (crying) occurs at unpredictable and often seemingly inappropriate times. Caregiving may be desperately sought and resisted simultaneously. Caregiving attempts *from* others may evoke hostility or fear. Caregiving needs expressed *by* others may be met inconsistently with expansive, even excessive, soothing or, alternatively, with hostility, fear, and retreat.

Healthy Crying

A good cry is restorative, creative, and cleansing. It can help us heal and regain a sense of hope. However, a good cry is paradoxical: it is about pain *and* relief, despair *and* hope, agony *and* comfort. No matter how good it is, it does not have the power to undo loss and pain. It does not make our lover come home, release us from the sting of a cruel remark, or give us a better grade on our algebra final.

A good cry does not necessarily even feel good—it may hurt deeply. We do not seek "a good cry" because it is pleasurable, although we may welcome it as a friend. It is good like a cast on our leg is good because it helps support us when we are in pain, while helping the injury to heal. Crying helps us recover from the hard things that happen to us.

I have long thought that the somewhat old-fashioned ego-psychological concept, "regression in the service of the ego" (Hartman, 1958), fits well with healthy crying. Crying is always in the broadest sense "regressive," in that it takes us back to our preverbal, bodily expressed distress states. The meaning behind Hartman's original idea about regression is that it requires a healthy ego to surrender to a certain level of vulnerability. Healthy crying for adults does require a healthy self-concept, security, and the ability to tolerate and, more importantly, to demonstrate vulnerability.

Healthy Caregiving (and Care Receiving)

If the purpose of healthy crying is to bring about a healing connection with a caring attachment figure, it is necessary that the crier be able to accept and benefit from it. It is also necessary to have close relationships with people who are willing and able to give care. In her book, *Lost Lullaby*, author Deborah Golden Alecson (as cited in Aronson, 1995) describes just such a situation that occurred during an agonizing period of grief following the birth of her severely brain-damaged daughter. One night when her husband was out for dinner with his parents, she had several glasses of wine, "sprawled out on the carpet in the living room, dressed in a skimpy negligee with candles lit" and cried. When her husband returned and saw her there, she said that he "poured himself a glass of wine, stripped down to his underwear, and joined me on the floor. He held me as I continued to cry" (p. 7). The tenderness, comfort, and closeness that her narrative communicates is an example of caregiving (and care receiving) at its best.

Being able to give care sensitively and to receive care gratefully is far more difficult than it might seem. The ability to seek and benefit from caregiving in adulthood requires that the crier feel at least some degree of trust and security with the caregiver. The crier must also have the capacity to be soothed interactively (within a relationship), which is a struggle for the insecurely attached. Sometimes, it is also a struggle for securely attached people who have come to prefer self-soothing because that was the preferred method in their families or because they have acquired a more independent style of soothing as adults.

A complete clinical assessment of crying must also include the conscious observation (and internal experience) of the caregiving side of an interaction. Crying and caregiving are intertwined and thus must always be considered in tandem and intersubjectively. Both also depend in large part upon attachment style.

The Clinical Assessment of Crying

The assessment of crying in psychotherapy can be approached in two ways. One is to listen to accounts of crying and caregiving experiences that patients relate from their lives. The content of the stories—the precipitants and the outcomes, the use of self and others—and also the language used to describe crying and caregiving are full of clues about attachment relationships, past and present. The second, more immediately available assessment tool is the crying and caregiving that take place within the therapeutic relationship. When the patient cries with the therapist, both have a direct experience of attachment and caregiving in the moment. For both people, the experience resonates with the state of their attachment and caregiving bonds in the past and the present, as well as within the current therapeutic relationship.

Accounts of Crying and Caregiving Reported in Psychotherapy

A number of factors are relevant in assessing crying and caregiving when experiences of each are reported in psychotherapy sessions. Is the crying described proportionate to the degree of loss? Was the person able to artic-ulate the losses (or some of the losses) being grieved in a particular crying episode? Does he or she describe reaching out for comfort and being open to receiving care? Did the soothing work and were there signs of reorganization or healing? Are there signs of disappointment in others or unrealistic expectations of self or other caregivers? Is the crier judgmental or self-critical?

Millie, who came to see me for psychotherapy 6 months after she returned from France, where she had been an American student at the Sorbonne, told a story about a crying and caregiving experience while she was abroad. She had studied French for 5 years before enrolling in school there. She could read the language well, but did not have confidence in her conversational abilities. One day in class the professor asked her a question about an assignment and she froze. She could not think of how to reply and, to make things worse, she started to cry. After class she ran into her friend, JoAnne, another American student whom she had known since high school. They went to the park and Millie tearfully told her about her sense of helplessness in class. JoAnne sat with her on the bench and sympathized with her, "You're right. It hurts to lose something so basic as opening our mouths to speak." As they sat together Millie continued to cry and tried to express to JoAnne what she had been feeling.

Millie said that she felt she had lost more than her speaking ability; she had lost her self-confidence and her sense of being an intelligent, competent woman with extraordinary skill at communication. She could not even function as a university student any more, never mind excel as she usually did. She missed the comfortable familiarity of moving through her classes with ease and speaking without needing to search for words or tripping up on strange grammatical constructions and worrying about making a fool of herself.

After listening for a while, JoAnne recalled their high school French teacher's words of encouragement: "You have studied. The language is in you. Just relax and it will flow," and Millie realized that her fear of making mistakes was paralyzing her. By responding to her tears with comfort and counsel, JoAnne helped Millie regain a sense of personal mastery and the image of herself as a competent, intelligent person. As they talked, Millie remembered how she had felt helping a French exchange student at her school learn English. She expected him to make mistakes—how could he be perfect when he was just learning? She never felt critical of him.

Gradually, Millie's despair turned to relief and resolve: she knew the words and the grammar well enough to express herself and be understood and now she felt determined to take the risk and do so.

Millie's tears that afternoon in Paris took her through all the stages of the grieving process in one sitting. She went from protest and frustration: "This is too much—I can't do it!" to sadness and despair: "I will never feel at ease in this language like I do in my own," to hope and reorganization: "Okay, so I make mistakes, I can communicate my basic ideas and just keep trying to learn more." Her crying, coupled with JoAnne's response, enabled her to connect with the confident sense of herself that she had lost. Working through the grief over her loss in this way even helped her to grow; she gained a sense of strength and resolve to face a challenge, even though it might include stumbling and making mistakes along the way.

It was too early in our relationship to be certain, but I noted that many aspects of Millie's story contained markers of secure attachment. She cried appropriately in grief over her loss of mastery. Of course, it was not ideal that she cried in class in front of her professor and the other students, which was socially embarrassing, but she recognized that being so far from home and her usual support system was another part of the loss. She did not dwell on, or even mention in the account she gave, any shame at having to return to class the next day. She had also been able to connect with an attachment figure, an old friend who was familiar with her home and with her. She was not only open to sharing her vulnerability, but she was open to comfort.

Crying and Caregiving in the Therapeutic Relationship

Dave, a man I was seeing in couples therapy, illustrates how crying that takes place in the here and now of a therapy session reveals much about attachment and caregiving styles and dynamics. The key to assessment is that the therapist pays conscious attention to crying within this context, rather than allowing it to remain on the periphery unexamined or thinking of it merely as the discharge of painful affect.

Dave cried in a session as he talked about missing his family in another state since he had moved to California to be with his new partner, Robert. Robert and I expressed understanding of his loss and how difficult it must be to have his large and close-knit family so far away. We felt with him and for him. Robert's face showed compassion and concern. He put out his hand to cover Dave's and occasionally patted it in sympathy. Eventually Dave's mood lightened and we went on to talk about their plans for a trip to see his family over the holidays. On the way out of my office Dave stopped to drop his tissues into the wastebasket and said to Robert, "She's got quite a collection of tissues in there! She must be good!" and we all had a good laugh together as they left.

What I could see from Dave's crying was that he accepted it and comfortably acknowledged the healing potential of his tears. Clearly, he was also open to the caregiving offered by his partner and by me and was able to recognize that we truly felt with him what it is like to live far away from family. From the way in which he gradually moved through his pain enough to talk about his trip with eager anticipation, I also could see that he was able to use interactive repair and was secure in receiving care.

I later reflected on my reactions to Dave's crying as a way to assess his attachment and caregiving. I realized that his losses resonated for me as they would for many people in this highly mobile society. One of my adult daughters lives in New York City and my sister and her family in Washington, D.C., and I miss them all the time. His sadness touched another level of my grief as well. I had quite deliberately moved far away from my parents because I could not at that time withstand their pressure and censure about leaving the church of my childhood. I grieved for what was missing with my parents rather than simply because I missed them. I knew from my self-examination that my caregiving urges toward Dave as he cried came from a place of personal understanding and loss as well as empathy specific to his situation. His crying invited me in on multiple levels, which I took to mean that he and I were open and on the same attachment/caregiving wavelength.

I also reflected on Dave's joke about my being a good therapist and could see that it might mean several things. I think he consciously meant it as a sideways compliment to me, letting me know that he appreciated what had happened that day. His joke was a way to "give care" to the therapist. I also considered that his comment might mean that he had the idea that crying in therapy is "good" because it is "expected" or because it signifies that we are "working on" things. In that case, his joke could have been an acknowledgment that crying had lightened his mood or a way to seek my approval by lightheartedly calling my attention to his crying as he disposed of his tissues.

It also occurred to me that seeing other patients' tissues in the basket might have made Dave feel a little less special. However, that was something to keep in mind for the future of our work together, not the thrust of his conscious comment at that moment. Finally, revisiting the humor from a different angle, I made a little wordplay joke to myself. I noted that "tissues" rhymes with "issues," which I, the crying scholar, had never noticed before. I took that as a parallel to Dave's joke, which meant that I too felt a little better after our mutual grieving (internalized for me) and caregiving that day.

Healthy Crying in the Insecurely Attached

I do not mean to imply in the preceding discussion that only securely attached people demonstrate healthy crying and caregiving. Insecurely attached people may also do so at some times and in some relationships. They may also, in the context of healing adult relationships, develop an attachment style that has been called "earned secure" (Hesse, 1999).

Sad cries of despair involve letting go of control and surrendering to loss, and they require the presence or inner experience of, or the wish for, a caregiver. Crying in psychotherapy, even in insecurely attached people, may represent a move toward a more secure caregiving connection with the therapist. Successful experiences of crying in despair in the context of caregiving from close friends, family, or adult romantic partners may also gradually enable the insecurely attached person to approach "earned" security. In my experience as a therapist, this kind of change does not come easily or quickly; however, for some people, it does come.

Peggy

Following more than a decade in treatment during which time she cried frequently, but always with shame and self-criticism, Peggy began to cry about a particularly hurtful exchange with her mother. She had been helping her mother shop for a new outfit when her younger sister called on the cell phone to say she would take her mother to pickout the dress. Her mother immediately rejected Peggy's help (and, by implication, Peggy) and said that she would wait until that evening and shop with her younger daughter. As Peggy recounted this incident to me, her tears flowed but she no longer called herself "stupid" or seemed ashamed as she had previously. I sat quietly. My caregiving took the form of shaking my head in dismay at this overt, undisguised preference for the younger sister. I nodded toward the box of tissues sitting near her and she took one, although in the past she had rummaged in her purse to find one of her own. In this small symbolic way, taking my tissue, she was able to accept my caregiving openly. I finally said a few words about how unbelievably blatant her mother was and how intrusively her younger sister had inserted herself into the situation. Then I added in a sympathetic voice how painful this was for Peggy and how this unfair treatment had had an impact on her self-esteem over her whole life.

Peggy's crying this time had all the components of healthy crying and caregiving: feeling her sadness and despair, letting me be there with her and receiving my caregiving. She was no longer trapped in the anxious-ambivalent cycle of attachment: crying easily but being unable to take in my caregiving or to self-soothe comfortably. She was not yet at the point of consolidating her gains and "earning" security, but one day a few years later she came in from the waiting room bursting with joy and said, "I just saw the green grass." She repeated for emphasis, "The green grass! Something is happening to me! I'm finally able to see!" Her internal world was beginning to shift in a positive direction that she could feel and identify.

Bill

After long, unsettling, painful years trying to understand the therapeutic relationship and its formalized (though potentially genuine) attachment relationship, Bill's avoidant attachment style softened enough that he was able to cry. His tears had been visible to me before but, up until this point in treatment, he had fought them back with wrenching (and equally visible) determination. He also resisted all my efforts to show that I was with him or understood or cared about his pain. He openly rejected empathic comments or responded with sarcasm. Sometimes, he would simply say, "I don't get this" (meaning the therapeutic relationship and my caregiving).

On this particular day, Bill was telling me how his girlfriend had been criticizing him for not being sufficiently attentive to her. He reported some of the cutting things that she had said to him and he began to cry. This time, he let the tears come instead of fighting them. His face was relaxed and his body slumped into abject despair. I felt a deep sense of compassion for him, but I held back from expressing it verbally. My silence seemed for the moment to be all the caregiving that he could tolerate. Here was a man whose insecure, avoidant attachment style had left him feeling confused about what others wanted from him, yet yearning for something he could not name or accept. Those first tears of despair shed in my presence were a significant indicator that something different was beginning to transpire in his attachment and caregiving system.

Bea

Bea was in the early months of her therapy when she reported an incident that made her feel mystified and uncomfortable, even a little angry. She had been on the telephone talking to an insurance agent she knew slightly, and in the course of the conversation, he had called her "honey" in a kindly parental way. She immediately started to cry and of course felt embarrassed and upset about it. Her crying puzzled her so much that she brought up the incident in her therapy session.

Bea was just beginning to allow herself to feel the grief of her massively misattuned and emotionally abusive childhood upbringing. Her mother would rage at her when she cried and call her a baby. Her father's method of soothing was to tell her that she was not in fact feeling afraid or lonely or whatever vulnerable emotion she seemed to be expressing. The appearance of this unannointed caregiver, the insurance salesman, at this moment in time caught her off guard. His use of the intimate word "honey" and his kindly tone unleashed her grief in a way that made her feel the tiniest bit hopeful, even as she said that the man was a patriarchal jerk for presuming to call her that. My soothing took the form of helping her to see that he had tapped into her wish in childhood to have a soothing somebody somewhere care about her. When he came out of nowhere with his kindly, though misplaced, parental remark, she was able to cry in sadness and despair for what she had been missing all her life.

Symptomatic Responses to Healthy Crying

Even healthy crying over appropriate losses may cause criers to respond negatively. Self-deprecating remarks, such as "I'm losing it here" or apologies, "I'm sorry, I told myself I wouldn't do this," signal internalized judgments about crying. People with avoidant attachment styles may be uncomfortable with any crying in any setting. However, securely attached people who cry comfortably alone or with a few intimates may also express similar negative feelings about crying in front of others.

When assessing whether social discomfort is coloring complaints about crying, a direct question will usually elicit the answer. Most people know and can readily say if they do not like crying or think it causes problems for them socially or personally. Follow-up questions about the sources for their feelings will also help to clarify their significance in relationship to the complaint. It is also important to listen to the particular language used to describe crying to see if it is negative or self-disparaging, even in subtle ways.

When negativity about crying is observed early in treatment, the questions could be a matter-of-fact part of early exploration and assessment. I did that with the woman cancer patient, Sharon, when she was so determined to stop crying after her chemotherapy treatment. I quickly learned that, for her, resistance to crying was related to her attachment style rather than to internalized social judgment.

In another instance, the mother of a newly diagnosed developmentally disabled infant apologized profusely for crying as she told me about her child in the first session. When I asked about her hesitancy to cry, her answer was much different from Sharon's. She said that she had been crying daily ever since her child had been diagnosed. Her grief was understandable, she knew, but she saw her consultation with me as the time to start learning to cope. There were complicated self-expectations in her explanation and an understandable wish to put the painful aspect of the sadness, grief, and despair behind her. However, her crying was appropriate and her caregiving and care-receiving behaviors seemed to reflect secure attachment. I came to the tentative conclusion that she resisted crying because her loss was so difficult to bear. She also feared that her feelings would immobilize her. Knowing that, I could reassure her that the two are not mutually exclusive; she could cry *and* cope.

Healthy Solitary Crying

Solitary crying works when we feel sufficiently secure to draw on our own reserves and when it is used to signal ourselves that we are in need of care and nurturance. As one woman put it using attachment terms, "When I cry alone, I feel a sense of connection with myself." I would add that solitary crying at its best also enables the crier to connect with whomever (or whatever) has been lost.

In a rush to finish her errands one day, 70-year-old Virginia forgot her ATM password and found herself crying in her car in momentary despair over her failing memory. She recognized that her crying signaled a need for self-nurturance. She sat there for a few minutes in the sun feeling sad. Then she thought,

> I have been pushing myself too hard. I'm just going to stop right now and take care of myself this afternoon. I'll go to the park, walk in the rose garden and sit on a bench. I'm too old to stress over the little things when there is so much beauty and life around me.

Virginia is a person who has built a network of personal connections filled with many friends and loved ones. Any one of Virginia's many friends would have been glad to comfort her in this moment of despair about aging but, because she was secure that they were there, she could make the choice this time to perform that function with and for herself.

In the years immediately following my divorce, I lived 10 miles up a steep and winding road in the hills above the Napa Valley. Driving up from town through the madrone and oak trees was a soothing journey after a busy day. I often played music—and I often cried. My car became a safe little time capsule where I relived and grieved the 23 years of good times when the girls were young and we were a tight family unit. I was deeply in touch with the joy of that past, which made its ending doubly painful. I wept for what was so incredibly gone and the pain of losing it. I also cried in a kind of melancholic reverie as I summoned up memories of the wonderful ways in which we had "been there" together and for each other. By the time I got home, I could remind myself that, even though the family as we had known it then was ended, I would always feel connected to my daughters and former husband internally and in ways we were all in the process of discovering, in letters, e-mails, phone calls, and visits.

Healthy Inhibited Crying

The absence of crying is sometimes obvious though often it is not visible to an observer, which makes it difficult to assess. Is the observer merely thinking that he or she would cry under the circumstances or that most people would shed tears? Also, many losses are totally subjective and it is impossible to impose any kind of objective view. Is the person in denial or is he or she truly not feeling threatened by what might be considered a loss to someone else?

Some people never cry yet fit healthy psychological profiles (Frey & Langseth, 1985). The term "inhibited crying," suggested to me by a colleague, Dr. Saul Rosenberg, is an appropriate description for people who never cry and who have no desire or ability to do so. Some people complain of periods or occasions when they would normally cry but find themselves unable to do so, which is a situational form of inhibited crying. When people who can and do cry suppress tears consciously, the term "prohibited crying" seems more appropriate. People who prohibit crying do so by diverting their thoughts, smoking, eating, taking deep breaths, laughing, or distracting themselves. Because so many personal and social factors go into the choice to prohibit crying on specific occasions, for purposes of assessment, we will only consider people with inhibited crying.

Healthy inhibited crying is possible when people feel and express their sadness, despair, and grief in ways other than crying. They talk about their losses, write, or sing about them. They are also able to comfortably turn to people around them for comfort and solace. After her mother died, Dana was sad and low-key even though she never shed a tear and could not imagine that she would because she had not done so in years. Her explanation was that she had "outgrown" crying when she founded her fashion design business and hired numerous employees to work for her.

After she returned home from the funeral, she thought of her mother often and told her husband how sad it made her not to be able to pick up the telephone to chat with her about a situation at work. In the evenings during the first month, Dana curtailed her social activities and chose to stay home with her husband and 6-year-old son. She began to work on a special scrapbook with photographs and keepsakes from her mother's life and she told her son it was to help them remember his grandmother. Then she would tell him she was sad and missed her mother and ask him for a hug and a kiss to make her feel better. She would ask her husband to sit with her on the sofa after dinner and would snuggle close to him and tell him when something on the television evoked her grief. She sought and took solace from the comfort of her family in the immediate aftermath of her loss. Her care-receiving functioned fully even though her attachment behavior was thwarted. Hers was a healthy version of inhibited crying.

Assessing Crying and Bereavement

Healing from grief is not about getting over the pain; it is about getting over the despair, recovering from what may feel like a threat to survival. We cry when we lose a loved one because of the permanent separation and the huge, unimaginable loss that we face. Like infants separated from our parents, we cry instinctively then.

Sudden waves of grief and tears are typical responses in the months or years following a major loss. Emotions may be tranquil and manageable for hours or days. Then something will come along that brings the loss to mind and the pain and tears will return unforeseen and unbidden. Knowing that this can be expected can sometimes bring relief to people suffering a major loss. A mother in grief over the death of her infant daughter was upset because she would start crying over little things when she was not even thinking about her daughter's death. Once it happened when a Pampers diaper commercial came on television and another time when she went to buy a new camera. It was as if the pain of her loss was lurking just out of consciousness and could hit her at any time. When she realized that this is the way in which grief works, she stopped feeling so crazy for crying at odd times.

When theorists and researchers first began to study the course of grief after a major loss, they focused on the first 6 months, believing that to be a reasonable time frame for recovery. They found that crying continued throughout that period but decreased over time. More recently, however, studies are looking at the long-term effects of grief. In one such study, 40% of bereaved people checked the response, "At times I still feel the need to cry for the person who died," years (up to 10 years in this study) after the loss of their loved one (Zisook, DeVaul, & Click, 1982).

Conventional wisdom has it that crying after a death helps to get the grief "out," thereby releasing the tension and stress that drains energy. But why would we want to *get rid of* feelings caused by a loss? Why would we want to empty ourselves out when the problem is that losing our loved one has already left us feeling so empty?

Author David Macfarlane (as cited in Klinkenborg, 1992) interviewed his great-aunt Kate for his book, *Come From Away: Memory, War, and the Search for a Family's Past.* She still shed tears of grief 50 years after her three brothers, Ray, Stan, and Hedley Goodyear, died in World War I. Her tears were a way to honor her lost loved ones, keeping them present and "alive" after they "passed away." Crying is a wonderful testament to the longevity of her relationship with them—a positive way of holding onto them even after so many years. If losing them still hurts and still matters, so do they and so does her love for them. Because crying is about separation *and* connection, loss *and* love, it helps us acknowledge the person who is missing while recognizing that he or she is in fact gone. Crying helps us to heal by letting us remember in the deepest part of ourselves.

Looking at the timeline of grief another way, however, some contemporary research is beginning to question the efficacy of openly encouraging people to talk—and openly grieve—in the aftermath of a traumatic loss. The technique known as "special incident debriefing," whereby grief counselors meet with those who have experienced or witnessed a traumatic loss within the first 24 to 48 hours after the event, is now being questioned on the basis that it may further traumatize people. Instead, it has been suggested that the passage of time in the presence of the person's usual support system and affect-regulating style is the best course. It would appear that having options available after a trauma, including grief counselors for those who wish to talk, is a better option than routinely prescribed grief counseling. Perhaps attachment style has something to do with the differing responses to formalized caregiving.

Recent studies have also shown that the bereaved elderly who do best are those who grieve quickly for their losses, perhaps because they do not have the energy to invest in prolonged grieving at that stage of their lives. I recently saw an 88-year-old woman who had been crying several hours a day for weeks over the sudden death of her beloved cat. After a few weeks in which I offered sympathy and comfort, I shared with her the research findings about the elderly. That next week she resolved that she had cried enough over the cat and began to work to distract herself and go forward with her life. Within a few more weeks, she had changed her mind about not getting a new cat and soon was deeply attached to him. Perhaps this kind of grief is a speeded-up process that enables the elderly to reorganize and reattach quickly so that they are able to recover and survive.

Whether grief is short or long, includes crying or is dry eyed, it is about a ruptured attachment bond, and it is best accomplished within a close circle of caregiving intimates. The differing attachment styles and related styles of affect regulation of the bereaved dictate that no single expressive or, for that matter, repressive style for healthy grief can be prescribed. More than crying, successful healing is determined by the availability of close attachment/caregiving relationships.

A "Good Cry"

A good cry is circular: it takes us from disconnection and loss, through feelings of grief, and back to connection again. A good cry is liberating; fully facing our pain enables us to let it go and release the energy that can be bound up in ignoring and resisting it. However, we cannot do that alone. That is what families, lovers, friends, and therapists are for: to give us the care and energy of their presence, or at least the memory or the promise of it. When we feel the most disconnected, we cry, and when someone reaches for us—or when we feel his or her presence in our despair—that connection, not our tears, helps restore faith, hope, and balance.

CHAPTER 8

Symptomatic Adult Crying and Inhibited Crying

At first glance, it seems strange to think that an innocuous, inborn behavior such as crying could be dysfunctional or symptomatic. Crying is associated with vulnerability and carries with it the presumption of a certain childlike innocence. It is also, for the most part, beyond conscious control, which lends it a sense of inevitability that has mostly rendered it off limits for conscious clinical assessment. However, once we postulate different kinds of crying, different social attitudes toward crying, and an association between crying styles and attachment/caregiving styles, it becomes clear that some crying—and some inhibited crying—might be maladaptive, dysfunctional, or immature. Symptomatic crying and inhibited crying may also be associated with psychiatric or physical disorders. What might be called "insecure" caregiving styles may also be dysfunctional, maladaptive, undeveloped, or abusive in response to healthy, functional crying or to symptomatic crying.

The Assessment of Symptomatic Crying

The signs to be considered in the assessment of symptomatic crying include the following:

- protest crying that elicits apathy or irritation instead of sympathy or empathy
- crying accompanied by infantile behaviors or sounds, or by stereotyped, repetitive body movements

- crying in the absence of a clear or appropriate evoking stimulus
- prolonged or frequent crying that is not associated with grief over a significant loss
- dramatic crying with shallow emotion

Any clinical assessment of crying also requires that the therapist have a good working understanding of his or her attachment and caregiving styles, along with consciousness of any social biases for or against crying.

Protest Crying

Protest crying may be assessed in three ways: the crier's words, body language, and impact on the observer. The words that accompany protest crying are often tinged with anger, frustration, and helplessness. This crying is more intense than weeping in despair. Vocalized sobs, rare in adults, will in all likelihood be cries of protest. The character played by Diane Keaton in the romantic comedy, *Something's Got to Give*, has a long, drawn-out, protest crying scene as she writes a play about her own recently "broken heart." She is overacting because it is comedy, but she is definitely overacting protest crying. She even, at one point, creates the square-shaped open mouth that Darwin (1872/1965) described as characteristic of an infant's scream. It might be possible to feel some pity for her, but the only thing that would truly soothe her at that point is to have her heart "unbroken" by reuniting with her lost love.

As with most protest criers, she is not receptive to any other form of soothing. As discussed earlier, protest crying is understandable in the immediate aftermath of a profound loss when the crier is unable to take in or accept the reality of the loss. Only when protest crying persists, without ever resolving into despair over the permanence of a loss, would it be considered symptomatic of an unresolved grief reaction. Attaching a time frame to the transition from protest to despair is difficult because it depends upon the nature of the relationship to the lost one; the age and stage of the crier; and the patience, understanding, and tolerance of the caregivers. The norm for some sad crying of despair to appear would be within a few days or, at most, a few weeks following a major loss. The exceptions that I have seen were both in mothers who lost children unexpectedly—one an infant to SIDS and another an adolescent in a car accident. In both situations, the traumatic, unexpected nature of the loss and the state and stage of the attachment/caregiving maternal bond made it particularly difficult to move beyond the protest stage, although both did eventually do so.

Grief experts generally agree that the stages of reaction to a major loss are not linear or sequential, but rather may overlap each other—despair this hour or this day and protest another. I have also thought that protest and despair might intermingle in a single crying episode. Although it was difficult to be objective, I noticed that my crying during and after the death of my 95-year-old father seemed on one or two occasions to combine both. When he was in his final days of life, it became clear that the palliative medications given to him at the residential hospice were probably going to hasten his death. I was alone with him when the nurse administered yet another heavy dose of morphine even though he was already comatose from earlier medications. I sat there sobbing, feeling helpless and angry and thinking, "That shot is going to kill my father." I knew he was going to die, but I hated having to stand by and feel so helpless. I simultaneously protested the process and grieved in despair over losing him.

Grief over losses other than death may also be protracted. When anger is associated with a loss, protest—and protest crying—may become a fixture of the grief reaction for years. I am thinking in particular of divorce when one party feels wronged by the other in the undoing of the attachment/romantic partnership. A woman came to see me several years after her husband of 47 years announced he was leaving her for his secretary just as they were about to retire to their dream home in Hawaii. She complained that she had not been able to get on with her life and cried in anger and frustration as she ruminated on the details of his betrayal and the divorce. She also complained that her adult children and her friends practically hung up on her when she started crying about this with them. Instead of feeling drawn to comfort her, they were impatient with her demands on them for caregiving and with her inability to move beyond bitterness and anger.

Predictably, my early attempts at soothing and comforting were rejected and the protest crying continued unabated through our brief relationship. I did not feel particularly impatient with her, but I did feel mild frustration that my ability to respond was severely restricted: she could not be soothed and became impatient with me when I tried. On the other hand, had I confronted her in any way, she would have felt rejection from me as she did from her friends and family. My only recourse was to try empathically to educate her about grief and how it is sometimes hard to move on after a loss such as hers, especially when feeling so angry and betrayed.

A typical response to another person's protest crying is to feel pushed away or devalued, blamed, inadequate, or guilty. At times, however, when a patient is beginning to grieve significant losses, crying in protest will actually bring an internal feeling of relief to the therapist. Protest crying here is welcome because it represents the onset of dealing with grief that was previously denied or otherwise defended against.

Protest crying is a hallmark of the anxious-ambivalent attachment style. For the person with this style, crying, especially protest crying, is easily activated, even over minor everyday breaches. Soothing is resisted or rejected even though the person feels desperate for the presence of their attachment figures from whom they chronically fear rejection. In the case of the woman whose husband left her late in life, her fears of rejection were realized by her husband's departure and played out afterward by her children and friends. This further destabilized her and left her spinning hopelessly in the protest phase of grief.

In attachment research with infants (Ainsworth et al., 1978; Belsky, 1999), the anxious-ambivalent style has been associated with caregivers whose responses are inconsistent or unattuned. This unpredictability in caregiving leaves the child chronically insecure and anxious. Protest crying, designed to engage the caregiver maximally, is repeatedly activated, even though the results are uneven at best. Caregiving is not trusted and is therefore not effective because of its unreliability. (Anxious caregivers may also directly impart insecure-ambivalent/resistant attachment styles to their children through their anxiety-tinged affect attunements and misattunements and affect regulation.)

Overgratification in response to protest cries in childhood (what is commonly known as "spoiling") by indulgent or distracted caregivers might also lead to overuse of protest crying in adulthood. Overgratified children learn to rely on an immature pattern of protest, expecting and demanding that caregivers rescue them from their losses. Of course, this type of response is rare in adult life.

Another psychological dynamic that might leave a person prone to protest crying in adulthood is intolerance for the direct expression of anger because of a family culture that prevents its expression or because of the anger-aversive values (especially for females) in the culture at large. Aggressive behavior or words might be threatening to a person with anxious-ambivalent attachment who fears that his or her anger might provoke rejection. Angry tears of protest might serve to obscure the underlying aggression in an effort, largely ineffectual most of the time, to protect the fragile security of the attachment bond. Some writers have suggested that gender role socialization (anger is acceptable for men but not for women; tears are all right for women but not for men) might also lead women to channel their aggression into tears.

Paulette, a recently married young woman, suggested marital counseling to her husband because she found herself crying every time they had an argument. Her family had been calm and upbeat most of the time; her parents' disagreements were brief and always handled with a light touch.

She realized that she was not accustomed to protracted disagreements and saw them as threatening to the relationship. After discussing her fears with her husband, however, she became increasingly able to express her anger directly during arguments without becoming fearful and without shedding tears. A securely attached person, once she understood the source of her tears and her fearfulness, she began to practice speaking up during arguments rather than crying.

Sometimes protest crying occurs in solitude. Typically, these tears do not provide relief or healing. As one woman complained after losing her job because of a personality conflict with her boss, "I cried at home that night but afterward I felt worse, if anything. I am so angry, and I just can't seem to get over it. It is all so unfair!" Because crying in protest is a demand for change, it does not allow the crier to grieve the loss. It may be necessary to go through the anger as a first step, but unless angry tears are the beginning and not the end of the grieving process, the loss will not be absorbed and integrated. Prolonged protest crying is symptomatic of a stalled grief reaction.

Infantile Crying

Perhaps a training video would best illustrate the infantile type of symptomatic crying to distinguish it from usual adult crying, which always resembles infant crying in some way. Darwin was the first to point out this resemblance. He outlined the various facial muscles and the parallel expressions in infant and adult crying. This type of symptomatic crying has a developmentally "early" feel to it that experienced clinicians and other astute observers of crying might intuitively feel is "off." One feature might be an exaggeratedly quivering lip prior to crying, which is seldom seen after childhood. Another might be intense sobbing with gasping respiration or habitually vocalized crying. In general, the feeling is that crying behavior has "frozen" at or regressed to an earlier stage of development.

An exaggeratedly infantile crying pattern is not a frequently encountered symptomatic crying style. I have seen it in a chronically ill young adult whose disability kept her from being able to gain her adult independence. She was most prone to regressive crying at the times when her illness became acute. At other times her crying fit the more typical adult picture—quiet weeping rather than fractured sobbing. Another young woman whom I saw had survived a violent crime and a long recovery from the injuries suffered. Her caregiving needs in the aftermath of the trauma severely overtaxed her support system, leaving her vulnerable and defenseless.

A different form of infantile adult crying is even more rare. That is when adult criers demonstrate stereotyped movements similar to those of children with autism or developmental or attachment disorders. Schore (2003) refers to the fact that some of the behaviors of infants who are classified as having disorganized styles of attachment "... take the form of stereotypes that are found in neurologically impaired infants. These behaviors are overt manifestations of an obviously impaired regulatory system, one that rapidly disorganizes under stress" (p. 251).

I first learned of this symptom in adults from a colleague who reported to me that a female patient of his, who was a functioning professional in a scientific field, would shake her arms in a manner sometimes seen in autistic children when she cried. It alerted him to the possibility of more severe underlying developmental or attachment disorders. It was a long time before he had the understanding and the words to go with his initial impression from the crying, but it helped him to listen and attune at a different level early in the work.

I have seen one or two people who held themselves and rocked as they cried in the self-soothing manner of some children. With intense, traumatic losses such as death of a close loved one, self-rocking is not particularly unusual. However, when it is commonly associated with weeping over less intense losses, it may signal a number of different attachment difficulties. Avoidantly attached people might develop various self-comforting maneuvers (smoking, eating, alcohol or drug use are more typical). However, because they rarely cry, it is unlikely that stereotyped self-soothing behaviors would be demonstrated in the presence of others, unless severe grief breaks through the usual pattern of control. When it does, their self-hugging and rocking is self-contained with no hint of receptivity to caregiving from others. In people with anxious-ambivalent styles of attachment, rocking or other visible self-soothing behaviors might serve the opposite function: to draw greater attention from caregivers.

Crying in the Absence of a Clear or Appropriate Stimulus

Whenever I teach or present to clinicians on the assessment of crying, I am careful to emphasize that unprovoked crying and frequent crying may be symptoms of a physiological disorder as well as a psychiatric one. At a clinical social work conference in Los Angeles, a young therapist in the audience came up after my talk to tell me how, at age 19, she had started crying for no discernible reason. At first she wondered what was making her so upset, but after thinking it through, she concluded that this crying felt different. The only way she could describe it was to say that it felt "physical." Fortunately, she had the maturity and presence of mind to make an appointment with her physician and, even more fortunately, he did not dismiss her with a pat on the shoulder and false reassurance that she would feel better soon. Instead, he did a thorough workup and discovered that she had thyroid cancer.

Physicians and psychotherapists are apt to assume that crying "for no reason" represents undiagnosed depression, which is indeed often the case. However, it is important that potential physical disorders be ruled out, including hormonal imbalances or neurological disorders such as brain lesions, strokes, cerebral tumors, multiple sclerosis, or seizures, before it can be safely assumed that crying is a psychological symptom. Unprecipitated crying is also a side effect of certain drugs, including sodium pentathol and, for some women, birth control pills. On the way home after dental surgery, my daughter cried for several miles, but she was puzzled. She said, "I have no idea why I'm crying because I'm not upset, I'm not in pain, and I'm not afraid." We quickly concluded it was the anesthetic and waited for it to wear off.

Clinicians need to be particularly observant because often people who have physiologically induced crying "for no reason" search far and wide for some loss to explain it. Women with PMS, for example, can almost always find a loss or threatened loss to explain their excess tears. One day I blamed my crying on our cat, Petunia, who had just dug up my new flowers—a loss to be sure, but not one that normally would have brought me to tears.

Also, sometimes family members will speculate about "reasons" that have not been articulated by the crier. For example, a friend's mother had a severe stroke and had to be placed in a nursing facility. She cried for several days and, because she could not speak, my friend assumed her mother was crying because of having to leave her home. According to the doctors, however, her mother's cognitive abilities had been severely damaged, so I explained that it was equally, if not more, likely that nerve damage from the stroke was making her mother cry. This was of some comfort to my friend, who was strugling with her own grief about her mother's illness and placement.

Once physiological causes have been ruled out, unprovoked crying may turn out to be linked to depression, an unrecognized grief reaction, or unacceptable and unrecognized attachment needs. People with avoidant styles of attachment strongly prefer to be self-reliant and not to activate attachment behaviors that signal their need for care. However, sometimes their losses are of such magnitude (or touch on an earlier ungrieved but significant loss) that they cry in spite of themselves. This can produce tremendous distress and, in the case of a smaller loss touching off an earlier big one, confusion.

Brian stopped crying when he was 12 years old and never looked back. He had been labeled a "cry baby" by the much older brother responsible for "babysitting" him while both parents were away at work all day. Shortly after Brian's marriage to Patsy, her mother died. Brian felt that he barely knew her and he said he felt no real sense of loss; however, he cried at the funeral home and the burial and decided he was "losing it," even though Patsy and her family seemed to think it was fine. As he talked about his feelings a bit with his physician, he mentioned that the one time he had met Patsy's mother, she had been very "mom like" with him right away. She told him to call her "Mom" and asked what his favorite foods were so that she could make them for him. At the time, he thought that was strange, but now he wondered if something about that "stirred [him] up." His physician recognized that Brian's grief about his own absent mother was activated by his mother-in-law's death and gave Brian a referral to a therapist who could help him understand his reaction.

Securely or anxiously attached people might also cry without knowing the reason if the loss or threatened loss makes them so anxious that they cannot face it consciously. For example, when Todd cheerily told Alicia early in their dating relationship that he was thinking of applying to graduate school in Hawaii, she was embarrassed because she started to cry "for no reason." She apologized to Todd and blamed it on allergies, but it kept nagging at her. When she got home, she called her best friend to talk about it. Janice helped her to recognize that she really liked Todd and was harboring some secret hopes that their relationship could "go somewhere." Hearing of his plans to study so far away crushed her unspoken dreams for their future.

Prolonged or Frequent Crying

Once physiological causes have been ruled out, complaints of prolonged or frequent crying may represent one of three conditions. In increasing order of severity they are: social discomfort with appropriate crying, an unresolved grief reaction, and/or clinical depression.

Because complaints of too much crying are subject to individual interpretation, the first questions to ask are how often and for how long. Some men and women cry up to several times a day without evidence of any physiological or psychological disorder (Frey & Langseth, 1985; Green, McAllister, & Bernat, 1987; Hastrup & Baker, 1986). The average crying frequency found in a survey of adults (Frey & Langseth, 1985) in the

Midwestern United States with no history of psychiatric illness or depression is 5.3 episodes per month for women and 1.4 for men.

The International Study of Adult Crying (Becht, Poortinga, & Vingerhoets, 2001) surveyed a sample of 1,470 men (mean age 24) and 2,100 women (mean age 23) from 29 countries about their crying frequency in a 4-week period. In the United States the mean frequency over 4 weeks was 3.5 episodes for women and 1.9 for men. The highest mean crying frequency for women was 3.6 in Chile and the lowest was 1.6 in Peru. Men in Nepal matched the 1.9-mean frequency of crying for men in the United States; the lowest male mean was 0.4 in Bulgaria.

Another important initial question to pursue in regard to prolonged crying is its actual duration. People tend to be vague and global in their descriptions of duration, with comments like "I cried all day yesterday" or "I cried all last week." In surveys that look at duration (Frey & Langseth, 1985), 1 minute of crying is the length most often reported for both sexes. Here, as with crying frequency, the range of individual differences varies widely, ranging from 2 seconds to 2 hours. These differences occur as patterns between people or in the same person, depending on the circumstances and the precipitants.

Once the factual data about the frequency of the crying and its duration have been determined, two comparisons are helpful. The first is done by keeping in mind the wide range of individual differences in crying frequency, as well as the averages and means cited earlier. Second, and most important, is to ascertain whether or not the frequency and duration represent a change from this person's usual pattern. Changes in patterns in the direction of more crying for longer periods, particularly in the absence of any significant loss, are indicative of problematic crying, and the crier should be referred for physical examination and evaluated for clinical depression. Depending on the clinician's judgment, people who report frequent and prolonged crying as their usual pattern might also be considered for further evaluation.

Social Discomfort With Appropriate Crying. If a person complains about too much crying, it is important to understand how he views crying frequency. Is any amount of crying too much, as it was for the cancer patient Sharon? Is he comparing himself to someone else who has experienced a similar loss? Have others expressed concern that he is crying too much? If so, who was it and what is their view of an appropriate amount of crying? Perhaps the social discomfort may come from the fact that the crying in question is protest crying, which is less acceptable to the crier and to

others. In that case, perhaps it is the type of crying, in combination with
the amount of crying that is the problem.

Unresolved Grief Reactions. When protracted protest crying follows a
significant loss, it prohibits the resolution of grief. Unresolved grief may
present clinically as prolonged and frequent crying. In order to clarify the
relationship between the crying and grief, it is sometimes helpful to focus
on making an inventory of the crier's losses (Simos, 1979). The place to
begin is with major losses in the present and in the recent past, followed by
less significant ones in both time periods. Anniversary reactions to previous losses may stir up grief that is not consciously connected to its original
source. Loss and grief may also be cumulative, so multiple losses, even if
none of them is major, might lead to unexplained frequent crying.
Changes, even for the better, may be grieved without their being recognized or acknowledged because they are presumed to be "good." Finally,
grief over what the conscious mind sees to be a minor slight or threat may
also contribute to crying that seems excessive.

Early in my career, I wrote a manual and taught a class in crisis intervention techniques for volunteers working on hotlines, and I continue to
coordinate that program for mental health paraprofessionals in a variety
of settings. Part of the training is to learn to assess crises quickly by role-
playing with other trainees. Assessment in these circumstances depends on
keeping an active mental checklist for uncovering stress, loss, and change,
which includes looking for it in unlikely places and from unlikely sources:
for example, the evening news threatening job layoffs in another city, or
television programs about the Holocaust, or medical emergencies. Because
the volunteers practice creating the callers' situations, as well as assessing
the simulated calls from each other, they develop a high level of consciousness about where to search for losses. They learn that even a broken-down
car, an overdue bill, or a husband who forgot to say good-bye that morning can be a loss.

Frequent Crying and Depression. People who suffer from dysthymia, the
less-severe form of depression, and those who suffer from major depression may present with one of three complaints related to crying. The
first is to cry all the time for "no reason." The second is related to the
first—being afraid to cry for fear of never stopping. The third is to be too
numb, apathetic, or beyond caring to cry at all, even over serious losses.

Leah, a long-term patient of mine in her late 30s who suffers from the
most severe form of major depression, has paid close attention to her crying patterns in relation to her episodes of depression. She reports three cry
conditions that she believes relate directly to the severity of her depression.

The first is when she is between depressive episodes and crying in what for her is a normal pattern: she only will cry over significant losses, such as the death of her uncle or a life-threatening illness in her pet. As she begins to become more depressed, she notices that her crying increases in frequency (up to multiple times in a day) and duration (for up to an hour or more without interruption) and that it will be triggered by inconsequential stresses that normally would have little impact. For example, she might cry because the sprinklers got the newspaper wet, her dogs are playing too roughly, or the television is too loud in the other room. Finally, however, in the throes of major depression, she becomes "numb" and does not cry over even serious losses. "I can't even care enough about anything to shed tears," she says.

The item relating to crying on the Beck Depression Inventory of self-reported symptoms reflects Leah's experience of changes based on the severity of depression. It begins with a score of zero for the item, "I don't cry any more than usual," followed by one point for "I cry more now than I used to" and two for "I cry all the time now." Finally, the choice given a value of three (for the most severely depressed) is "I used to be able to cry, but now I can't cry even though I want to." Clinically, that sequence seems to fit the experience of many people. However, research to date has not supported the association between inhibited crying and major depression or between excessive crying and dysthymia on the Beck Inventory (Steer, Beck, Brown, & Berchick, 1987), or between a lowered threshold for crying and depression (Rottenberg, Gross, Wilhelm, Najmi, & Gotlib, 2002). The latter study did, however, suggest that being depressed over time may serve to "blunt the crying response: those individuals who had been depressed the longest were the least likely to cry" (p. 309).

Kraemer and Hastrup (1986) found that moderately depressed people had significantly elevated crying frequencies. However, it would appear that many, if not most, of the people who are frequent criers are not depressed. In the end, excessive crying or, conversely, the inability to cry in a person who formerly could cry, may serve as a clinical indicator pointing to the need for physical evaluation and for ruling out depression. An evaluation for antidepressant medications, which may help with excessive crying as well as depression, may also be indicated.

To further complicate matters, clinically depressed people may also be having grief reactions in which crying due to biochemical and neurological changes may co-exist with attachment-based crying. To deal with these interconnected phenomena, which to one degree or another may always be a factor in depression, I have devised a simple pie-chart method of assessment. I draw a circle representing the depressed mood in total and, together with the patient, label wedges of the pie with a particular stressor such as "bad evaluation at work" or "fight with boyfriend." The percentage allocated to each pie wedge is done by following the patient's intuitive sense, along with my observations and feedback. If there is a history of clinical depression, one of the wedges will always be "biochemical depression" so that it is factored into the mix.

This assessment is clinically useful and therapeutically beneficial in helping to make visible the often frightening and overwhelming internal experience of despair. In other words, by drawing the chart, I am serving as an external regulator of negative affect by helping to contain and master an affective experience. The process also increases the patient's awareness of the subjective differences between feeling the physiological aspects of biochemical depression and dealing with stress, loss, and grief.

Dramatic Crying With Shallow Emotion

"Sobbing uncontrollably on minor sentimental occasions" appears in the fourth edition of *The Diagnostic and Statistical Manual of Mental Disorders* (*DSM IV*; American Psychiatric Association, 1994, p. 655) as a diagnostic feature of the histrionic personality disorder. One of the diagnostic criteria for that disorder is "rapidly shifting and shallow expression of emotion" (p. 658), which could, and often does, refer to crying.

In Victorian literature, when sentimental weeping was at its height, this type of crying was referred to as "crying at the death of the canary." Present-day attachment theorists, who take the human–animal bond seriously, might not consider the loss of a pet bird to be such a minor precipitant, which is a good reminder that one person's shallow emotion or minor sentimental occasion is another person's deeply felt loss. Nonetheless, clinicians are sometimes called upon to make judgments as to levels of severity and the appropriateness of the response to the precipitant.

Some individuals who cry "dramatically" might not have the ability to regulate affect internally and therefore appear over-ready to externalize it. This could be the result of overgratification of protest crying in childhood—or the opposite: undergratification that required high levels of attention-getting signals to succeed. In most instances, however, the person who cries in this way would be likely to fit the anxious-ambivalent style of attachment, whose attachment behavior of crying is easily activated and difficult to soothe.

The Assessment of Symptomatic Inhibited Crying

Inhibited crying that is symptomatic is detached and avoidant, cutting off potential caregivers at times when vulnerability and loss are obvious.

To be considered symptomatic, prohibited crying, when the urge to cry is conscious and the efforts to control it deliberate must also include detachment from caregiving, rather than merely being a temporary defense or soothing strategy.

Situationally Inhibited Crying

The shock and numbness that accompany sudden grief or trauma are familiar examples of situationally inhibited crying in people who are otherwise able to cry. When Marta's husband was killed in an industrial accident, she was stunned and silent. Her family quickly gathered around to offer support, but she preferred to stay in her room alone. She stared into space, responding only cursorily to their questions and not participating in the funeral arrangements. Marta continued in this tearless wooden state until after her husband's burial. She did not return to work for a month and continued to isolate herself. Her mother stayed with her, however, and eventually, she began to talk about John and the accident. One day, putting away his fishing boots, she began to cry.

Prior to John's death, Marta had been an upbeat person always ready to lend a hand or an ear to someone who was suffering. She said, however, that she had never experienced anything like this trauma. She was the youngest child of four, the object of great affection and even pampering by her three older sisters. She and John married just out of high school and she felt their marriage had always been secure. He protected her, she said, from worrying about anything, even the bills. Her attachments seemed secure, but her affect had been externally regulated so much that her internal resources were overwhelmed by this external tragedy. Her inhibited crying was a symptomatic response to her loss but it resolved eventually through the persistence and availability of her family.

Other people who have just lost a loved one may also find themselves temporarily unable to cry because of ambivalent feelings about the lost person. If a marriage was rocky before the loss, or if the lost loved one died because of long-standing self-destructive behaviors such as alcohol or drug use that had previously been a source of struggle in the relationship, feelings of anger (or guilt about relief) may cloud the ability to experience sadness.

Detached Pervasive Emotional Control

Many, if not most, people who inhibit crying as part of a pattern of detached pervasive emotional control do not complain about the inability to cry. In fact, if asked, they think that crying would cause them much more distress than not crying ever does. In other words, the wish for control pervades consciousness to the exclusion of other options. Typically, it will be other family members or romantic partners who complain.

People who fit the criteria for obsessive-compulsive personality disorder and people with an avoidant attachment style are most likely to be associated with this type of pervasive emotional control. No specific criteria relate to inhibited crying in the *DSM-IV* (1994) description of this personality disorder. The associated features, however, include the following rather unusual description: "they are stingy with their emotions," along with the more typical "tend not to express their feelings" (p. 355).

Ronald was a successful chemical engineer who had been divorced for several years when his grown children suggested that he go for psychotherapy because, they said, he was "too uptight" and they were afraid he was going to have a heart attack. He said that they also complained, as had his former wife, that he was cold and aloof. Ronald mentioned in the early weeks of therapy that he had "forgotten how to cry." He recalled being a sensitive and somewhat anxious child but said he learned early that, to get approval, he had to be well-behaved and high-achieving. Any show of vulnerability was met with ridicule, at best, and banishment or threats of punishment at worst. Both of his parents traveled a lot as part of their academic careers, leaving him and his younger sister with a series of babysitters hired from the college placement office.

Ronald's style of detached pervasive emotional control also fits with his avoidant attachment style. His wife had pursued him when they were chemistry students and he asked her to marry him because it seemed as if it was expected of him. She had complained that he was too distant and would not let her in emotionally and, similarly, that he was never really "there" for her. Ronald understood that he was not "very good" at expressing his feelings, but believed his qualities of being a steady, good provider and his professional achievements should be taken into consideration, especially by his adult children.

Ronald's style of rigid and pervasive emotional control often is paired with difficulties in responsive caregiving. He was not comfortable in his role of emotional caregiver, with his former wife or with his children when they were young. He did not understand feelings. He said that on the occasions when his wife cried, he would busy himself with something around the house until it was over. His children, understandably, never turned to him for comfort when they were upset.

In a painful article, Harold Brodkey (1994) described his reactions to having AIDS and to the grief and caregiving responses of his wife and doctor. When the doctor brought up counseling and medication to help him with the "shock, despair, the natural grief," he answered with a little joke. He wanted to make his wife and doctor laugh and admire him, but he also wanted his wife to stop "that inward shaking." He said that he had an "odd cowardice toward grief" and would just as soon suffer without it (pp. 9–10).

He also described his discomfort with receiving their care. "The two of them were watching me, ready to sympathize and comfort." However, he said, "I have never, since childhood, really expected to be comforted." He explains his situation this way: "... you see, a traumatized child as I was once, long ago, and one who recovers, as I did, has a wall between him and pain and despair, between himself and grief ..." (Brodkey, 1994, p. 36).

Brodkey might be said to suffer from pervasive resistance to receiving care, a close relative, I believe, of detached pervasive emotional control. In his description of his adult struggles with grief and caregiving, we hear the echo of childhood trauma, the absence of comforting caregivers, and an insecure attachment style.

Defensive Substitutes for Crying

Alcohol and drugs lead to increased crying for some people; however, for others, they blunt emotions and numb the pain of losses that might trigger grief and crying. Wallerstein (1967) describes working with two women who had uncontrollable alcoholism and totally controlled feelings. A friend who has been in recovery for 10 years told me that when she was using drugs she never cried at anything, no matter how significant the loss. At the time, she said, she felt guilty about not showing her grief, especially at the death of family members, but the tears simply did not flow. Not until she was in recovery did her pattern change to what had been normal for her: appropriate crying in response to serious losses.

Suzanne, the fictional character in Carrie Fisher's novel *Postcards From the Edge* (Fisher, 1987), describes day 6 in a drug rehabilitation program:

> After not feeling anything for years, I'm having this Feeling Festival. The medication wears off and the feelings just fall on you.... These are the feelings you've been specifically avoiding—the ones you almost killed yourself to avoid.... I talked to my agent and ended up in tears ... I tried very hard not to, but I didn't have a chance. I've used up all the Not Cry I was issued at birth. Now it appears, it's crying time (p. 14).

Other methods for maintaining cry inhibition include cigarette smoking and eating, which are soothing but also provide a physiological barrier to crying. Cigarette smoking is particularly effective because it involves deep inhalation, which is the physiological opposite of crying with its brief inspiration and long exhalation. Eating is also in physiological opposition to crying. It is impossible to swallow and cry at the same time. I know because I have had the experience of eating dinner in front of the television and trying to cry at a sad moment in a movie at the same time.

Laughter and smiling are also attachment behaviors. When they are used as substitutes for crying, they may bring loved ones closer without "burdening" them with negative affect. A colleague who is very comical said that she had been the family entertainer, always trying to get a smile out of her depressed mother. She told me that she had had to look long and hard for a therapist who would not laugh at her jokes, who realized that underneath she needed to cry. She was desperate to find a caregiver who would recognize that fact.

Some people who are uncomfortable with crying and/or caregiving feel more comfortable with a sexual connection than a caregiving one. I have seen more "B" movies than I care to think about in which a woman begins crying, her lover hugs her as if to comfort her, and immediately it becomes sexual. I understand that some feminist film critics point to sexual power politics in this dynamic—men taking sexual advantage of an emotionally vulnerable woman—that may indeed be represented. However, I am also struck by the sad fact of how uncomfortable many people are with giving and receiving emotional care, quickly diverting into the more acceptable sexual arena instead. Sexual encounters not only provide a physical release in orgasm that is somewhat akin to the physical release some people feel with crying, but also include physical touch and closeness that may substitute for nonsexual caregiving.

CHAPTER **9**

Tears as Body Language

By its very nature, crying contradicts mind–body dualism. Emotional weeping is a complex blend of mind and body. As such, it provides a rare and valuable opportunity to experience body and mind simultaneously and consciously. When tears are shed for emotional reasons—and sometimes when they are suppressed—the body speaks. With little, if any, conscious effort and virtually no conscious control, thoughts, feelings, and images translate into a visible bodily secretion. Nerve impulses that stimulate the lacrimal nucleus in the brain stem (ultimately causing tears to flow) travel along numerous pathways, from the frontal cortex (in the case of conscious thoughts that evoke tears) or from within the limbic system, the so-called "emotional brain," the basal ganglia, and the thalamus (van Haeringen, 2001). From the lacrimal nucleus the signal to stimulate tear production goes along the seventh cranial nerve to the lacrimal glands, where tears are produced. Eventually, the lungs, diaphragm, and muscles that control breathing and facial expression are also involved in crying (Frey & Langseth, 1985).

Tears are secreted by the main lacrimal gland and the many (about 60) little accessory lacrimal glands underneath the eyelids. If a sufficient quantity is produced, some tears spill out of the eye onto the cheeks. Some of the excess tears produced may also pool and drain into the nose through the tear ducts in the corner of each eye, the so-called "tear drainage system."

When I first began wondering about the body side of the crying equation, I talked to an ophthalmologist and a neurologist. When I began to get specific about the physiology of emotional tears, however, I met head on with the mind–body split in Western medicine. The ophthalmologist said that he only knew the eye as a structure, unrelated to thought and emotion. The neurologist said, "People just don't realize how little we really understand about the nervous system." In medicine and in psychotherapy, adult crying is generally categorized as emotional behavior, leaving the body out of the equation altogether.

Hoping to find a model for a more comprehensive view of crying than that offered by Western medicine, I took questions about crying and the mind–body connection to several practitioners of Chinese medicine. Acupuncturist Irit Weir, who studied extensively in China, helped me locate reading material and understand more of the Eastern perspective. A holistic view so thoroughly permeates the thinking in Chinese medicine that it is difficult for practitioners to isolate a behavior like crying. Any idea of a mind–body split is unfathomable to them. Health, they believe, represents a balance of body organs, secretions, seasons, colors, feelings, and even food. Healthy crying, like eating, breathing, heartbeat, glandular secretion, and elimination, is simply a part of that balance. To a practitioner of Chinese medicine, too much *or* too little crying would be considered a manifestation of imbalance, not an isolated symptom.

Weir did recall that when she studied in China she took a class in which programmed—even forced—laughing and crying (on alternate days) were used to promote health and healing, almost like exercise. She said the laughter was far easier to produce spontaneously than the crying because the contagion factor in group laughing worked much better than when the group was trying to cry in unison.

Finding neither Eastern nor Western medicine adequate to explain my view of emotional crying as a relationship behavior with varying degrees of biological and social influences, I conceived of a continuum to represent all of the elements holistically. An episode of crying then might be seen as occurring along a continuum based on the proportion of physiological, emotional, cognitive, gender, familial and cultural influences. One end of the continuum is heavily weighted toward the physiological, as with crying that occurs because of brain injury or stroke or during a seizure. To distinguish this type of crying, I use the term "somatic tears." Even purely physical tears, however, may include social and emotional forces, interpretations, and judgments that influence how the crier and those around her or him perceive and cope with the behavior. At the opposite end of the holistic crying continuum is the purest form of emotional weeping, which is, of course, also always a complex physical process.

The proportions of emotional/social and physical elements shift developmentally or individually and with each crying episode. Early infant crying is predominantly physiological, bearing in mind that attachment behavior is part of our inborn physiological equipment for obtaining and ensuring the caregiving necessary for survival. Adult emotional weeping is much more heavily weighted toward the psychological in the broadest sense. However, at times of greater physical vulnerability, as with illness or fatigue, the physiological threshold for adult crying may be crossed more easily.

Referring to the International Study of Adult Crying (Becht et al., 2001), researcher Ad Vingerhoets said,

> What surprised me was that people often cried for seemingly very trivial and trifling "causes." One person wrote that she cried when she was trying to sew curtains but did not succeed in her plans. Another cried when she was trying to learn a new dance and made mistakes with the steps. This made me aware that very often the physical and/or mental state is probably far more important (Vingerhoets, personal communication, February 22, 2004).

Some people are disturbed by their crying, even when it falls at the physiological end of the continuum. They feel better coming up with a convenient explanation for it. Humorist Erma Bombeck (1980) said that during menopause she would start crying when she threw out the garbage or found the date on the package of yeast had expired. I especially like these "reasons" because they are symbolic of some of the emotional side effects of aging: feeling outdated and ready for the trash bin. Bombeck acknowledged this too in her column. She said, "Maybe it's meno—" (a word that she could not bear to utter in full).

Tear Physiology and Biochemistry

Whenever the eye registers a physiological emergency—onion fumes, a squirt of grapefruit juice, being hit on the nose with a baseball, eating hot pepper, or laughing really hard—reflex tears start to flow almost instantly, protecting the eye by diluting or washing away the offending problem. This tear fluid, along with continuous tears distributed by blinking, helps to cleanse and maintain the eye surface for vision and moisturize the mucous membranes to prevent infection. However, as far back as Darwin, scientists believed that the tears secreted during emotional weeping served no biological purpose. Some early psychoanalytic theorists speculated that when we are emotionally traumatized, our eyes respond in the same way as when they are physically traumatized: tearing up and symbolically "cleansing" the psyche of emotional pain, as if it were a cinder in the eye (Heilbrun, 1955).

Biochemist William Frey (Frey & Langseth, 1985) theorized that the chemical composition of tear fluid might contain clues about its function. He showed that tears, like urine and perspiration, can excrete potentially harmful chemicals from the blood or body tissue. Perhaps, Frey reasoned, because tears are associated with stress, they may rid our bodies of some of the chemicals secreted when we feel anxious, angry, or under attack. He enlisted 106 people (80% of whom were women) to collect their tears in test tubes held on their cheeks when they sniffed onion fumes and when they watched sad movies.

Reflex and psychic tears—onion versus sad movie—did turn out to be chemically different. Frey also found traces of several of the chemicals known to be produced with emotional stress in the sad-movie but not the onion tears. On the basis of these findings, Frey proposed that emotional tears evolved to eliminate certain chemicals from our bodies and to help restore our equilibrium after stress. The popular notion that it is good to "cry it out" takes on new meaning with Frey's theory, if it turns out that tears are literally excreting the chemicals that our bodies secrete when we experience stress.

Does Crying Have Health Benefits?

It has long been assumed that crying is psychologically and physically "good for you" and that, conversely, chronically suppressing tears is "bad for you." A group of researchers in the late 1980s hypothesized that weeping would "release tension, reduce toxicity, and thus buffer the effect of negative events on mood disturbance" (Labott & Martin, 1987). To everyone's surprise, this study, like most others to date, found that instead of improving moods, relieving tension, or enhancing the immune system, crying did the opposite: it left people feeling more depressed and weakened the immune system.

Even though these researchers refined and repeated their study three times using hundreds of subjects, they consistently found that high weepers of both sexes showed more mood disturbance than low weepers. Humor, it turned out, *did* help to enhance health and well-being, including the immune system (Labott & Martin, 1987). Levels of immunoglobulin A—an antibody in the saliva that protects against respiratory and gastrointestinal tract infections—increased in a group of women when they laughed watching a Bill Cosby comedy and decreased when they cried at *Peege*, a sad film about an elderly woman in a nursing home (Labott, Ahleman, Wolever, & Martin, 1990).

If crying does promote physical health—and many people, including me, continue to assume that it does—it is difficult to demonstrate in laboratory research and even more difficult to isolate outside the lab. I believe that crying is complex enough to bring us down in mood and suppress our immune systems in the short term while, over time, helping to restore our physiological equilibrium and enhance our overall health.

It may be that crying is more like running a fever. It lets us know that we are grieving some loss, as a fever indicates that we have an infection. Fevers and crying may eventually help the body restore its equilibrium, even though we might be weak and wobbly for a while after they end. I cannot help wondering, too, whether research outcomes might be different if it were possible to study tears triggered by real-life losses rather than sad movies; weeping that takes place in the context of a comforting or supportive relationship rather than under laboratory conditions; or weeping that lasts longer or is more intense than crying about a movie.

A good cry may also provide physical release—a secretion of body chemicals, a decrease in muscle tension—in the same way in which deep breathing or having an orgasm can help relax a stressed body. However, as with sex at its best, body, mind, and spirit are all involved in the kind of good cry we are talking about here. Also, like sex, crying is most meaningful in the context of an intimate connection with a loved one. Neurobiological research has also suggested that physical contact and comfort release oxytocin, a brain chemical that helps in the management and reduction of stress.

Reminding ourselves that crying is attachment behavior designed to signal those around us that we are in distress and in need of care and comfort suggests that its positive benefits may come not so much from actually shedding tears, but rather because the tears bring us physical contact and solace from others. The connection and comfort that crying helps to bring our way, in reality or symbolically, may help to make our bodies feel better and heal sooner.

The Physiology of Gender Differences in Crying

We have myths, stereotypes, and value judgments about male and female crying, but until recently very little data. The assumption has been that sex-role training determines which gender cries more and why. I started from that point when I began looking through the meager research findings to see if I could discover the age at which boys begin to cry less than girls. I thought that would show how quickly the "boys don't cry" messages take effect and I expected it to be quite young.

In the early weeks and months of infancy, it turns out, there are no sex differences in crying frequency. However, I did find some confusing data: parents of infant boys expect them to cry *more* than infant girls do.

The "boys don't cry" edict was not operating in the crib. Even in infancy girls are apparently expected to be quiet, sweet, and demure, rather than outspoken and demanding like the boys.

In the preschool age group, still no statistically significant gender differences in crying frequency appeared. However, again I was surprised to find a curious and consistent tilt toward more crying by toddler boys (Blurton Jones & Leach, 1972; Smith, 1974). Are little boys crying more because they are more physical and get into more confrontations? Are little girls socialized early to be soothers and caretakers?

Finally, I found a study—and to my knowledge, it is still the only one—that specifically charted children's crying behavior from ages 1 through 16. It was conducted by the Gesell Institute for Child Development Research (Gesell, 1946; Gesell et al., 1956) in the 1940s and 1950s. Gender differences in crying frequency, I learned to my surprise, did not show up in early childhood. Even at age 11, they noted that "boys are just as apt to cry as girls" (Gesell et al., 1956, p. 86) and, at age 13, "both boys and girls may cry because they haven't been asked to a party" (pp. 121–122). Not until age 16 was a dramatic sex difference apparent: "No boys admit to crying now, nor are they said by parents to cry," while girls were said to be "apt to cry on occasion" (p. 263). In this post-World War II period, famous for some of the most intense sex-role training in our century—Gesell (and his female coauthors) included this sexist comment about the crying of 16-year-old girls: "A sad movie will invariably bring tears from a certain type of empathic girl, more often on the rotund side" (p. 263)—girls and boys cried with the same frequency until they reached puberty.

Subsequent studies in the 1980s, by which time many parents and schools were consciously trying to change the traditional gender-based messages about crying, found the same thing: no gender differences in childhood crying frequency (Hastrup et al., 1985). Boys cry as often as girls, if not more often, until puberty, at which point crying decreases for both sexes. In the mid-teen years male crying drops off sharply to well below the average for girls, a pattern that continues throughout adulthood.

I was shocked by what I discovered. If girls and boys cry at the same rate until puberty, even though study after study shows that sex-role socialization begins within minutes of birth, I knew I must be staring at a biologically influenced gender difference. I had taken issue with Freud's often quoted maxim, "Anatomy is destiny." Now I was forced to amend it with scientist and historian Carl Sagan (1977, p. 189), who said, "Anatomy is not destiny, but it is not irrelevant either." If crying frequency is the same until puberty, then differences in our reproductive systems are the obvious place to look for an explanation. Here, more than anywhere else in our body, we have clear gender differences—anatomically, functionally, and, of course, hormonally.

As part of his biochemical research, William Frey found the hormone prolactin—related to lactation—in the lacrimal gland and in tears. In the early weeks of life, prolactin levels are high in infants of both sexes. By 3 months of age, it decreases and levels off in girls and boys—corresponding to the decreased crying frequency consistently found in 3-month-old Western infants. It is not until adolescence, between the ages of 13 and 16, that female prolactin levels outmeasure those of males by 50 to 60%. That is also the age of puberty, the time when male crying declines sharply in comparison to female crying.

Looking back at the junior high and high school graduations that I attended when my daughters were in school, I can visualize that change dramatically. Redwood Junior High graduation was on a sunny June day in 1982. Because I was working on my crying research, I could not help noticing with a glad heart that the 13-year-old boys in Cynthia's class were crying and hugging every bit as much and as openly as the girls; this was not the case at her high school graduation a few years later. Only a few students cried at that milestone and not one of them was male.

Frey suggests that higher levels of prolactin may lower the crying threshold so that emotional tears flow more easily. Abnormally high prolactin levels in people of both genders are believed to be associated with excessive crying. One woman, whose prolactin level was 155 (normal is 25) until drug treatment reduced it to 40, cried for hours and sometimes even days over insignificant things. After treatment, she wrote to Frey (Frey & Langseth, 1985): "I still cry sometimes but only with a good reason—because I am upset, hurt, sad, or angry over something specific" (p. 52). Subsequent research (Vingerhoets, Assies, & Poppelaars, 1992), however, found that people with high prolactin levels were not more prone to weeping compared to a control group without "hyperprolactinaemia."

The association between increased female crying and menstruation, oral contraceptives, pregnancy, childbirth, and the early postpartum weeks and months is well known medically and anecdotally. Changes in crying patterns in conjunction with pregnancy or childbirth are familiar to many women, although, statistically, crying presents a problem for very few. A study of over a thousand women at a gynecological clinic found that premenstrual depressive symptoms, which included "excess crying," affected less than 25% of the women and only about 2% of them severely (Hargrove & Abraham, 1982). Although it may not be a "problem" to many women, an increased tendency to cry in association with their menstrual cycle is probably familiar to a far greater percentage than is reflected in this study.

When we look at the possible biological component of gender differences in crying frequency, we see that from the standpoint of attachment and caregiving, it is powerful, deeply logical, and crucially important. Honoring the role that our bodies play in the gender differences in crying helps us appreciate our differences and be kinder to ourselves when we cry and less judgmental of others who shed tears, as well as of those who cannot. Because our bodies also respond to conscious choice and learning, men and women who are uncomfortable with their crying can work to alter their crying patterns, leading to healthier emotional balance and healthier intimate relationships.

Excess Crying

Physicians and psychotherapists too often assume that unexpected or excess tears are a sign of an emotional problem, not a physical one. Criers think the same thing and may not even mention unusual crying to a doctor or therapist because they do not realize that it might be important. Shedding copious tears is not physiologically harmful, but the stakes are high if it is an unrecognized or misdiagnosed symptom. We risk missing hormonal imbalances, malignancies, or neurological disease or damage.

Patricia, a woman in her early 40s, came to see me complaining of crying several times a day at work. It was interfering with her managerial duties and her tasks. Her physician tested everything that might be physically related, (including, at my request, her prolactin levels). Fortunately for Patricia, everything that her doctor checked turned out negative. In the therapy sessions, we looked at all of her stresses, crises, and losses—past and present. Still, the crying seemed to us disproportional to the stimuli and we theorized that it might be a symptom of biochemical depression. Her doctor prescribed an antidepressant, which quickly brought her crying back to manageable levels while we worked on the emotional issues in her therapy sessions.

Certain medications may also cause physiologically induced weeping, sometimes called pharmacologic lacrimation. A young man whom I saw was prescribed a new medication to deal with some severe neurological symptoms and he reported to me that he was crying "all the time." I suggested that he check the list of side effects that came with his new medication for that symptom. He was relieved as well as upset when I saw him the next time because increased tearfulness (and depression) had been listed there: relieved because he now knew what was happening, but upset because he did not like it.[1]

A New England Veteran's Administration hospital research team looked at 300 middle-aged men hospitalized for medical–surgical reasons, who were referred for a psychiatric evaluation because of "prominent" crying. The researchers tried to see if they could distinguish whether the crying was related to neurological dysfunction, a psychiatric disorder or both, or whether it was simply normal crying in response to loss and grief (Green et al., 1987). Only 20% of the men turned out to be suffering solely from a psychiatric disorder (primarily depression); more than 30% suffered solely from a neurological disorder. Almost half of the men had *both* a psychiatric and a neurological disorder. A small percentage, whom the research team labeled "essential criers," had no disorder at all. They just cried often, perhaps in response to grief over their medical conditions or at being separated from home and family.

The research team identified several typical signs of neurologically based crying. First, it is more likely to have an abrupt beginning—"push-button" crying, they termed it—and it is not tied to any particular emotional trigger, externally or internally. Each episode is also stereotyped, in that it is exactly like the ones that precede it, instead of the more usual pattern in which crying episodes have varying levels of intensity, from sobbing to quiet weeping, and last for differing lengths of time, from a few seconds to a few minutes.

The VA research team found that two things were essential in the treatment of crying related to physical disorders. First was education—explaining to the men and their families that crying can be triggered physiologically as well as emotionally. Then antidepressant drug therapy helped reduce some of the neurologically based crying, as it did with Patricia's crying associated with depression.

Tear Deficiencies

Some tearlessness, like some crying, may also have a physiological basis. More common than excess tearing, dry eye—inadequate or absent tearing—is potentially harmful to vision and can be painful and frustrating as well. Sufferers say it feels as though they have sandpaper in their eyes. Dry eye may be a disorder in itself or part of another syndrome such as Sjögren's, where it is one of a triad of symptoms: dry eye, dry mouth, and arthritis. Some people with dry eye are able to shed emotional tears, while others lose this ability as well. Hormonal deficiency of estrogen or prolactin is a suspected cause in many of the more than 4 million cases of dry eye in the United States. Of the people who have dry eye, 90% are female and many of them are over 50.

Congenital absence of tears, alacrima, is rare. A colleague and both of her sons were born without the ability to shed tears. My colleague says that doctors always insist on doing the painful test for tear function, which involves tucking a strip of paper in the lower eyelid and seeing how wet it gets in a prescribed period of time. My colleague now tells them that they must take her diagnosis on faith because she does not want to repeat the test, which is painful and always shows the same thing: the paper stays dry.

I was curious about how the other physiological processes involved in crying manifest in my colleague. I learned that she does get a lump in her throat, followed by the prolonged exhaled breaths that normally accompany crying. Her tearless weeping provides some physical relief, she said, but sends a confusing signal to those around her. Her mother, thinking she was in physical distress, had made her drink water to stop her tearless crying episodes. Swallowing naturally interfered with the long exhaled breaths, but left my colleague feeling frustrated and misunderstood. The atypical physiological presentation obscured the relationship message that crying is meant to convey.

Her two sons also had the experience of having their cries of distress misunderstood when they were away from home. One of them was hurt by another child on the playground but was told by his friends that he was "faking" because he did not cry with tears. When he told them that he was not able to shed tears, his playmates demanded to see a note from his mother supporting his claim. She sent it with him the next day.

Damage to the right hemisphere of the brain can cause a more complicated form of tearlessness called "aprodasia." This involves the inability to express feelings or interpret the feelings expressed by others. One 39-year-old stroke victim was unable to laugh or cry and could not shed tears at her father's funeral. I mention this condition, even though it is uncommon, because it offers promise in terms of helping neurological researchers to unlock the physiological mysteries of tear production and its absence. It might also help unravel the basis for empathy with others, which underlies caregiving.

Just as medication can have an impact on crying frequency, it can also contribute to its absence. Antidepressants, for example, may alter a person's usual crying patterns. Sometimes the person may experience this change as a loss. Lorraine, for example, said that she had never been much of a crier, but she missed the occasional cry, especially as her chronic illness became increasingly debilitating. She theorized that Prozac was responsible. She had been quite depressed and benefited from the medication but mourned the loss of her crying ability. For other people who have felt plagued by overly frequent crying or who fear it, this side effect is, of course, welcome.

Displaced Crying

Dr. Henry Maudsley (1996), wrote, "The sorrow which has no vent in tears may make other organs weep." British author Kay Carmichael (1991) said that as a young child she was sent away to a convent school. "I didn't cry when I was left.... Instead I wet the bed. Every night my body wept at the wrong end" (p. 192). In popular and in professional writing, we find the idea that noncriers substitute other physical symptoms for crying. Clinical literature is full of examples, most of them linking suppressed crying to a variety of disorders: respiratory (asthma, sinus headache, allergies, and the common cold); skin (hives and eczema); urinary; gastrointestinal (colitis and gastric ulcers); and circulatory (heart disease).

When Kay Carmichael was denied the natural outlet of protest crying after being left alone at the convent, wetting the bed could have been a symptom of blocked childhood grief, a way of protesting her abandonment and symbolically crying out for her parents to come back and take care of her. When presented with such a physical symptom that can result from many conditions, however, we cannot assume that it is psychosomatic without first ruling out other possible physiological causes.

The term "psychophysiological" is an attempt to move from dualistic mind–body thinking, but it is best used to imply coexistence rather than causation in a particular direction. My hunch is that psyche or soma may lead to or "cause" certain physiological disorders in ways that cannot be directly observed or completely understood.

One of the clearest examples of potentially displaced crying—involving the fewest logical leaps (because of the well-established link between crying and the respiratory system)—is a condition in which inhibited crying, a significant loss, and a respiratory, sinus, or laryngeal/throat problem coincide. I have the daughter of close family friends to thank for one example. Then age 7, Katie and her older sister were staying with us for a week following their summer camp session, awaiting their parents' return from New York. On the second day, Katie complained of a sore throat. Not seeing any visible signs of illness or a red throat, I wondered if her problem might be that she was missing her parents. I decided to approach the subject obliquely and created an elaborate story about an Indian princess and her family preparing to go on a trip that would temporarily take them to separate villages. The day of their departure dawned and they began their journeys down the river. At the exact moment when their canoes reached the fork in the river where the little Indian princess and her parents would go their separate ways, Katie grabbed her neck and said, "My throat hurts! My throat hurts!" indicating to me that I had correctly diagnosed the sore throat as displaced crying.

Choreographer Paul Taylor described in similar terms his reaction to the death of 96-year-old Martha Graham, in whose company he had once been lead dancer. His first reaction was relief that she no longer had to suffer, but about a week later, Mr. Taylor said, "I woke up feeling lousy. A bothersome lump had got stuck in my throat. I thought maybe a cold was coming on or some strange type of knobby depression. Then something reminded me of Martha's passing and I realized I was having a delayed reaction" ("Dance," 1991, p. 8).

In her book, *Your Mind Can Stop the Common Cold*, Lucy Freeman (1973) describes how she had chronic sinus trouble and from childhood onward got a dozen colds a year. In desperation she decided to try psychotherapy. In her third session, "… as I was talking about how much I thought my mother hated me, tears flooded my eyes. I started to sob. I seized a Kleenex and blew my nose" (p. viii). Twenty minutes later she walked out breathing deeply "as I had not done in years" (p. ix). After several years of treatment, her colds diminished to one or two a year.

Freeman points out that a cold can symbolize a grief reaction. Bruce Ruddick (1963) points out that the word "cold" has a number of meanings, "including the loss of bodily warmth related to physical separation; the idea of separation as expressed spatially, i.e., cold = distant; and with the absence of emotional warmth" (p. 178). If we look at colds from the standpoint of separation and grief, the protest stage—loud crying to undo the loss—is represented by a swollen red nose, runny eyes, and sometimes sneezing and coughing; the sadness and despair of grief are represented by the loss of energy during a cold, and healing and recovery by the return to health. Of course, like many other physical symptoms that may substitute for crying, colds also enable people to receive nurturance and caregiving from medical professionals or loved ones, the same healing forces as those ideally generated by crying.

Globus hystericus is a frightening sensation of choking and being unable to breathe or swallow that appears to be linked to suppressed weeping. Several doctors theorize that this symptom may be a chronic version of the "lump in the throat" that often precedes crying. A psychiatrist (Weinstein, 1987) wrote that he asked his patients suffering from globus hystericus, "Have you felt like crying lately?" He received one of two replies: "Yes, but I can't" or "I cry all the time and for no reason" (p. 529).

When he made the association between their symptom and crying, his patients felt reassured and, with psychotherapeutic help and antidepressant medications, many improved significantly.

Because of the frequent association between a "lump in the throat" and crying, I have attempted over the years to investigate what, if any, physiological purpose the "lump" serves; however, to date, my research has been inconclusive. Most medical people whom I ask about it look at me as if I were daft. About half the lay people whom I ask, including those who actually cry on occasion, say they have never experienced that feeling. "Engorged laryngeal tissue" was a psychiatrist friend's best guess as to what it is, but that does not answer the question of how and why it happens and whether it physically facilitates the shedding of emotional tears. My best analysis, based on personal experience, is that the lump precedes crying by a quick moment and feels like it may help to "express" tears physically. I have also noticed that suppressing tears causes the "lump" in the throat to grow, which may account, over time, for the "sore throats" and the sensation of being unable to swallow for people with a diagnosis of globus hystericus.

Symptom as Symbol

Our eyes are literal and symbolic; they have functional and emotional meaning. "Windows to the soul," our eyes are central to our being, as is crying. Eyes are how we see and are seen, how we connect and become intimate, and how we are attracted to—or repelled by—each other at the most visceral level. Our eyes are also one of the most valuable parts of our body and one of the most vulnerable. A patient who read an earlier article of mine about weeping said that as he read about crying, he realized that, since childhood, he had been protectively hiding his eyes and his tears behind his eye glasses.

Psychoanalyst Phyllis Greenacre (1965) calls weeping an "affair of the eye" because it is with the eye that we establish by "looking and seeing" or "looking and not seeing" the presence or absence of a loved one. She wrote, "The disappointed eye, failing to find the lost [loved one], behaves very much like the physically irritated or traumatized eye which defends itself with the soothing tear lotion" (pp. 212–213). I like this formulation because it ties in directly to attachment behavior and crying at separation from the caregiver in infancy and the loss of a close loved one later in life.

Although we need to be cautious about assigning specific symbolic meanings to crying or crying inhibitions, underlying experiences of grief and loss could help to explain the symbolism behind some symptoms. When the skin is said to "weep," as it does with hives or certain rashes for example, there is a linguistic (and possibly symbolic) connection with crying. Skin conditions may be associated with weeping and early loss or with present-day stress, usually in close relationships (Kepecs, Rabin, & Robin, 1951a).

In 1951 (when research protocols were less closely scrutinized for potential harm to participants), researchers induced blisters on the skin of 12 people, 6 of whom had skin disorders and 6 of whom did not (Kepecs, Robin, & Brunner, 1951b). Next, the researchers removed the top of the blister, hypnotized the subjects, and tested the fluid output from the blisters. When the subjects were relaxed, the blister fluid remained constant, but when they were induced to cry under hypnosis by asking them to talk about sad subjects, the blisters exuded more fluid. When the researchers suggested that the person would feel like crying but not allow himself to do so, the amount of fluid coming from the blister decreased initially, but was shortly followed by an increase. These findings, which applied to those with and without a pre-existing skin condition, are unique because they directly show how weeping and suppressed weeping can be transferred to another part of the body—here, the skin.

Because urination also involves a physiological excretion somewhat beyond conscious control (especially in childhood), it seems particularly symbolic of crying related to early grief. In the psychoanalytic literature (Yazmajian, 1966), I found an article describing three adults with excessive urination related to suppressed weeping. One of the people described, a young man, urinated so frequently as a child that his friends nicknamed him "the pisser." All three patients, it turned out, had suffered the loss of their mothers prior to the age of 5—two due to illness and one because her mother emotionally rejected her, blaming her for her marital conflicts and unhappiness. All recalled, during the course of treatment, that at the time of their losses in childhood, they cried and sobbed for prolonged periods. However, they stopped when their crying brought no response. Each then developed urinary symptoms and lost the ability to weep, even in adulthood. The author concluded that the frequent and urgent urination, which would occur at times when grief was touched upon in their psycho-analyses, was a symbolic expression of the wish to shed tears.

The act of crying is a miraculous dance between the cognitive and the neurological. It gives us a unique opportunity to understand intuitively a puzzle that thinkers and scientists have struggled with forever: how body and mind work together. We are each walking research projects on how that takes place. We can observe ourselves in the act of acknowledging grief;

watch ourselves cry; and notice what our bodies do, where our thoughts travel, and in what order. We can watch for signs that we are dodging pain and sadness and notice what our bodies do then as well. Do we get tense shoulders, have a headache or a sore throat, get nauseated or short of breath? Crying humbles us with its mystery and complexity, but it is a wonderful teacher if we open ourselves to its lessons.

PART III

Crying and Inhibited Crying in the Therapeutic Relationship

CHAPTER 10

Crying in the Clinical Hour

The words, facial expressions, gaze, and body language of patient and therapist during the moments that make up the clinical hour can only be fully known and shared by the two intimates involved. Crying is a particularly delicate visceral, nonverbal experience, one that merges into their individual and collective memories, a part of their mutual history that can never be recreated or fully expressed in words. Attempting to capture these particular clinical moments and their meaning is then an exercise in poetry, not science.

My goal in taking up the topic of crying in the clinical hour is to bring a fresh consciousness to what is often overlooked: the attachment and caregiving messages that crying conveys. To that end, I have been asking myself the same question for several decades: how does looking at crying as attachment behavior that evokes caregiving behavior affect my understanding of crying in the clinical moment? My answers may be grouped into four categories:

- Crying may be seen as an intersubjective, two-person relationship behavior mutually generated and mutually regulated.
- A crying episode represents layers and stages of grief.
- Crying in psychotherapy is an indicator of the state of the attachment bond in the therapeutic relationship.
- Crying reflects the patient's attachment style and caregiving style, which suggests certain principles that the clinician may use to inform responses to crying and inhibited crying.

My clinical and theoretical perspective will probably be obvious to most practicing psychotherapists by now, but this is an appropriate time to make it explicit. I am a clinical social worker practicing from a contemporary psychoanalytic perspective. I began my career in the 1960s doing psychotherapy within the framework of traditional psychoanalytic theory and practice, grounded in social work principles and values. In the 1970s I integrated into my work the newly emerging psychoanalytic theory of self-psychology, with its revised view of intrapsychic conflict and the transference relationship. Currently, I am most identified clinically with the branch of contemporary psychoanalytic theory known as "relational" or "intersubjective."

Attachment theory has informed my clinical thinking for many years as a developmental theory with implications for understanding the patient's past wounds, current struggles, and transference dynamics. Attachment theory and research are now gradually being incorporated into contemporary psychoanalytic theory and practice. I hope that this book and these clinical chapters in particular will contribute to that integration.

A large portion of my work over the past three decades has been long-term, intensive psychotherapy with adults, although I do brief psychotherapy and couples therapy as well. I am grateful to the many patients and colleagues who have so generously shared with me their stories and experiences of crying, grief, pain, connection, and disconnection in psychotherapy. I have removed or altered identifying information to protect confidentiality. For purposes of illustration, I have also used some composite or elaborated examples.

Incidence of Crying in Psychotherapy

There is no way to know how frequently crying occurs in psychotherapy, but one 1988 study of 227 clinical psychologists and social workers reported 21% of sessions involved clients with watery eyes, 9% with many tears, and 3% sobbing (Trezza et al., as cited in Labott, 2001, pp. 213–214).

Coombs, Coleman, and Jones (2002) studied the occurrence and management of painful affect (which included crying) in transcripts of psychotherapy sessions with depressed patients. The therapists were either cognitive–behavioral therapists specially trained for consistency in approach or interpersonal therapists similarly trained. Coombs et al. hypothesized that painful affect would be expressed less in the cognitive–behavioral group (because of their focus on cognitive distortions behind the affects) than in the interpersonal therapists (with their emphasis on exploring, clarifying, and "ventilating" painful emotions). They were surprised by their finding: no significant mean differences between the two therapies on the "painful affect" measure. Their conclusion was that "the presence of high painful affect in patients is more independent of technique than one might expect" (p. 241).

The authors also found, to their surprise, that "… some therapists, when faced with painful feelings (including crying) in their patient, added techniques and responses to their usual approach." For example, in one cognitive–behavioral session in which a client persisted in manifesting "high emotional upset," the therapist shifted into more empathic listening and responding (which was not consistent with the research condition) before returning to focus on looking for patterns of "faulty thinking" (p. 243). From an attachment perspective, it would appear that the caregiving needs of the patient expressed through crying were so powerful that they derailed the therapist's conscious intentions and, in a sense, "demanded" caregiving in the form of affect attunement before the more cognitive work could be done.

Crying Is a Two-Person Behavior

I have come to see attachment behavior and its corresponding system—caregiving—as synonymous with intersubjectivity. Crying, representing both of these systems, becomes by definition a two-person intersubjective behavior (as opposed to being seen as a "one-person" behavior in theories of affect discharge that focus on its internal individual dynamics rather than relationship ones). In a given crying, or caregiving, experience, the interlocking nature of the two systems makes it impossible, at most times, to know where one person's attachment and caregiving begin and the other person's end. Crying and caregiving are inseparable: attachment behavior (the patient's and the therapist's) and caregiving behavior (the patient's and the therapist's) are a mutually interactive cycle in adult psychotherapy.

The attachment/caregiving bond, as may be seen in the accompanying illustration of attachment and caregiving behaviors in psychotherapy (see Figure 10.1), goes in both directions: from therapist to patient and patient to therapist. However, as a professional caregiver, the therapist, like a parent, has a responsibility to put the attachment needs and vulnerabilities of the patient at the center of the relationship, to function as the primary giver of care. Therapists, like parents, also form bonds with those to whom they give care. However, the therapist's attachment behaviors, especially the vulnerable ones that solicit caregiving directly, like crying or asking for help, are rarely manifested openly with a patient.

Crying that takes place in psychotherapy reveals volumes about a lifetime of attachment and caregiving successes and failures. Crying sheds

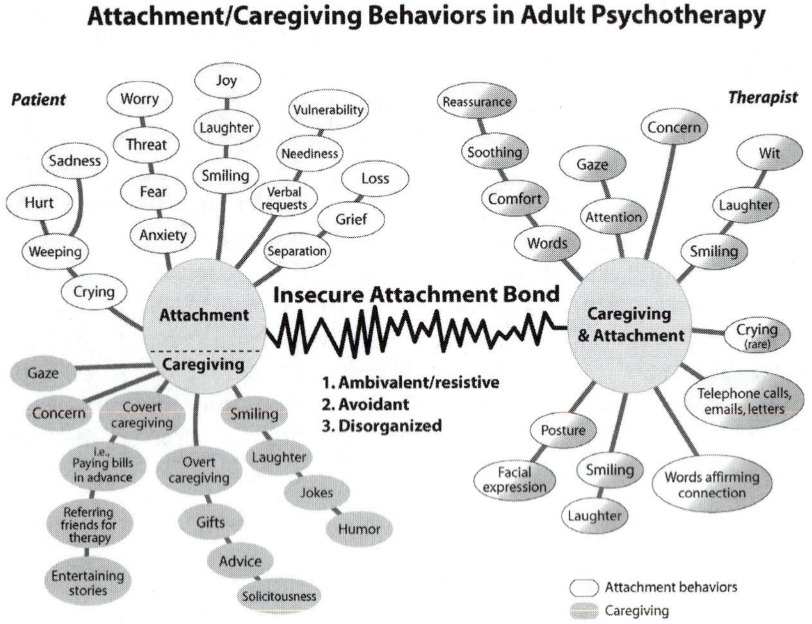

Attachment/Caregiving Behaviors in Adult Psychotherapy

Fig. 10.1 Attachment and caregiving behaviors in adult psychotherapy.

light on the interplay between the child–caregiver bond of the past and the patient–therapist relationship in the present and helps to provide a bridge between these two related pair bonds. Tears in psychotherapy bring loss, grief, and an appeal for caregiving alive in the immediacy of the therapeutic connection. They carry the entire stream of attachment experiences from birth onward, but they do not simply represent grief about the past. They also represent hope because they are triggered and shared within the context of an entirely new caregiving relationship.

Therapist and crying patient, like mother and crying child, enter each other's internal worlds in ways that defy language, involving parts of the brain and the being far more basic and powerful than words. Once, searching for a poetic image, I wrote, "one tear is worth a thousand words," although I was then forced to admit that what I am trying to do by writing about crying is to describe in words what crying does so powerfully without them. In discussing the intersubjective nature of the crying experience in psychotherapy, whether in this book, in the therapist's mind, or in open discussions with the patient, we face the same dilemma: we are attempting to express in words something deep, vast, and essentially indescribable. Still, this translation represents affect regulation and is part of the healing process as it awakens, or reawakens, our consciousness to the powerful potential in this basic yet often overlooked, oversimplified, and marginalized behavior.

A careful exploration of crying in the therapeutic relationship gives the therapist an opportunity to better understand some of the mysterious, often unexplained choices made in responding to affect-laden material in the clinical hour, including some of what seem to be "intuitive" interventions. The process of unraveling the intersubjective strands in a particular crying/caregiving episode is akin to backtracking through a chain of associations to see how I happen to be driving down the road thinking about the pink recital dress I had when I was 8. It is just as impossible and imperfect, although it is always interesting and instructive.

For example, when a patient cried, was I, in my role as caregiver/affect generator, unconsciously or deliberately helping the patient to embrace some aspect of grief and loss? Did I, in effect, "make" her cry? If she began crying, did I, in my role as caregiver/affect regulator, begin to empathize and soothe? Did I do something to distract her focus and thus help her, as it were, to turn down the volume on her grief, or interact in such a way that she did not cry in the first place?

To use a clinical example, I wonder if it was something I said or did not say that triggered Karl's tears when he was telling me about his birthday surprise for his girlfriend: airline tickets to Hawaii. Overtly, I had been attuned to his excitement and expectation, showing how I would feel if someone brought a similar surprise to me. That positive affect, I felt, could be affirming for him, and it was genuine. I would be jumping for joy if someone surprised me with tickets to Hawaii, and I was genuinely happy and hopeful for Karl.

Perhaps, however, his tears were tears of grief over the contrast between my response and those he had experienced in the past—his tears in the present joyful moment acknowledging his past wounds—together with the overlay of hope for repair and healing in the therapeutic relationship and in the relationship with his girlfriend. If, however, Karl's birthday gesture were to be seen as a repetition of his over-giving in relationships—a symptom of his wounds rather than an attempt at healing them—he could be crying because my positive response was a misattunement to the surface gesture, rather than to the underlying compulsive-caregiving one.

Alternatively, Karl's grief could have been more about our mutual, though unspoken, fear for him—based on his early experiences of grave disappointments with giving care in order to receive love—that his girlfriend's response would be understated or even rejecting. Without consciously realizing it, I might have been worried that Karl would be rewounded by her reaction to the surprise. Perhaps part of my helping to regulate his affect was to respond positively at one level while preparing him for the possibility of a disappointing outcome at another—preparatory grief for the future threat and grief for his many disappointments in the past when his affection and caregiving gifts were spurned or spit back at him—thus his tears of grief in what appeared to be a joyful moment. Perhaps Karl could feel a little grief of my own behind the positive enthusiasm that I expressed openly because, as the designated trip-planner in my partnerships, I had never left room for anyone to surprise me with tickets to Hawaii. I had to ask myself if I might feel guilty for envying his girlfriend or if he might feel guilty for "wounding" me.

If reading the preceding paragraph was dizzying, so was thinking it through and writing it down. I could probably go on, see-sawing back and forth to Karl's feelings and then to my own, from his attachment needs and my caregiving to my attachment needs and his caregiving, trying to identify the mutually generated source of his tears and the affect-regulating, caregiving aspects of my soothing of him and his, perhaps unconscious, soothing of me. Were his tears an artifact of his connection with me or part of his healing process in the context of my caregiving, or both? In the end, the best I can say is that Karl and I were in this experience together, and in that particular, clinical togetherness lay the experiences that could help him heal and, if mutuality is the paradigm, might bring some healing to me as well.

Layers and Stages of Grief

Layers of Grief

As we have seen, crying physically acknowledges and interpersonally communicates feelings of loss and grief. By doing so, it provides an opportunity to surface, explore, and explain feelings of loss and their origins in the present and in the past. Part of the healing process in the therapeutic relationship is to formulate the words and thoughts that go with attachment-generated affect. From an attachment standpoint, words serve as powerful caregiving conduits with affect-generating and affect-regulating functions. When therapist and patient explore the layers of grief expressed in a particular crying episode, it is done as part of the caregiving and attachment process, not simply to uncover the content of the layers. It is important to recognize, however, as we look at what might be called the "content" behind the crying—the attachment wounds over the course of a lifetime that may be compressed into one crying event—that verbalizing those multiple, layered losses *is* caregiving, a necessary and valuable aspect of affect regulation and the therapeutic attachment process.

The psychoanalytic term "condensation," used to refer to the layers of memories, feelings, and associations that may be found in a single dream image, is a liquid metaphor that seems particularly apt for the layers of meaning in an episode of crying. Like a dream image, a single experience of crying *condenses* many different feelings, experiences, levels of consciousness, thoughts, and fantasies from the present and the past. So much is going on at once that, again using a liquid metaphor, the crier may fear being inundated or flooded with painful affects related to loss.

Melissa, a former patient, described an episode of crying that illustrates the multiple layers of loss and grief that may be represented. I use this example because Melissa was aware of several layers of loss as she described the experience to me. Not all of these layers would be dealt with at once in a therapy session, of course. At the time she related this to me, I speculated internally about some of the earlier wounds condensed into this crying episode rather than openly discussing them with her. My internal process was, however, helpful in understanding her and the future directions our work—and our relationship—might take.

Melissa had been vacuuming one Saturday morning, in the aftermath of a painful breakup with her boyfriend, when she heard the noise of grating metal. She quickly turned off the vacuum and discovered her silver cat pendant dangling from the brushes. She sat right down on the floor, covered her face, and began sobbing. Melissa loved the necklace, but at first she questioned how something so small and easily replaceable could trigger such a strong reaction. Perhaps, she thought, the little silver cat symbolized her real cats and she cried all the harder, imagining how she would feel if they were ever injured or killed.

Slowly, as she grieved for the actual loss of the necklace and the imagined one of her cats, it began to dawn on her that she was also crying because of Brad, her former boyfriend. Not only had he given her the necklace in happier times, but he had also said that the cause of their breakup was her devotion to her cat family. To save their relationship, he had insisted that she banish all of the cats to the back yard or, better still, give most of them away. Melissa was struck by a new wave of despair over the emotional gulf between her and Brad and cried even harder.

That is as far as Melissa's analysis of her crying episode went, but it was my sense that the core of Melissa's grief went even deeper. She felt that Brad had trampled on and misunderstood the essence of who she was—a person whose bonds with animals were central and familial. I wondered if earlier wounds and rejections from parents, friends, and lovers who did not understand who she was or, if they understood, ran roughshod over her needs and wishes, were also being revived during this new loss. Melissa was grieving viscerally, through her sobbing and tears, the misattunements from caregivers and attachment partners in the present and perhaps also in the past. I was not certain, but I wondered if such wounds were what led her to establish such an intense bond to her feline family with their unquestioning devotion and readily available comfort. The "vacuum" indeed held many losses.

Unraveling experiences and associations is part of therapy, but what makes it possible and potentially healing is the presence of the caregiver/ therapist. Melissa saw me as a caregiver with whom to share her pain; however, later, if I made a caregiving misattunement, I might also become a disappointing and wounding caregiver as had others before me. I had to watch my countertransference even at this point because, in all honesty, I could identify with her former boyfriend's point about the difficulty of living in a house with so many cats.

At this relatively early stage of her work, Melissa was telling me about her crying, which is one step removed from actually crying in my presence. Relating a crying episode that happens outside therapy sometimes feels like a safer way for the pain, grief, and loss of misattunements, ruptures, or traumas to be experienced, understood, and shared—a way to cry without actually crying. The "regulating" or comforting presence of the therapist is a step removed from the actual experience, unlike those times when crying takes place within the clinical hour and the caregiving needs are more immediate.

People with insecure attachment styles—anxious-ambivalent, avoidant, or disorganized—take a long time to work through their insecurity enough to be able to trust in the safety and reliability of the therapist's care-giving. Telling the therapist about crying rather than actually doing it is a way to begin to build the relationship. Over time, gradual and repeated attachment/caregiving experiences in therapy may have an impact on the internal attachment organization of the patient in the direction of greater security and an increased ability to tolerate and regulate negative, as well as positive, affect.

Stages of Grief

In addition to the layers of grief represented in a single crying episode, it is also helpful in terms of affect attunement and affect regulation (caregiving) to be conscious of the stage of the grieving process that the patient is experiencing and expressing: protest, despair, detachment, or reorganization. The therapist may best gauge where the patient is in the grieving process by observing the body language that accompanies the tears, listening to the verbal context, and monitoring his or her own internal responses (assuming that personal work and self-examination are ongoing).

The first thing to notice internally is whether there is a desire to comfort, which most often represents the stage of despair. The therapist's feelings of irritation or apathy may signal protest. An urge to support protest crying or relief generated by it would likely mean that the crying represents protest-on-the-way-to-despair, that is a necessary part of the patient's grieving process. Feeling shut out, frustrated, or pushed away is often the caregiver's experience of detached inhibited crying. Finally, the therapist's feeling of deep satisfaction (or even joy) when the patient cries may be seen as a sign of reorganization and connection.

In long-term therapy with severely injured or traumatized patients with insecure attachment styles, the therapeutic process may include all three stages of grief and types of crying as the patient moves through the process in the presence of the therapist. Along the way, insecurity must be overridden so that trust, or the hope of trust, in the caregiver may develop, along with the ability to experience, even to "withstand," affect attunement (see Kalsched, 1996).

Catherine, a long-term psychotherapy patient of mine, had been severely wounded in childhood by a distant, emotionally unavailable mother and a sadistic father. She described spending long days and weeks isolated in her bedroom on a separate floor of the house when she was ill, playing endless games of solitaire. Her only reliable attachment companion was the family dog. Her mother's lack of attunement was vividly illustrated when Catherine brought me an old postcard found when she was going through her mother's papers after her death. The message on the card, written by her mother to her father, said that 5-year-old Catherine had been so "happy" when she left her at her aunt's house for 2 weeks that "she didn't even notice when I snuck out of the house." Catherine remembered the occasion well and said that she recalled feeling terror that she would never see her mother again.

Her father's abuse was more overt and attacking than neglectful. His shaming misattunements came in the form of attacks if she showed fear, neediness, or vulnerability, telling her that she was "making a mountain out of a molehill." She recalled one occasion when she was about 12 and had just had dental surgery. She was holding her jaw and complained aloud that it hurt. Her father came over and slapped her on the cheeks and told her that she needed to learn to be tough "like an Indian." When she discovered quotes from very old German parenting manuals in Alice Miller's (1983) book, *For Your Own Good*, Catherine theorized that, as some of these old texts suggested, her father (abused as a child by his

German immigrant father, raised in the same generation as the old parenting manuals) had tried to "get control" of her early infant crying by loud commands or even corporal punishment.

Catherine could viscerally recall being shaken, hit, or admonished loudly for crying as a very young child and perhaps as an infant. She said that she had been a noncrier for as long as she could remember. She was skittish, as if fearing attack when she became at all vulnerable. In my office she would startle at a loud or unexpected sound—so much so that she asked if she could install an on/off switch on my telephone. I allowed her to install the switch for literal reasons and symbolic ones: to show that she could regulate her environment and, on another level, that I would help regulate the incoming stimuli as she began to experience the affect connected with her early trauma.

In the beginning years of treatment, Catherine was numb or detached. She told me her story with no affect, giving evidence of what I suspected was an avoidant attachment style. I listened to her stories and internally attuned to their content, but I made only mild affective comments. I might, for example, shudder quietly at a particularly painful memory and say, "How awful," or "Parents have no right to do that." I saw this phase of treatment as an opportunity for Catherine to establish a connection with me that was safe enough and secure enough to tackle the frightening deeper layers of negative affect. This phase lasted several years.

Gradually, as the rage and hostility toward her parents came to awareness, she started to make tearless crying sounds that had an infant-like quality. Curiously, she would startle in fear at her own sounds in the same way that she did to environmental ones like the telephone. This lent credence to her theory that her infant crying had been associated with attack instead of soothing.

During this early protest crying phase, I helped to regulate Catherine's affect by calmly, empathically supporting her feelings of anger and suggesting various ways in which she might express them. At home, she wrote journals and worked in modeling clay and brought these to show me at her sessions. She was easily overwhelmed by this process, and much of my work was to help absorb her negative affect and help her to contain it. The protest crying was clearly associated with her anger, so it was easy to identify this stage of grief. My internal response was of mild relief that she had begun the process, mixed with a determination to remain calm, steady, and available as she needed me.

Gradually, Catherine was able to express her early unmet needs in our safe, attuned relationship and she felt safe enough to begin to shed a few tears with her cry sounds. One of my close colleagues, who saw Catherine while I was away, commented to me later that Catherine cried in a strange way that did not evoke sympathy or empathy: it was more like seeing someone with a runny nose or "the sniffles," she said. She also noticed, as had I, that Catherine worked very hard to keep visible evidence of her tears from spilling onto her cheeks; I assumed that this was a holdover from her father's attacking response to them. I had a different take on those early protest tears because of my closeness to Catherine's process: I knew they were hard won and represented early steps away from detachment into feeling and showing her painful grief in the safety of our relationship.

At some point further on we entered a new phase in which her protest grief focused on our relationship rather than her parental one. In particular, she protested my travel and vacations and would cry and attack me in anger for leaving her. One time, in angry protest, she said that I was being "abusive" for going away because I knew how hard it was on her. Needless to say, my internal reactions to her protest tears became much more difficult for me to bear during this phase. Internally, I would feel annoyed and unappreciated (she said that she was going to get a new therapist who did not travel so much), defensive, and unjustly accused. My overt behavior, however, was aimed at affect regulation—hers and my own. I attempted to soothe both of us by explaining the reasons for a particular trip and the alternative arrangements for her care while I was away.

It helped me and, eventually, her to withstand this phase to remind ourselves that she was grieving the many abrupt departures for travel (including a month-long separation from her mother shortly after she was born) that she had experienced as a child in the here and now of the therapeutic relationship, where she could be soothed. I helped her to frame her feelings as post-traumatic stress reactions to the absent, traveling caregivers in her past and to being left with the harsh, older nanny, whom she was asked to call "Stoney"—a derivation of her surname that Catherine thought to be an apt description of her personality and caregiving skills. My departures gave her a new, more hopeful opportunity to show her anxieties and be soothed about separation and loss.

Eventually, Catherine did come to shed quiet tears of despair over her many losses in the present and the past. At this stage of her work, a nurse asked her during a medical evaluation whether she ever cried. She replied, "Yes, twice a week when I see my therapist." Later, she was pleased to report to me the first time she cried outside therapy in the early months of a new relationship. It was in the presence of her caring lover at a movie that focused on a painful relationship between a mother and daughter. One day quite recently she was quietly and appropriately crying over the many losses related to a chronic illness. I chimed in, being with her in her grief by gently helping her recall all the things in her life that had been affected by her illness. She could feel despair and seek and accept caregiving without any anxiety.

Catherine's treatment went on, uninterrupted, for more than 20 years. Stages of grief in those who have suffered the earliest and most destructive of attachment wounds are not passed through lightly or quickly. Crying has been part of our work and our open discussion from the very first hour I met Catherine. Not knowing of my interest in crying, she brought a news magazine from the waiting room with the picture of a crying infant on the front. She walked in the door, showed it to me, and said that it frightened her to see it in my office because that was what she had come to therapy to talk with me about. It was as if the intersubjective process began even before our first meeting: I was to be the new caregiver who accepted and understood infant crying.

Crying and the Patient–Therapist Attachment Bond

Crying in psychotherapy is a gauge, not only of the patient's grief about attachment and caregiving issues and wounds, but also of the state of the attachment bond with the therapist. Catherine's crying throughout the years, for example, gave me a reading on our relationship as she struggled with trusting me and being able to accept and use my caregiving to regulate her overwhelming affect and to grieve her early (and ongoing) traumas.

In the beginning, Catherine was avoidant and detached and, as is typical for those with avoidant attachment styles, she did not ever cry. She was married and had numerous people who considered themselves friends, but she felt alone in spite of them. Her only real sense of attachment was to her son and her decision to enter therapy came about because she feared she would not be able to manage her anxieties about separation as he was getting older.

Initially, she told me her history without really understanding its significance, how I could help her, or where our relationship might go. Once she began to know and trust me a bit in the early years, she brought me all the lyrics to the Foreigner song, "I Want to Know What Love Is," and said that was what she hoped she would come to understand from me. Since adolescence, she had seen that other people felt a sense of connection that was alien to her, and she wanted me to help her figure that out and maybe, someday, to feel it.

In the middle phase of treatment (the protest years), Catherine showed more of the qualities of anxious attachment: easily aroused negative affect that was difficult to soothe. Those were the rocky years, hard on both of us, although they were essential in terms of healing the grief over her early losses and traumas. She was learning how to cry and learning how to receive caregiving.

In the final phase, the years of despair when her attachment style has been on the way to earned security, our relationship has been smooth and steady. We each feel a mutual sense of the reliability of the other. She misses me when I am away ("missing someone" was a revelation to her), but she is not worried or traumatized by the separations. Catherine is able to use interpersonal affect regulation with me, friends, family, and colleagues and to self-soothe when she is stressed in her daily life. She is divorced now, but she has a circle of friends and a close relationship with her now-adult son. She no longer cries in protest but states her anger or frustration directly in words. When she cries in despair, as she did over her chronic illness, it is linked to present-day loss rather than overburdened by the traumatic ones of the past. More than 6 months ago, she reduced her sessions (originally twice a week) to about once a month. She is comfortable now seeking out my caregiving only when she senses or fears that she might be overwhelmed.

As with Catherine over these many years, I pay such close attention to the attachment and caregiving messages that crying in therapy delivers that at this point it is hard, if not impossible, for me to know what difference it would make if I did not do so. I believe that, with her, it has enabled me to hone my responses, to adjust and fine-tune them continually, and to bring to them a greater conscious understanding of what she is experiencing, what I am experiencing, and how the therapeutic relationship is proceeding. This consciousness, in turn, has an impact on the state of the intersubjective process and the state of the therapist–patient attachment bond.

More conscious awareness of the attachment messages as they are conveyed through crying—or inhibited crying—might not change the course of work done by a self-aware, emotionally attuned therapist. What it can do, however, is to bring to the therapist increased insight about the nature and vicissitudes of the intersubjective bond. It can also help him or her to withstand the feelings associated with a difficult, protracted protest phase. Careful attention paid to the attachment/caregiving aspects of a crying episode can also help the therapist to understand the source, meaning, and impact of an intervention that has gone badly or can shed light on an unusual or particularly "intuitive" intervention that brings a patient to tears.

As an example of an effective, intuitive, affect-generating intervention, Christopher Bollas (1992) writes of a time when he chose to share a fantasized image with a patient. His image moved her to tears for the first time in her analysis and seemed to signal a turning point in their relationship. From his description of the work leading up to and following the crying episode, sharing the image helped to regulate the patient's affect so that she was able to move away from a frustrating period (for both of them) of protest grief and into more connected grieving in despair. Her crying not only helped to signal the change in her grieving posture, but also represented the changing connection to her analyst.

Bollas's (1992) descriptions of the clinical work prior to sharing the image that evoked the patient's tears are tinged with the frustration and helplessness often felt by analysts or therapists dealing with prolonged protest grief. For example, he notes that his patient was "listlessly moaning about the many disappointments in her life" and that she persisted in "hysterical denigration" of her husband, "describing in minute detail how wimpish and repellent" he was (p. 120). At the same time, she rejected Bollas' interpretations, even though they did identify the "despair" underlying the protest grief (p. 120). Bollas writes, in words that resonate with frustrated caregiving, that his interpretations "were unable to reach her." She was not able to risk letting herself feel her despair or allowing Bollas to soothe and comfort her, even though he attempted to point her in that direction. The connection with the analyst and the more hopeful, working-through form of grieving were fended off through the persistent protest grief.

At this point, Bollas chose to share the following image (it was fictional and not based on her actual history) with his patient: "You know, as you are speaking I have a picture of you, a little girl of 3 in tutu and ballet shoes, asked by Mummy and Daddy to perform for guests, and who, warmed by the applause, believes the world will always be like this." At that moment the patient responded by "bursting into tears for the first time in her analysis" (p. 121).

Bollas attributed his image to a kind of "unconscious rapport" between the patent and himself. He was intuitively connected to her attachment wounds, in the here and now as well as in her past, and made his exquisitely crafted and timed intervention based on the nuances of the intersubjective processes going on between them: hers as endlessly protesting (albeit tearlessly) her losses and his as frustrated caregiver. Focusing on this first occasion of crying from the standpoint of attachment and caregiving helps to shed light on the source of some of what Bollas called his "unconscious rapport."

As with Bollas's example, it is sometimes appropriate and helpful to "regulate" affect in the direction of intensifying it by helping a patient to face more pain or a different kind of pain. Bollas knew that despair was beneath the protest—he had mentioned it to her in an earlier interpretation—and he was able to encourage her to experience that despair by using the fictional image of her childhood, perhaps the source of the original losses and wounds that underscored the present-day complaints about her attachment figures. As Bollas (1992) put it, the image "captured something about my patient that I had previously put in the abstract" (p. 121). Tears came for the first time ever in the therapy. She was able to let in the reality of the sadness and despair over her loss and to let her analyst be there for her as well.

Crying, in this instance, provided the means for establishing the attachment—letting Bollas actually be with her in her active despair—and the evidence of its existence. Now there was hope that in the context of the therapeutic relationship she could move forward in grieving for the disappointments and losses that she had experienced throughout her life. A year later she had a dream incorporating Bollas's fictional image of her as a ballet dancer—confirmation of her growing internal attachment to him.

Affect Regulation

Thinking about crying from the standpoint of attachment and caregiving not only helps us to understand (that is, attune better to) the patient's experience, but also can help to guide us in our regulating responses, even the intuitive, in-the-moment ones that come without conscious planning. In this way, attachment theory (like other clinical theories) can provide a "secure base" from which the clinician branches out to work clinically, just as the mother provides a secure base, in Bowlby's language, from which the child moves comfortably to explore the world.

Affect attunement, empathy deeply felt and freely shared, can also be affect regulating, a form of caregiving most effective for the securely attached person. The insecurely attached person often cannot heal through attunement (empathy) alone because empathic caregiving too often arouses anxieties and insecurities. People whose attachment style is anxious-ambivalent are difficult to soothe. Their vulnerabilities and crying behavior are easily aroused, and they readily seek care but have difficulty making use of interactive regulation because it always stirs up more anxiety and a fear of rejection. People with avoidant attachment styles, on the other hand, are in large part unable to open themselves and share their attachment vulnerabilities; they feel safe only when they suppress their needs or rely only upon themselves for care.

In therapy, as in infancy, the growing ability to regulate affect intersubjectively within the attachment/caregiving relationship is the key to growth, healing, and stabilization. Much of the neurobiological research reported by Allan Schore points to psychobiological affect attunement and regulation as "the mechanism that mediates attachment bond formation" (Schore, 2003).

Crying—and inhibited crying—serve to signal where we are in the attachment/caregiving therapeutic relationship and process (I emphasize "we"); what is happening in the moment; how I am contributing to its unfolding and its valence (positive or negative); and how I might best respond. Crying is a clear, openly visible signal of arousal, and the ability to distinguish its nuances (protest or despair) and the attachment style of the crier guides the therapist in responding and regulating the arousal. Sometimes it is important to turn the volume up—that is, to intensify the affect; at other times it is important to turn the volume down—that is, to calm, soothe, or distract. In the following clinical cases, I will give examples of each. There is no exact guide, however, because emotion is not static. It moves and changes—emotion is always *in motion*—so that the therapist's responses mirror and change even as they are helping to move the affective process along. We are attuning and regulating and, while we do that, *because* we do that, we are bonding.

Deintensifying Negative Affect

Jackie was a patient whom I had been seeing for about 2 months. She cried in the initial session and in many of her sessions over the next few weeks. Her insecurity was palpable; her grief and tears were always on the surface as she discussed the traumatic loss of both parents in a plane crash when she was 10. My early image of her brought to mind the archetypal grieving woman with an endless stream of tears, like the princesses in folk tales around the world whose flowing tears of grief have been said to create lakes, rivers, or springs. These felt like eternal tears that would never diminish no matter how much comfort and caregiving Jackie received from me. Her permanent grief seemed to fit the anxious-ambivalent style of attachment. In other words, her affect was easily elicited but difficult to soothe. She could ask for help but not take it in.

Although I believe that crying in despair is the road to healing from grief, in some instances, it may be the road to more despair. Jackie was not permanently protesting her loss—a more common unresolved grief reaction; instead, she was drowning in the despair of it. I suspected that, in large part, this was because she had not been able to connect successfully with a caregiver after her traumatic loss. Her despair became a way to hang onto the lost caregivers, although it kept her from reorganizing and forming new attachments.

At the beginning of the third month of treatment, Jackie told me she had seen a film about Flight 93, the hijacked airplane that went down in Pennsylvania on September 11, 2001. This film catapulted her into a raw, tearful despair. It felt to me that she was sinking fast and needed a life preserver from me. I empathized briefly with her tragic loss and then reminded her how seeing traumatic events in the present can instantly revive traumatic grief, "like Vietnam veterans hearing a bus backfire re-evokes their experiences in the combat zone." Then I asked a few questions about the film: when and where she had seen it; who she was with; who made the film; and what she thought of its quality.

My affect attunement (empathy) quickly moved to affect regulation (education about post-traumatic stress disorder; questions that would help her to move slightly, though not completely, away from the raw intensity of her grief to thinking about the film). I did this based on my belief that the road to healing for Jackie was not to feel her despair endlessly but rather to be able to accept and benefit from caregiving in the therapeutic relationship. By helping to deintensify her crying (arousal), I was giving her care and helping her to soothe and build a new caregiving relationship with me.

This kind of affect attunement and affect regulation requires a lot of self-awareness on the part of the therapist. In the moment, I had to read and respond to her crying. I had to trust my internal barometer, which said this outpouring was too overwhelming for her and that she would not be able to take in or benefit from pure empathy in view of her anxious attachment style. I was relying on everything I know about attachment, crying, and grief and I was using my internal process as a guide: her grief expressed in this way at this time felt like too much *to me*. Of course, I had to ask myself later whether *I* was overwhelmed by the pain of her loss and needed some distance from it and therefore initiated my responses to help distract her. It was excruciating to enter into her despair in that moment as an image of the passengers on Flight 93 flashed into my mind, but what was excruciating for me, I believed, was overwhelming for her, especially because it was early in our relationship, and she could not yet directly take in pure empathy and comfort from me.

One potential pitfall that I had to keep in mind was that by choosing to de-escalate her crying, I had replicated the foster family that she had joined after her parents' death, who always tried to distract her from any expression of her grief. I made a mental note to bring up that possibility with her at some later time when our relationship was more established. When I gently steered her into talking about the film instead of her own loss (and in subsequent sessions), I did not detect any signs of what self-psychologists call a "break in empathy." For the moment I felt comfortable that my affect-regulating strategy was not experienced as a misattunement.

Later, she might turn her protest toward me for having done this, protesting the misattunements that she had earlier endured with her well-meaning foster parents. Uncovering this "break in empathy" at a later stage of our relationship might actually help facilitate her adult grieving process, contributing eventually to reorganization and healing because she would be able to take up her protest safely with me, whereas it had been impossible with her deceased parents and her subsequent guardians.

At this stage of our contact, I felt I needed to be open to her grief but not encourage her to plunge in too deeply and too quickly. I hoped that my "rescue" of her on this occasion might be one of the things that would help her learn to feel gradually more secure in our bond. I would help her to regulate her overwhelming feelings of loss while acting as a protective caregiver rather than one who insisted that she ignore her feelings. I would be with her and make sure that she felt safe.

When a person persists in protest crying that alienates potential caregivers and keeps him or her from moving into despair over his or her loss or losses, my therapeutic affect regulation takes a different form. Then, I attune and empathize only with the anger in the protest, not with the tears. If a man divorced for 10 years is telling me, through gritted teeth, albeit tearfully, that once again his former wife has pulled a fast one financially and now he must go back to court, I might say, "How upsetting! She just can't seem to let you go in peace." I would not respond soothingly to the tears, or even acknowledge them, but rather help to emphasize the appropriate anger that might help to mobilize him rather than keeping him mired in protest, unrealistically waiting to be rescued by someone who would make the whole thing go away.

The preceding examples of deintensifying crying relate to patients with anxious-ambivalent attachment styles. Even for the securely attached, however, sometimes it makes sense to effect an attuned "rescue" from overwhelming affect. One such situation might occur because it is too soon in the relationship for an experience of such depth to be integrated. Another would be if profound social shame is attached to crying so that tears signify interpersonal struggle rather than comfort.

The securely attached are those for whom humor often lightens a tearful moment, although on occasion that occurs with other patients as well. It is natural for me to move in and out of tears and laughter because that is a caregiving style with which I grew up and that I find very comfortable. Recently, a long-term patient was crying in a hard-earned moment of despair over her anxious, uncertain early relationship with her mother. I sat quietly nodding, proud that she had come to this place of acknowledging her loss in my presence, after years of getting annoyed or sarcastic with me when I would relate anything in her life to her relationship with her mother. After a minute or two of focused crying, she said, "I suppose my mother quit breastfeeding me too soon," and we burst out laughing. It was a reference to a funny conversation that she had overheard and a nod to her former resistance to my discussions about her relationship with her mother. I thought that perhaps, after so many years, our caregiving styles were now finely tuned to each other and we could connect *and* caregive by laughing through tears in the same moment at the same thing, in much the way that my family does.

Encouraging Crying

For many people, crying is a dangerous and frightening prospect. "I never want to let myself go and cry; I'd be afraid I would fall into this deep well and drown," was the way a woman whom I saw briefly years ago put it. A long-term male patient could not even acknowledge that crying frightened him. He just told me that he compared emotion to static electricity. "You gather it up as you cross the carpet. If you reach out and touch metal, sparks will fly but if you just stand there a few moments and wait, it will go out slowly through your shoes." These two people represent cry-aversive people: those afraid of crying because no caregiving can soothe them and those averse to crying because it shows a need for caregiving when, for them, survival means being compulsively self-reliant and never showing their vulnerability.

In the first instance, the woman with anxious-ambivalent attachment had suppressed her ever-ready tears as a coping mechanism for so long that she felt they would drown her if the dam ever broke. In the second, the avoidantly attached man expressed his ideas about affect couched in mechanistic, depersonalized terms. In neither case would it make sense simply to "encourage" the person to cry. The caregiving wounds must first be addressed and a platform for caregiving established within the therapeutic relationship, which is a long, painstaking process for the insecurely attached. Only then might crying begin to emerge as it did with Catherine after years of treatment.

I rarely, if ever, actively encourage a person in therapy to cry. If I think he or she is ready, my encouragement takes other forms. I might, for example, ask a pointed question that goes to the heart of a loss, such as "Wasn't your birthday around the time of your Dad's funeral?" Here, I am highlighting the most painful aspects of a loss rather than steering away from them as I might when someone is too flooded with crying despair.

Another way in which I have observed myself encouraging tears is by giving a hypothetical parental caregiving response when hearing about an early wound. For example, a young woman was telling me about the confusion and grief she felt as a young girl when her mother began to date after her parents' divorce. I said, in a tender, parentally soothing tone of voice, "No one said to you, 'Honey, this is going to seem strange and uncomfortable for a little while until we get used to it'?" and she began to cry. My caregiving at this stage of her life accomplished two purposes: it showed that I was attuned to her childhood affect as she related it to me as an adult, and it highlighted the caregiving that had been missing for her back then, thus touching directly into her grief.

A Caregiving Conundrum

Writing about his work with a patient whom he calls Donald, Stuart Pizer (1996) raises one last significant point regarding crying in the clinical hour; this relates to the centrality of physical contact in affect regulation with infants and young children and throughout life. In infancy, crying is a signal that physical proximity to the caregiver is urgently needed and, as might be expected, touch is the most powerful terminator of infant crying. Physical touch continues throughout life to be the most powerful affect regulator. However, it is not available to psychotherapists because of the need to maintain professional boundaries.

It is important to recognize that, because our caregiving must be done without touch, in a figurative sense, we are working with both hands tied behind our backs. Caregiving must always be translated from its native language of physical connection into words or some other form of distal caregiving. Fortunately, we still have access to other powerful, although nonverbal, caregiving behaviors of infancy, including gaze, facial expression, body language, and tone of voice. These enable us to respond in a right-brain way to the right-brain distress mutually felt when a patient cries.

Donald, who had been abused as a child, had gone through a long period when, Pizer (1996) writes, he "painfully and persistently *protested* [italics mine] my failure to be a father to him" (p. 689). After a while, Donald broached the subject of crying, saying that he felt he needed to cry but did not think he could ever do so unless Pizer would actually hold him, although he knew the rules of therapy forbid this. At that point, Pizer writes, "I chimed in with, 'That's right; no holding'" (p. 699).

Later, Donald again raised the issue and asked why Pizer "had flatly said, 'No holding.'" This time, Pizer, reflecting on that prior moment, explained why he had jumped in so quickly and suggested that they might "leave the question of holding open between us without *a priori* assumptions, to see what this might entail, what we might learn, and what might actually help him" (p. 699).

Immediately, Donald said he felt better. He tried on the idea of going to a psychodrama group in which it would be all right to hold people. "Maybe then I could cry like I need. But it wouldn't be with you" (p. 699). The next week, he reported an even more direct caregiving fantasy: coming to the analyst's office during a crisis where he would, Pizer writes, "lie down on my couch and I would sit on the floor next to him and cradle his head as he cried" (p. 700). When the analyst followed up with an attuned remark about Donald's inner experience, Donald responded "with immediate, *tearful* [italics mine] relief," saying that the analyst's understanding helped him "hold this experience together" (p. 700).

At this point, Donald could safely reveal his attachment behavior in the knowledge that the analyst was "open" to holding him rather than distancing about it. Donald's words, that the analyst helped him "hold this experience together," show that symbolic, verbal, and emotional caregiving was possible: "the metaphorization of holding" (p. 700), as Pizer calls it here.

As the case unfolds, we have the opportunity to watch the attachment and the caregiving deepen and to note the increased presence of attachment behavior (crying) and openness to the real and symbolic caregiving of the analyst. Gradually, Donald could experience the full despair and sadness of the severe abuse he had experienced at the hand of his stepfather, shedding tears as he did so in the comforting, caregiving presence of the therapist. Donald progressed from an "initial requirement of concrete, skin-to-skin bodily holding ... to the eventual emergence of his inner capacity to symbolically register holding as a useful metaphor representing our relationship in the service of his self-regulation" (Pizer, 1998, p. 38).

CHAPTER **11**

How Therapists Deal With Crying and Caregiving, Including Their Own

Crying in psychotherapy takes place in the context of a newly formed or forming therapeutic attachment bond that stirs up attachment and caregiving issues and wounds, not only for the patient, but also for the therapist. Crying and caregiving take root in our earliest experiences in life and carry over into the present, echoing throughout all of our close relationships, including therapist and patient. How could they not when they are embedded in our very beings? Crying opens a window into a patient's attachment and caregiving core, as well as into the therapist's.

In our role as professional caregivers, it is imperative that we recognize, grieve, and struggle with our attachment and caregiving issues. We must do this because they are the stuff of which our caregiving responses, interventions, questions, feelings in the moment, and even our enactments are made. Indeed, they may also be the stuff of which our very professional selves are made, bearing as they do on our choice of career, colleagues, and theoretical orientation.

In looking at the impact of the therapist's attachment and caregiving behaviors on the relationship with the patient and on the therapist's own internal process of that relationship, we focus on what in psychoanalytic theory is called "countertransference." We will be looking at countertransference in terms of its traditional meaning of conflicts within the therapist that may bias or derail the work of the patient, as well as in the broader sense as everything the therapist as a person brings to, experiences within, and contributes to the therapeutic relationship. From this broader

173

standpoint, we see that the subjective experiences of the patient are complexly interwoven with the subjective experiences of the therapist to create the feelings, conflicts, attunements, and misattunements of the intersubjective therapeutic connection.

Increasing our awareness of attachment and caregiving countertransference is necessary because therapists must be able to take a reading of internal responses to a patient's crying in order to assess the type of crying and what it signifies about the state of the therapeutic attachment bond. If, as we have discussed, affects are mutually created and mutually regulated, then we must bring a great deal of consciousness to bear on the affects that we evoke and why we evoke them, as well as on those evoked in ourselves and why. Do I feel irritated or apathetic toward a patient's crying because it is protest crying aimed at distancing or devaluing my caregiving, because I have difficulty with seeing older women cry, no matter the reason, or because I am distracted by a conflict in my family and unable to attune to the patient's demanding or blaming protest? To make this determination requires that therapists continually examine and expand awareness of their attachment and caregiving issues, past and ongoing.

The case examples in this chapter come from my practice, those of colleagues, and the literature. They highlight a variety of clinical experiences with crying to encourage therapists to think consciously about these issues. The examples also show that, because crying by the therapist is complex and multilayered, no guidelines can anticipate every situation. In the end, crying by the therapist must be examined and understood one relationship at a time. However, an attachment and caregiving perspective is invaluable in doing so. The cases here are intended to help the clinician determine on a case-by-case basis when suppressing tears is optimal (assuming it is a choice) and when sharing them openly might be the wiser course. Furthermore, if the therapist does cry, there are guidelines to help the therapist decide whether and how to process the experience openly with the patient. Guidelines, however, are always a work in progress that must be addressed anew with each individual patient.

Do Therapists Cry With Their Patients?

Crying by the therapist is a subject that is rarely discussed in the literature or informally among clinicians. In talking and consulting with colleagues over the years and in a recent informal survey that I conducted, I have found that crying during a session is an experience familiar to many, although it is unusual behavior for most of those who do cry. Among therapists who have cried in a session (about one in three said that he or she never cries), most say that it is a rare event, occurring on only a few, usually memorable, occasions in their professional lives. The most frequently checked category was "three to five times" in periods ranging from 9 to 40 years. For example, I have cried during a session only four times in almost four decades of clinical practice, which is comparable to many of those who responded to my survey question.

Among the group of therapists who do cry, a number said that they feel *like* crying frequently but suppress or put off their tears until later. A small number of therapists said that they do, in fact, cry frequently during a session, which for them meant once or twice a month. One of these therapists wrote that she often gets tears in her eyes but because they feel "like such a natural part of the work, I don't really notice." Another said, "It is such a common experience that I don't have too many distinct memories." This therapist said that she tends to process her crying with patients when it occurs and finds that most are comfortable and appreciative. They take her tears to represent empathy, as does she.

No one who was in touch with me said he or she cried in almost every session, although I heard through a friend about her therapist in another state who apparently did so. My friend said that at first she thought it was sweet, a sign that the therapist felt her pain along with her. Later, however, it occurred to her to ask another woman who was also a patient if their mutual therapist ever cried. When the woman responded with, "all the time," my friend thought, "My god, that woman must sit there crying all day long!"

Although it is impossible to know how the therapist viewed this experience, it is hard to imagine how this much crying would not be burdensome to the patient. My friend adapted to it well in the beginning, but eventually did not feel comfortable with it. From a clinical viewpoint, processing the experience would be the most logical place to begin, for patient and therapist. If crying easily and often is uncontrollable but not based on grief or symptomatic of a physical disorder, sharing that with new patients might help to stave off their confusion and misunderstandings. I know of a nurse who cries multiple times a day at slight provocations, especially during allergy season, and lets her students and patients know this so that they do not become alarmed or otherwise misinterpret her tears.

Among those whom I surveyed, the half dozen (including one man) who said that they have never cried in a therapy session are all in long-term practice (9 to 28 years). Three of them said that they do occasionally feel like crying, but when they do, they suppress their tears or, as one person put it, "I hold back my overt tears." One said that, a few times, she has "welled up" enough to be noticeable to her patient.

I should have asked an additional question about whether these therapists ever cry outside therapy. Three of the respondents who never cry in therapy are people whom I know well. Two of the three told me that, in fact, they never cry in *or* out of a therapy session (one is physically unable to shed tears). The third said that she cries only on rare and extreme occasions and then only in solitude.

Therapists' Attitudes Toward Crying in a Psychotherapy Session

I also asked therapists in the survey whether they think crying by the therapist is helpful to the patient, interferes with their process, or is sometimes helpful and sometimes interferes. Among the group who never cry, most said, "I think crying by the therapist interferes with the patient's experience." Among those who cry on occasion, most said that they believe that crying can sometimes help and sometimes interfere, which is also my view. One clinician wisely pointed out that the therapist's crying may also have mixed results: helping (or interfering) in the moment and interfering (or helping) later. For example, she writes, "If I cry, it can cause a narcissistic patient to see me as a person, which they may resent at the time but come to value as they develop the capacity to see others as separate people."

I hear echoes of the traditional psychoanalytic ideal of neutrality in comments indicating that the therapist's crying *necessarily* interferes with the patient's process. Those of us who were psychoanalytically trained prior to the late 1980s learned that strict neutrality was to be the goal for the therapist's demeanor and behavior. All personal feelings were to be worked through, suppressed, or masked. This ideal of neutrality, representing what we now call a "one-person" psychology, was so that the therapist should contribute as little affect as possible to the therapeutic exchange in order to keep the air clear, so to speak, for evoking the patient's transference projections. We were striving to be a "blank screen," open to reflecting, absorbing, and analyzing the patient's material, unclouded by our own. Crying in that formulation would have been out of the question because crying, as one therapist points out, is "involuntary self-disclosure." The therapist's crying shows that he or she is feeling something personal, even though the tears may be evoked by the patient's words and experiences.

I have come across only two articles that discuss crying by the therapist (or health care professional). Both caution against it while acknowledging that at times it might be helpful. One was written by a nurse and the other by a group of cognitive therapists. The first, published in the journal *Canadian Nurse* (McGreevy & Heukelem, 1976), says of crying along with a crying patient: "It can be assumed that this is acceptable and may be beneficial to both, as long as the nurse's needs do not exceed those of the patient and she maintains a degree of objectivity" (p. 20).

In a similar vein, Beck et al. (1979) caution that therapy is not "for the therapist" and that, therefore, crying by the therapist must be carefully monitored.

> On occasion we have heard of therapists who were so empathetic with the patient that they started to cry along with the patient. This kind of interchange apparently had some therapeutic value in building a bridge with the patient. Nonetheless, this type of response occurred with highly experienced therapists who knew when to give vent to their own feelings (p. 41).

I have wondered why crying by the therapist is so rarely mentioned in the clinical and theoretical literature and why it is not, in my experience, openly discussed in any formal way in training programs. I have had the feeling that, for some reason, even among therapists, crying is often experienced as vaguely shameful, perhaps going back to the tradition of maintaining analytic neutrality.

Crying *is* "involuntary self-disclosure," a sign that we are having and showing feelings (and perhaps attachment or caregiving needs). We need to ask ourselves whether an admission of crying might make us feel vulnerable to criticism or professional embarrassment. Through a colleague, I learned of a meaningful experience of crying by her male therapist when she was in treatment. Years later, the therapist told her that he had written about the experience in an article. In the disguised version, however, it was not the therapist who cried, but someone else in the patient's life. As all of us who do clinical writing and thus disguise cases realize, much of the authenticity of the here-and-now experience in the therapeutic relationship must be sacrificed for confidentiality. I did wonder, however, if altering that detail served more to protect the therapist's confidentiality than the patient's, and I speak as a writer who can identify with the self-exposure component of clinical writing for the therapist.

In some of the therapists' responses to the survey, I hear evidence of a gradual move into a more relational stance, combined with lingering ambivalence about crying in therapy. A noncrying therapist in practice for 9 years writes, "I have become more open to the idea of letting my clients see my emotions in that way, but I believe strongly that suppression of the tears is often in the best interest of the client." The theoretical viewpoint has changed with the advent of a more relational, two-person psychology. The goal of maintaining a strictly neutral stance has been called into question, as a therapeutic ideal and because it is now believed to be impossible to maintain. Nonetheless, crying may still be somewhat stigmatized because it is a clear display of the therapist's affect (or attachment needs), which might at times "interfere" with the patient's therapeutic work.

Because of the attachment/caregiving wounds of so many patients, therapists may choose to resist crying in therapy for good reasons. I agree with many of my colleagues who say that crying early in a treatment relationship is especially problematic. Once the therapeutic attachment is well established and the issues well understood, the therapist's tears may be processed within the context of the patient's attachment and caregiving needs (and, to whatever degree necessary and relevant to the treatment, of the therapist's attachment and caregiving needs as well).

However, it is also possible that resisting all crying in psychotherapy might be defensive. A firm "no crying" policy might represent a belief that crying is too risky (for the patient) and too much self-disclosure (by the therapist). Such a policy, however, might also represent defensive avoidance of self-exposure for the protection of the therapist. Furthermore, it could be that a refusal to allow oneself ever to cry with a patient represents an entrenched need to maintain the role of caregiver and a discomfort with the idea that the patient may at times serve as caregiver to the therapist, to the benefit of both.

Another potential source of reticence and perhaps even shame about crying by the therapist may be tied to the social stigma that crying suffers in parts of society at large. Therapists cannot assume that they are immune to social values, even those that they do not consciously espouse. An awareness of one's upbringing and family and social mores regarding the open expression of attachment needs and vulnerabilities through crying is therefore essential.

One of the "never cry" therapists told me that, when she first began to practice, she was "dumbfounded" when her patients would cry, seemingly without any concern about it. She had been raised in her large family to think crying was making a "fuss," which made it an imposition on others. Disapproval of crying, she had come to believe, was part of her family's immigrant posture of never drawing attention to oneself, which crying would definitely do. In her family, if crying could not be avoided, it was to be done in solitude. She recalls that when she first began practicing as a therapist she was so troubled by her reaction to her patients' crying that she brought it up in consultation and was able to gain a different perspective. When social attitudes are more subtly ingrained, however, their impact may be hidden or translated into clinical terms that obscure their origins.

When the Therapist's Crying Helps and When It Interferes

An attachment/caregiving perspective on crying provides a framework for understanding why and when crying by the therapist may help and why and when it may interfere. On the problematic side, because most (though not all) crying represents an attachment appeal for caregiving, crying by the therapist may sometimes threaten the patient's ability to completely trust in or rely on the therapist as caregiver. Particularly for patients who had to give care to their caregivers in childhood or who compulsively do so in current attachment relationships, it may trigger an unfortunate reversal in the therapeutic relationship. The therapist's crying then dovetails with the patient's assumption that he or she must "shore up" the caregiver in order to receive care.

Crying by the therapist, even though it may be rooted in empathy rather than need, can be upsetting to the patient. Perhaps it is analogous to a child seeing a parent cry. Securely attached children may simply feel empathy for a crying parent. I have collected some wonderfully sweet photographs of children reaching out to comfort crying parents and a few in which the child and the parent are weeping and holding each other. In the insecurely attached, however, confusion sets in and, all too often, the child becomes anxious and senses that the parent is in need of care and that this must take precedence over the needs of the child. Another variable, of course, is whether the parents (as in some of the pictures I have collected) are grieving a particular loss or whether they are in a chronically needy state, which is far more damaging and difficult for children.

Several examples of situations in which the therapist's crying interfered with the patient's work have come to me secondhand from therapists reporting stories from patients who had left therapy with a previous therapist over this breach. The former therapists, perhaps thinking they were showing empathy, cried as they heard about a patient's wounds or traumas. The patients, however, took the therapist's crying to be a sign of neediness and a demand for care. In both instances reported to me, the therapy was abruptly terminated, although I believe that this is not an inevitable outcome. In the hands of a sensitive and experienced therapist, the misattunement caused by the crying therapist could be recognized and discussed with the patient and in that way have healing potential.

For example, a male therapist described an experience of crying with a long-term male patient (of more than 10 years) who was getting deeply in touch with what it was like to be "alone, frightened, and invisible as a child." The therapist wrote: "I think the experience he was having was close to those parts of me that are wounded in similar ways. And there was something about the two of us, both men, sharing this tender experience of vulnerability we felt as little boys. It was very real and alive." However, the patient was not comfortable and said to him, "Aren't I the one who is supposed to be crying here?" In response, the therapist bridged what could have been a caregiving misattunement stirring up the patient's insecurities about the strength and availability of his caregiver/therapist: "I told him that this work is for him but that I could not help but be moved by his experience and how he was able to share it with me." In this way, the therapist helped the patient to regulate his fearful response and maintain his view of the therapist as an attuned, present, and available caregiver.

In the diagram of attachment and caregiving behaviors of therapist and patient in chapter 10, I put crying by the therapist on the border between attachment and caregiving because I believe that it can represent a caregiving behavior or an attachment appeal. When it is an expression of the therapist's attachment vulnerability, at least in part, it may indeed represent an appeal to the patient for "care." However, in most instances therapists report (and in three of the four of my experiences this was the case) that the therapist's crying is an expression of the deep connection that they are feeling with the patient—crying in recognition of attachment rather than distress over a loss. In a sense, such a visible, visceral acknowledgment of attachment is the highest form of caregiving, a way of showing that "I am maximally attuned to your feelings right now." The case examples in the following section illustrate this optimal situation.

Crying as Connection

Perhaps the most compelling examples of the way in which crying by the therapist can successfully represent empathic care and connection and serve to solidify the therapeutic attachment bond are those given to me by three therapists recalling when they were patients and experienced their therapists' tears. In the first instance, the therapist and the patient were women:

> On two occasions over the course of my own recent 7-year, 3-times-a-week treatment when my therapist welled up with tears as she listened to me. I experienced this as deeply moving and very much about her experience of my emotional pain. In terms of attachment, I would say that these experiences increased my sense of a close bond between us.

This therapist/patient goes on to say that her therapist's tears did not occur until after they had been working together for more than 5 years. "Had it occurred early in the treatment I am quite sure it would have left me feeling very confused about my therapist's abilities and capacities to manage my own strong affects (which at that time were still quite scary to me)." In other words, early on, when she needed the steady, calm, and accepting presence of the caregiver, tears, even though they might have been truly empathic, would have delivered a different message to the struggling patient.

The next example is quite similar to the first except that, in this instance, the therapist was male. The female patient (also a therapist) writes: "About a half a dozen times during my therapy of 5 years, I saw his eyes fill with tears and it was very validating for me. I felt held and understood. It was very healing." Again, the crying is seen as serving a caregiving function that helped to solidify the attachment bond. The attunement of the therapist is underscored and the characterization of the "holding" function ("I felt held") of his tears points to their being experienced as effective caregiving.

A final example of crying shared by a therapist/patient is from a woman whose male therapist cried. It is an especially helpful example because it points out how the empathic and the personal layers co-occur when the therapist cries. However, it also points out how self-disclosure about the personal aspects may, at times, detract from the patient's experience of the therapist's caregiving tears. The therapist/patient writes that her therapist "cried later in the therapy when I was talking about the day my father died and how I learned about his death. At the time I was very moved. It felt good. I guess I felt that my sadness about my father's death was, in fact, sad." Later, however, she found out that her therapist had also lost his father early in life and she writes, "I actually wish I had not learned this because it takes away from the therapist being moved by my sadness."

For some patients, disclosing the personal information would have further cemented the empathy and the therapeutic attachment bond. For this patient at this stage of her life and her grief, it took something away. The "no self-disclosure" rule in traditional psychoanalysis avoided the latter problem but created other problems by subtracting something potentially valuable from the therapeutic attachment bond. Making differential choices about when and what to self-disclose is an ongoing challenge for the intersubjectively attuned therapist. Repairing misattunements growing out of self-disclosure or other aspects of the treatment, however, creates the interpersonal space where healing so often occurs.

The following examples describing positive caregiving and connecting elements of crying by the therapist are from the perspectives of the therapist (rather than the patient). In some instances, the tears were directly processed with the patient so that there was feedback as well as an intuitive appraisal of the outcome. I quote from the following three cases that have been shared with me in written form:

> The last time I cried with a patient was during the patient's shedding of some quiet tears over her inability to get pregnant and her recollection of her interrupted relationship with her mother who died when She was 15. My tears welled up quietly and I let them flow. I wiped them but kept my eyes on my patient. To me, the tears felt shared. I was touched by my patient's memories and dilemma but my tears were grounded in my own very difficult relationship with my mother and in the fact that I had tried for 6 years before I became pregnant with my son.

I especially appreciate this therapist looking at the intersubjective nature of this crying experience. The empathy that she felt for her patient was grounded in her own experience. It does not sound as if the therapist was actively grieving her own losses in that moment, but rather as though she was using her own experiences to attune empathically to the patient. The therapist does not indicate whether she shared her losses with the patient, but it is my impression that she did not. Instead, she let the tears speak their own language of attunement and caregiving without disclosing the personal information that might have then made them feel like an appeal for caregiving from the patient.

In the next example, the therapist was also aware of what had been touched in herself but did not share that with the patient. This occasion of crying occurred in a 10-year treatment relationship:

> In the previous session the patient was telling me that she knows that she has survivor's guilt but she has such a hard time acknowledging it. She asked me why this is so. I thought for a while and then said, "To acknowledge that you have survivor's guilt means that there was something awful or traumatic to have survived." (I teared up.) "You say repeatedly that your childhood was confusing because there were moments when things were good and normal. But you did not have a good childhood. Your mother often raged and at times the anger turned into physical violence. Your father was also depressed."

In thinking about the experience later, she writes, "I think I teared up because she has had difficulty feeling sad for herself as a child. Also because when I said 'trauma,' for a moment I went to Holocaust trauma, as I was immersed in writing about that at the time." Here the personal association not only helped to underscore the empathy, but also helped her to formulate the interpretation that her tears represented the patient's hidden abuse. By shedding tears for grief that the patient did not yet feel entitled to, the therapist affirmed the existence of the patient's trauma and loss.

The final example is especially poignant because the effect of the therapist's tears on the patient can be sensed just by reading about them. The patient was a strongly religious woman who, the therapist writes, "felt like a failure in her life. She believed that God had turned His back on her and didn't hear her prayers." As the patient described her feelings of abandonment by God, the therapist began to cry and as she did, she also had "a vivid image," which she chose to share with the patient. "I told her I thought God had turned His back to her to hide His tears." In the context of the therapist's tears, this caregiving response helped to soothe and regulate the woman's sense of loss and failure. The therapist writes that, following her tears and her words, the patient "seemed to gain an empathy with herself." The tears of the empathic therapeutic caregiver evoked the possibility of a positive connection with a compassionate and benevolent divine caregiver, rather than the harsh, negative, rejecting one that she had previously visualized (perhaps in reflection of her earthly caregivers).

Crying at Terminations

One of the therapists who responded to my survey says that she never openly cries but the times when she most feels like it are "when patients with whom I have a deep connection terminate." Three of my four experiences of crying in therapy were at abrupt or premature terminations. The end of a meaningful therapeutic attachment relationship inevitably triggers feelings of loss for both parties and thus might lead to tears. However, whether this is positive or deleterious depends on many factors unique to each relationship, its history, and the history of the individuals within it. Of the three times when I cried at terminations, two were solidly positive, while the third, I recognized immediately, was not.

I do not usually see children and adolescents, but the two instances in which I cried were with a 12-year-old girl and a 16-year-old girl. I think the fact that they were children highlighted themes of vulnerability. That the treatment relationship with each of them was suddenly and traumatically terminated further influenced the resulting attachment/separation behavior: my crying.

Twelve-year-old Jenny was the only child of a single mother who died suddenly in a car accident about 18 months after we began treatment.

Jenny was further traumatized by having to leave her teacher, her friends, and her therapist to live with relatives in another city. What she felt most strongly was tremendous fear; the multiple losses were too overwhelming to grieve openly at that stage. At our final session, I began to express my sadness about the end of the therapy and the fact that we would no longer be able to see each other regularly. As I talked about my feelings, I shed a few quiet tears. She watched me intently and I could see in her eyes that she also felt sad. As we said good-bye, she said that she would miss me too. It felt to me as if my tears reassured her that I cared and would miss her and also, I hoped, kept open the possibility that she would feel safe enough with her new therapist to express her sadness as well. I lost track of her after about a year, but was moved and gratified several years ago when I received a Christmas card that filled me in on the details of the intervening years and let me know that her adult life had finally come together in a satisfying way. Our connection had endured the traumatic rupture; perhaps, I mused, the power of those long-ago tears had something to do with that.

The termination with the 16-year-old was also completely unexpected. She had been having difficulties with her stepfather, especially after her brother left home to work in Los Angeles. He was barely 20, but knew of her unhappiness and offered to let her live with him and finish high school there. Her beleaguered parents agreed to this plan and it was set in motion immediately. At our last session, just 2 weeks after I first learned of her impending departure, I began to cry. I apologized to her, fearing she would see me as unsupportive or, worse, as wounded by her decision. She shook her head "no" and said, "Of all the people I have told that I'm leaving, you are the only one who has cried." Even though she wanted to go, her parents' almost instant agreement with the plan had felt like rejection. In my tears she found the comfort of knowing she was cared for and would be missed.

At this point it is important to reflect on how much raw pain we as therapists are exposed to in the course of our work. We absorb and attune to unimaginable human suffering and we are committed to remaining empathically open to feeling something of what our patients have gone through. Perhaps, at times when the wound is mutually experienced in the moment, as it is with a termination, it is much more likely to elicit a personal response. In the end, that is what deep empathy represents: truly feeling another's pain (as opposed to sympathy, which is understanding pain from the outside). With both of these young women, their loss also became my loss. The grief was mutually experienced, although in both instances, I was the one who was expressing it in tears. In this way, my attachment behavior was actually an extension of my caregiving role.

Another important aspect of crying by the therapist occurs when a mixture of personal pain and loss is represented by our tears, even though in the moment they may be triggered by empathy with a patient's loss. I will not go so far as to say that an underlying layer relating to personal attachment and loss is present on *every* occasion when a clinician sheds tears in a therapy session. However, I believe this to be true in the vast majority of instances, as most of the colleagues who have shared examples of their crying acknowledge and discuss.

In my own case, at the time I was working with these two young women, I was the mother of two daughters within a few years of my patients' ages. The traumatic losses of my patients were inevitably seen through the lens of my parenting and my vulnerability on behalf of my daughters. There was also a direct personal identification from my past. In the case of the younger girl, a significant personal detail corresponded with one from my childhood. In focusing on the complicated interconnections between us as I cried over these sudden terminations, it is clear to me how intersubjective my tears truly were and how complete neutrality was (and is) an impossibility.

Without question, my third experience in crying at a possible termination grew out of my countertransference conflicts, and my crying interfered with the patient's process. After a relatively brief 2-year, intense treatment, this patient decided that she had completed her work and began to discuss termination, which seemed to me to be premature. She had indeed worked through a number of significant issues in the context of what felt like a very solid connection with me. Ending in this way, I feared, might be an attempt to master her early traumatic loss of a parent, thus repeating the attachment rupture that she had worked so hard to grieve. As her therapist/caregiver, it just felt too abrupt *to me* and I felt comfortable using my reaction as my yardstick, but my tears did not help. It was too difficult for her to make sense of them. Was I showing that I cared or was I behaving like her needy surviving parent?

I had difficulty making sense of my tears as well. I believed that they were rooted in my sense of sudden loss after having been engaged in such an intense caregiving role with her during the previous months and recognized that the threatened loss of our relationship paralleled her sudden loss of a parent in childhood, so I immediately sought consultation. Once I did that, I was able to control my tears and return to a more helpful caregiving stance from which I could calmly help us try to understand together what had brought her to this decision.

Crying During Acute Grief Reactions

When therapists experience a loss and are involved in an acute grief reaction, their crying can raise complicated questions about attachment, loss, and caregiving in the therapeutic relationship. I have heard and read stories from other therapists who have worked during and after the painful loss of loved ones and I have learned how their vulnerability to crying has increased greatly during those times. Their stories illustrate some of the questions and issues that may arise.

At the most problematic end of the spectrum, I know of two situations in which therapists in the throes of acute grief (unknown to their patients) cried inappropriately, causing a rupture in the therapeutic relationship. In the first instance, a therapist who had just returned to work after her son's death was mildly confronted by a patient who took exception to something that she had said. The patient was shocked when the therapist burst into tears and she (the patient) made the decision to terminate the relationship. The patient never knew anything about the therapist's loss and was left to assume that the crying was a reaction to the confrontation. The second example is similar except that, in this instance, the patient was talking about the death of a family member when the therapist (who had also just lost a loved one, although the patient had not been told) suddenly began to cry and ran from the room. Again, the therapeutic connection was irreparably ruptured.

My assumption is that these were conscientious therapists unrealistically trying to contain their grief at a time when it was too fresh and raw. Crying is, at times, beyond our control, emphasizing the "involuntary" aspect of the self-disclosure. Three things might help to avert such unfortunate outcomes. The first would be to make certain that we have ample time to grieve after a significant loss before returning to the demands of our work. The second would be to acknowledge the basic fact of a major loss to our patients along with the suggestion that "I might seem a bit more emotional for a while." Third, if crying occurs unexpectedly, the therapist should explain in the moment, or as soon afterward as possible, what transpired so that it can be processed. By doing this, we acknowledge our loss and our feelings, and show that we are able and willing to risk opening ourselves up to concern and consolation from our patients (or, in some instances, to be prepared for hostile attacks while we are vulnerable).

Sharon Farber (2000) describes in detail an experience that occurred with the first patient she saw after returning to work following her mother's death. This particularly difficult, often hostile patient asked her if it had been her mother who died. When told that it was, the patient asked, in a kindly voice uncharacteristic for her, whether her mother had been sick. Farber writes,

> Her question triggered an immediate return to the vulnerable, anxious self-state that had been part of how I had lived for the past three years, catapulting me back to the pain of that time and so her kind inquiry felt instead like a knife in my heart. I feared being completely overcome by grief right then and there and just sobbing. Gathering the pieces of my destabilized self together, I took the only way I knew at that moment to fend her off (pp. 453–454).

With voice quivering and then breaking, Farber acknowledged that her mother had indeed been ill. Then, in what she describes as a "cold voice," Farber asked, "But I wonder in what way your knowing about this will be helpful to you?" (p. 454). This exchange triggered what Farber called "the big enactment," (which she defines as "any mutual action within the therapist–patient relationship that arises in the context of difficulties in the countertransference work"). Farber's response launched a hostile attack by the patient, beginning with a "thunderous 'Who the hell do you think you are?'" Stunned and barely managing to contain her overwhelming feelings, Farber nonetheless withstood the barrage for the remainder of the session, waiting until the patient left to "fall apart" in private.

In the following session, Farber brought up the exchange and told the patient that she had given her quite a "knockout punch," thereby opening the door for the patient to say, "I was being nice and you treated me like I didn't even deserve to live" (p. 454). This gave the therapist the opportunity to apologize and to explain:

> I told her that if I allowed myself to be moved by her words, I was afraid that I might feel my raw grief and become overwhelmed by it in her presence. I did not want to do that, I told her, for two reasons: first my grief was a deeply private thing; and second, I was afraid that her seeing me in the throes of grief would frighten or overwhelm her and I wanted to protect her from that (p. 455).

The patient listened raptly and then said that she thought she had heard grief in Farber's voice then and, furthermore, she thought that she heard it again now. At that point, Farber did well up with tears and said that maybe the "knockout punch" that the patient had delivered to her was something like what the patient had experienced as a child when her mother died and she was told not to cry or expect sympathy. This marked the beginning of the patient's slow and painful grieving process. Farber concludes by saying that if she had not struggled with and acknowledged how her own loss and her feelings toward the patient contributed to the enactment, the treatment would have been destroyed. Instead, the integrity of her therapy was preserved and, eventually, the patient was able to cry as well.

This open and painful description demonstrates that some therapist "breakdowns" that seem to interfere with the patient's process at the time may, in the hands of a skillful therapist, ultimately help to strengthen the attachment bond as affects are mutually shared and regulated. Two final case examples illustrate what can happen in a positive direction when a process of acute grief in the patient overlaps with acute grief in the therapist's life.

In the first, a colleague relates a painful and poignant example of work with a 20-year-old woman, Jenny, whose sister Sarah, aged 22, had just been killed in a crosswalk by a hit-and-run driver. The two sisters had been exceptionally close since early childhood and Jenny reported that she felt "completely lost without Sarah," as if "part of herself died" too. The patient cried in almost every session and, on three or four occasions during the year-long treatment, so did the therapist. I could understand why, because by the time I reached the place in the narrative at which the surviving family members gathered for the first Christmas after Sarah's death, hung a stocking for her, and "filled it with Sarah's favorite things," I was crying too. The therapist said of her own crying, "I felt genuine, honest and sincere in becoming teary eyed at times and allowing the tears to fall down my face. I believe this assisted in normalizing my client's experience and allowed for both of us to share the depth of this loss together."

Then, the therapist's sister died unexpectedly. They had also been very close in childhood and as adults. During the same period of time, for reasons related to managed care, Jenny was in the process of transferring to a new therapist. To manage the grief about her sister and to keep from having it interfere with the patient's process of transfer, the therapist returned to therapy and continued to work with a consultant who had supported her previously in work with this patient. During this phase, she did not cry. "Had I cried during … the transfer process, I felt this would have been a countertransference reaction." In other words, allowing her acute grief to emerge at this point would have clouded the patient's process by inserting her own.

A second example of a therapist who did cry when her immediate loss overlapped with a patient's loss shows that sometimes this can also contribute positively to the therapeutic relationship and to the patient's healing process. The therapist, a woman, had been seeing a 40-year-old man about a year when his father died after a 3-month struggle with cancer. They met for a few sessions after his death and then the therapist's husband died, also from cancer. The patient knew about her loss because of the message relayed by a colleague to explain her absence.

"Upon my return," she writes, "the patient was talking about his reaction to his loss ... and I recognized in the countertransference that he reminded me a good deal of my eldest son and this son's reactions to the death of his beloved father." The therapist was tearful, although neither she nor the patient commented on it then. In the following session, however, she brought up her crying and the patient said that "he felt understood and warm toward me, feelings he had had difficulty with in his relationship with his wife and mother." These gains, the therapist notes, have held throughout the treatment and through the current termination process.

Caregiving to and by the Therapist

As in the situation described previously by Farber in which she cried after a kind remark by her patient, it is often the caregiving response of the patient that complicates crying by the therapist. Caregiving urges toward the therapist may be part of a pattern of insecure attachment and compulsive caregiving and may accurately be seen or experienced by the therapist as seductive, defensive, or destructive. However, another side of caregiving is positive yet often difficult for a therapist to acknowledge or accept. Bader (1996) suggests that analysts (and this applies to other therapists as well) have a "bias against normalizing this dimension of the analytic relationship" (p. 742). This bias, he maintains, can impede treatment and prevent the healing and relationship-enhancing aspects of the moments when the analyst, "guided, in part, by an overall understanding of the patient should allow himself or herself to feel *and* express a genuine acceptance of and pleasure in being helped, bolstered and enhanced by the patient" (p. 742). To that list I would add: allowing ourselves, on occasion, to be "soothed and comforted" by the patient as well. The problem is that this is not especially comfortable for many therapists.

Because crying and caregiving are so inextricably linked, it is important that we as therapists examine our attitudes and comfort levels in the area of *receiving* care. Concerns about a patient's defensive or compulsive caregiving are justified and necessary, but after due consideration and experience, "pathologizing" patient caregiving may stand in the way. The value system of therapy that puts the patient's pains and wounds, not the therapist's, at the center of the therapeutic relationship presents one obstacle to the therapist accepting care from the patient. The attachment and caregiving experiences that we bring to our career choice of professional caregiver may also offer an obstacle. Bader writes, "Analysts tend to be helpers and have particular conflicts about being 'given to,'" which at times "can contribute to a subtle inclination to ward off a patient's need or wish to contribute to the analyst's well-being" (pp. 760–761).

Situations that may induce healthy caregiving urges in the patient may arise when the therapist is ill, stressed, tired, or experiencing acute grief, or during any number of other "involuntary self-disclosures" that patients see directly or intuit. Certainly, caregiving may be evoked when we cry. As a result, our needs, fears, and attitudes toward receiving care require the same conscious examination as that necessary when giving it.

One therapist shared with me a beautiful example of caregiving by a patient (of whom she is very fond), who one day brought two lattes to a session, "one for her and one for me." The therapist writes.

> I cried at her generosity. I remember the feeling, "She's thinking of me" and what an unusual experience that was at the time. I was under great personal stress and I don't think my crying had to do with her and her issues. It was the fact that I wasn't doing the giving at that moment. It was gratitude at being noticed, that I mattered to her.

The therapist went on to say that her tears were also a signal that she had to take some steps to deal with the massive stress in her life. She did discuss her crying with the patient, telling her only that she was "touched by her kindness at a particularly delicate time for me." The patient took in the explanation without comment and the treatment has continued to go well. Perhaps, we might speculate, being able to provide care to her therapist contributed to the positive outcome.

As we have seen earlier, children who are adequately cared for develop empathy for the distress of others and follow that up with caregiving gestures. A parent's affirming and accepting reactions to those gestures are crucial for the development of the child's attachment bond. As Bader (1996) writes, "By communicating a genuine receptivity to being 'touched,' comforted and gratified by the child, the parent confirms and recognizes something important in the child's 'being'" (p. 757). The same attachment dynamics appear in adult relationships, including the treatment relationship. Patients, too, may benefit from being able to care for the therapist.

In addition to the professional reasons that make us shy of receiving care, there may be personal ones. In the early years when I was trying to build a theory of adult crying, colleagues would often ask me why I was so drawn to the topic. What conflicts, they implied, was I trying to work through in this way? I could never think of any. I cry quite comfortably once or twice a month, often because I am pained or moved as I read a novel or watch a movie. However, as I began to build a theory of crying that combined attachment appeals and caregiving responses, I could not help noticing that my preference, by far, was to cry alone. The thing about crying that is the crux of my theory—that it is an interpersonal behavior designed to bring us closer together—was the thing about it that I most resisted. The care and comfort that crying brings out in others were the hardest for me to handle.

I was always given care and nurturance promptly, usually verbal and practical rather than hugs and soothing, but I was simultaneously praised for my strength in bearing up under pain. Once I learned to speak, the caregiving that I came to expect, rely on, and give was verbal rather than physical (and that is ultimately the kind of caregiver I became professionally). I learned that care was available, which did make me feel secure, but that self-soothing was also rewarded.

Understanding what crying means at the deepest level has made a difference in how I experience the pulls toward physical and emotional closeness that come with crying. Two dreams about crying and caregiving figure prominently in this process. The first dream was, in fact, the first dream in my own therapy. My mother was holding my then-toddler daughter and accidentally dropped her into a shallow puddle. I picked her up, wrapped her in a towel, and cuddled her close. I was comforting myself symbolically and, as in real life was also being careful not to "drop" my still needy toddler daughters as they reached the age when my mother "dropped me" (from physical forms of soothing, not verbal ones) because she thought I was old enough to manage on my own. The care that I received from my therapist was a crucial part of healing for me, as have been my adult attachments and friendships.

In a dream the first year that I was working on this book, I began to see a change. My Grandma Payne was crying, as she had so many times at farewells, but this time I hugged her and I felt like crying too. Now I was able to cry and give and receive care physically.

I conclude with a brief vignette of a time recently when I was able to accept and use appropriate caregiving in a clinical situation. Elsie is in her 70s and has been "a mental patient" (her term) since she was a young woman. Medication mostly helps to contain her disordered thoughts, but in myriad tangents and obsessions they creep into conversation regularly. One day shortly after my 95-year-old father became ill, I told her that I had to fly back East to see about him. She accepted it calmly, but on the way out turned at the door, looked me in the eye, and said, "But be sure to take care of yourself, too." As soon as the door was closed, I sat down, face in hands and cried, in sadness, but also in gratitude for this tender gesture from a person who has so little to give. Elsie somehow managed to get it just right, enabling me to feel closer to her.

For reasons that I am still trying to understand, caregiving from others triggers more tears for me than directly grieving a loss (a phenomenon that I have noticed in some of my patients as well; they cry when I make a soothing, caregiving remark more than when I empathize directly with their grief). Perhaps caregiving invokes a grief reaction for me related to a paucity of the body-to-body caregiving in my early years, or for the more traumatic early caregiving breaches and losses of my patients.

When Elsie made her caregiving gesture, I did not cry in front of her, perhaps because it was the end of the hour. However, I did let her know when I returned how "touched" I had been by her words.

PART IV
Attachment and Caregiving: Beyond the Personal

CHAPTER **12**

Transcendent Tears

Certain rare instances of crying transcend personal loss. These tears continue to represent attachment, but of a different order, signifying, instead of loss, a deep sense of connection with the human community, all of nature, the symbolic, the supernatural, and the universe at large—a mystical state that goes beyond human vocabulary. Tears that transcend the personal might be those shed when an orchestral performance of Mahler's First Symphony stirs a sense of love and awe; at a tropical sunrise witnessed from a *heiau* (ancient Polynesian temple) below the Napili cliffs at the tip of Kauai; or reading a poem that suddenly catapults from a detail of everyday life to the universal, such as "Shoveling Snow with Buddha" by Billy Collins: (1998) "This is so much better than a sermon in church/I say out loud, but Buddha keeps on shoveling./This is the true religion, the religion of snow/and sunlight and winter geese barking in the sky" p. 37.

In her doctoral dissertation, "Toward a Psychology of Tears," written in Leipzig, Germany, in 1935, Charlotte Spitz (as cited in Plessner, 1970) describes three different types of crying that develop over the course of a lifetime. The first, "elemental" crying, occurs in response to direct physical distress in infancy and childhood. The second, beginning at puberty, she calls personal crying. It arises from internal emotions, feelings, and moods. The third type, crying at its most mature level in adulthood, she calls spiritual (*geistig*) weeping.

The German philosopher Helmuth Plessner (1970) in his book, *Laughing and Crying*, describes *geistig* weeping:

> Here man first feels himself involved in his inmost being, yet no longer addressed as a personal I. The *thing itself* strikes him and moves him to tears—immediately, like the physical cause at the primitive level, but inwardly and without mediation by reactive feeling, without reference to the condition and situation of his own person (p. 121).

The "thing itself" can be as encompassing and sacred as a performance of Beethoven's "Ode to Joy" or as simple and direct as a dewdrop on a spider web. The essential feature is that these tears are about something other than personal loss or pain. They are tears that represent oneness and love, closing the circle of attachment and loss by returning to connection.

In the opening paragraphs of his book, *Civilization and Its Discontents*, Freud (1961) refers to a letter from his friend, Romain Rolland (a French writer who won the Nobel prize for literature in 1915), who had written that he disagreed with a passage in which Freud had called religion an illusion. Rolland said that in focusing on organized religion, Freud had overlooked the true source of religious feeling, what Rolland (as cited in Koestler, 1964) called "the oceanic feeling of limitless extension and oneness with the universe" (p. 273).

Rolland's remarks stayed with Freud. More than a year later he (Freud, 1927/1975) wrote back to him saying, "Your letter of December 5, 1927 … about a feeling you describe as 'oceanic' has left me no peace" (p. 388). Although Freud said that he could not discover the oceanic feeling in himself, he proceeded, with what almost sounds like a touch of longing, to speculate about its origins and meaning.

Freud (1961) first compared this "indissoluble bond of being one with the external world as a whole" (p. 12) to the merger of boundaries between two people in love, the "you-and-I-are-one" of songs and poetry. He then speculated that the union of adult love recapitulates the earliest merger in life, that of nursing child and mother. Adults, he theorized, retain from infancy "a shrunken residue of a much more inclusive—indeed, an all-embracing—feeling which corresponded to a more intimate bond between the ego and the world about it." The adult way of explaining an awareness of that feeling, he said, would be precisely "limitlessness and of a bond with the universe—the same ideas with which my friend elucidated the 'oceanic' feeling" (p. 15).

Crying does not always accompany the awareness of universal attachment, but frequently an association exists. Freud traced that association back to the cries that the child uses to summon the mother's breast, thereby creating that primal sense of oneness between inner and outer worlds that is source and symbol of universal attachment. Rolland's word, "oceanic," is a saltwater metaphor (suggesting tears and amniotic fluid) for the experience of union.

Science writer and poet Diane Ackerman (1990) describes a classic "oceanic" experience with tears that took place when she was scuba diving literally *in* saltwater in the ocean:

> As a human woman, with ovaries where eggs lie like roe, entering the smooth, undulating womb of the ocean from which our ancestors evolved millennia ago, I was so moved my eyes teared underwater, and I mixed my saltiness with the ocean's.... That moment of mysticism left my sinuses full, and made surfacing painful until I removed my mask, blew my nose in a strange two-stage snite, and settled down emotionally. But I've never forgotten that sense of belonging (pp. 20–21).

Arthur Koestler (1964) identified what he called "self-transcending emotions" that cause a "welling-up, a moistening or overflowing of the eyes" (p. 273). The source of this feeling might be, he said, "listening to the organ in a cathedral, looking at a majestic landscape from the top of a mountain, observing an infant hesitantly returning a smile." He called this type of crying a form of "entrancement," a "step towards the trance-like states induced by the contemplative techniques of Eastern mysticism." A 1906 article on crying in the *American Journal of Psychology* (Borquist, 1906) makes a similar point: "the feeling of being helpless, hopeless, forsaken, of having no desires ... suggests at once a relationship of the crying state to such conditions as occur in the surrender stages of religious experience" (p. 163).

Writer Christina Baldwin (1990) defines the state of surrender as the ability "to accept our unity with all life, and surrender our fantasy of separation.... The smallest piece is the whole and the whole is contained in the smallest fragment of itself" (pp. 227–229). This experience, she says, is not the death of the ego but rather the ego is "not experienced any longer as the center of the self" (p. 233). When I was working on this chapter, I found Baldwin's definition of surrender buried in some old notes in a file drawer where I was looking for something else and I began to cry. In this chance finding and in the words, I felt "the indissoluble bond" with the universe, a sense that something beyond my self and my brain was intimately involved in my struggle to find words to talk about these word-elusive feelings.

Psychoanalyst Carl Jung looked to the alchemical process (the ancient quest to transmute base metals into gold) as a symbolic model for psychic change. One part of the alchemical process called *solutio* involved dissolving the matter in its own water. Described in the words of Jungian analyst Edward Edinger (1978), *solutio* meant "the return of differentiated matter to its original undifferentiated state, i.e., to *prima materia*. Water was thought of as the womb and *solutio* as a return to the womb for rebirth" (p. 63). The term, "dissolving in tears," could be a modern-day description of *solutio*. Weeping is analogous to an alchemical agent of transformation; *solutions* present themselves and life-energy begins to flow again after dissolving in tears of grief—our own "water," our own wellspring.

Solutio is also a symbolic way to understand weeping that transcends the personal. According to Edinger, the psychological process of *solutio* takes place when something larger and more comprehensive than the personal ego overwhelms and dissolves it. From a Jungian point of view, a potential link always exists between the personal unconscious and the archetypal, so in that sense all adult crying could transcend the personal. When using the term "transcendent tears," I am referring to times when the experience is conscious. Crying may even help to bring the initiatory experience to conscious attention.

Symbolic representations of *solutio* include: baths, showers, sprinkling, swimming, drowning, immersion in water, and baptism. In Jewish tradition, the *mikvah* is a bath in "living" (natural, unpiped) water, a purifying ritual prescribed on certain ceremonial occasions. A patient told me about attending a mikvah before a family wedding in Mexico. The bride-to-be wept as she immersed herself in the bath and when the blessing was given by her mother. Soon all but two of the assembled female friends and relatives also wept.

My patient, who has a history of serious depression, joined with the others in the communal shedding of tears, but also wondered if at some point she crossed over into biochemically based crying as well. It felt by the end, she said, "like I was crying just to cry." These mikvah tears were a combination of the following types of crying: somatic (for my depressed patient, though not presumably for the other women present); personal attachment and loss, (marriage); communal attachment (by a group of women during the traditional ancestral ritual); and transcendent (at the symbolic ritual immersion in the water linking the spiritual and personal aspects of attachment: marriage, sexual union, and reproduction).

Weeping as part of spiritual practice and experience crosses religious boundaries. In Islam men called "weepers" shed tears as part of their ascetic practices (Carmichael, 1991). *Gratia lachrymarum*, "the gift of tears" (McEntire, 1991), was part of the early Catholic church doctrine of compunction. These tears were shed in contemplation of sinfulness and of God's love based on Psalms 6:6: "… all the night make I my bed to swim; I water my couch with my tears," and the words of Jesus in the beatitudes, "Blessed are those who weep." These "holy tears" were distinguished theologically from everyday tears of grief or, as one church father in the 13th century put it, "tears which necessity brings forth in the course of nature, tears which human weakness wrings out"—those that "slip out against our will" (McEntire, 1991, p. 35).

Kabbalah, the Jewish mystical text, describes 10 hidden aspects of God that, although essentially unknowable, can be felt in the world. One of these is a female principal, Shekhinah, who bridges the "abyss between the world of the divine and the human." According to psychologist Barbara Stephens (1991), "Reports of personal experience of Shekhinah come most frequently and dramatically when a person is suffering and weeping" due to a "deep, empathic connection with the plight of the Shekhinah" (p. 33), who is alone, alienated, and exiled.

The Shekhinah also guides and soothes the weeper, providing comfort as well as transformation. Stephens refers to this bond in suffering as "a sacred marriage of *myself and I, and I with other*," another description of attachment that transcends literal human relationships. Weeping in attunement with the Shekhinah's sense of separation, alienation, alone-ness, and loss—transcendent suffering as it were—is the human act that beckons her healing presence. Caregiving may go beyond the personal as well. Religious and spiritual traditions represent transcendent caregiving in varying ways, such as using parental names "Father" and "Mother" for deities or their human designates (such as priests and nuns), or assigning caregiving attributes such as compassion and comfort to the divine.

Transcendent Attachment and Symbolic Caregiving

For many people, spiritual meaning and a sense of attachment, oneness, or love may be found in nature—trees, mountains, the ocean, animals, or flowers—or in aesthetic experiences such as literature, music, dance, or the visual arts. Alfred Lord Tennyson (1847/2004), for example, describes a state of "divine despair" in which tears were triggered by gazing at "happy autumn fields":

> Tears, idle tears, I know not what they mean
> Tears from the depth of some divine despair

> Rise in the heart, and gather to the eyes,
> In looking on the happy autumn fields
> And thinking of the days that are no more.

Tennyson here refers to the cyclical nature of life and death symbolized by the seasons and the mixture of sadness and loss ("days that are no more") with beauty and joy ("the happy autumn fields"). Far from being "idle," these tears come from the "depth of some divine despair" in which happiness and sadness, death and life, loss and love are experienced simultaneously.

According to filmmaker Jacques Perrin (as cited in Nevius, 2003), who directed the documentary *Winged Migration*, the cameramen who photographed birds in flight from balloons and ultralight planes were deeply touched by the experience. At first, he said, they were "most concerned with angles, light, and shutter speed." Then they began to feel moved by their close communion with the birds. "Some of them cried, and not just the first day," Perrin said (p. D4).

Literature, paintings, music, drama, and films at certain times also tap into the oceanic feelings of universal attachment, love, and symbolic caregiving. A poem that I rediscovered recently, "The Collar" by George Herbert (1633/2004), brought tears as I recalled the personal anguish that I was suffering when I first read it more than 40 years ago. It also took me, as it did then, far beyond my pain to a deeply felt sense of attachment and love, which brought me immense comfort. The poem begins with what I originally described as a "spiritual tantrum," ranting against religious constriction. Herbert's struggle to break free of dogma—represented by collars, suits, ropes, and cages—echoed my anger in young adulthood at being trapped in the rigid religious doctrines of my childhood.

However, when I originally found it in college and again when I rediscovered it all these years later, the last four lines suddenly melted my anger into tears of relief:

> But as I rav'd and grew more fierce and
> wilde
> At every word,
> Me thoughts I heard one calling, *Child!*
> And I reply'd *My Lord.*

What I heard in the parent–child metaphor was reassurance that I could seek spiritual freedom without needing to sacrifice attachment and caregiving (not unlike the emancipation process of adolescents from human parents). I could have universal connection, caregiving, and comfort without being bound by the literal idea of God that I had been taught in childhood. I felt a sense of connection with a spiritual force outside the "cage" and the "collar."

I am inspired and humbled by the rich presence of weeping in the arts. Tears that the artist sheds in personal pain may be transformed in the creative process, thus capturing and communicating a sense of universal suffering that represents and underscores universal connection. Art succeeds by bridging the personal and the universal, connecting at both levels with the audience. Even art that is not "about" crying may evoke tears in the creator, the performer, or the audience, and sometimes all three, by reaching deep into each psyche and beyond. These are tears of recognition, acknowledgement, and mystery.

Inspired by his own mother's struggles, Alvin Ailey choreographed the dance, "Cry," for Judith Jamison. The theme is the suffering and strength of black women, but Jamison said that wherever she performed it around the world, even in countries, where black women were, as she said, a "romantic oddity," people still felt and understood the intensity of the suffering and the power of suffering overcome. In confirmation of that shared understanding, many people wept with her. As Jamison's biographer (Maynard, 1982) wrote:

> Time and again, when the curtain fell on "Cry," faces were wet with tears, as audiences became caught up in the convulsive revelation. More than once, Jamison, coming offstage in the wings, wiped something else than sweat from her cheeks. Many times, she found members of her own company weeping as they watched her (p. 139).

Ritual Weeping

Some cultures prescribe communal crying rituals to diminish isolation in a time of loss and help people as a group to deal with grief. Some societies, like the Kaluli of New Guinea mentioned earlier, also have crying rituals designed to honor and reinforce attachment. In his book on the Andaman Islanders (who live on part of a chain of islands between Burma and Sumatra), Radcliffe-Brown (1922) was one of the first anthropologists to write about ritual weeping. This type of weeping is unfamiliar to Westerners because we have no comparable social situations in which weeping is considered proper etiquette (funerals come closest) or in which it is a prescribed part of a social or spiritual ritual. People who remain dry eyed when ritual weeping is expected may be considered ill mannered or, worse, suspected of harboring evil motives or secrets.

The Andaman Islanders' ritual weeping took place at rites of passage (like menstruation and puberty), weddings, reunions after long separations, or funerals. The parties would face each other, one sitting on the other's lap (man on the woman's lap when mixed couples were involved) and weep. They also wept during conciliatory rites between groups that had been engaged in hostile combat. Men and women from each group would sit down and weep together in a renewal of friendship and an affirmation of their bonds.

Even though the weeping is ceremonial and people are able to cry at will, Radcliffe-Brown (1922) wrote, and modern observers have concurred, that the feelings are genuinely experienced, not faked or merely acted. (The Andaman Islanders, male and female, could also weep on demand on nonceremonial occasions.) "The man or woman sits down and wails or howls, and the tears stream down his or her face" (p. 117).

I was amazed to read Radcliffe-Brown's formulation of the meaning of ritual weeping decades before the advent of attachment theory. He saw it as emotion shared by two or more people serving to renew or modify *social attachments*. All ritual weeping, he wrote, is an expression of attachment and an affirmation of a social bond, whether for individuals weeping over personal loss or societies over collective ones. Whether spontaneous or ritualized, weeping is a way to connect with ourselves and symbolically, or in reality, with each other.

Anthropologist Greg Urban (1988) recorded and studied ritual wailing by men and women in three Brazilian tribes. In these tribes, all the occasions for ritual wailing have something to do with loss: death, departure, or separation. Even the so-called "Welcome of Tears," ritual wailing at a reunion that follows a long separation, is a means of expressing the sadness felt during the time apart.

In these tribes, ritual wailing is distinguished from spontaneous crying (they are expressed by two different words), although at times of loss the weeping occurs on a continuum between the spontaneous and the ritualized. The distinction between individual sadness and socially prescribed sadness, according to Urban, is that the latter is "meta-affect." Such emotions belong to the collective community, not exclusively to the individual, he says.

Rene Spitz (1965) pointed out that some societies use what he called "adjuvants" to inhibit the functioning of the ego or to evoke altered states with the aim of encouraging communal expression of emotion (which, in the case of crying, also serves to support attachment). The adjuvants that inhibit ego functioning, he wrote, are "fasting, solitude, darkness, and abstinence," all examples of stimulus deprivation, while the evocative adjuvants include "drugs, rhythm, sound, alcohol, and breathing techniques" (p. 137).

Spitz (1965) points out that in Western cultures, "adults who have retained the capacity to make use of one or several of these usually atrophied categories of perception and communication belong to the specially gifted. They are composers, musicians, dancers, acrobats, fliers, painters and poets ..." (p. 136). Instead of having communal rituals designed to evoke and honor spiritual weeping, in Western cultures crying is seen as a by-product of some other activity such as music, film, or literature that touches on oceanic or universal themes. Crying at a film or at a concert or over a novel is our version of communal meta-affect.

Literature

> On New Year's Day I was a deaf-mute
> walking down Tenth Street
> poetry streaming down my cheeks.

> (Nelson & Nelson, 1996, p. 15)

I agree with poet Maggie Nelson that crying is poetry. They have in common rhythm and sound, layers of symbolic meaning, the link between the personal and the universal, and, to my mind, the beauty of honest emotional expression. The themes of poetry and tears touch the deepest levels of human experience: love, loss, death, growth, pain, survival, triumph, divinity, and immortality.

A metaphysical poet who wrote in the late 16th century in England expressed the relationship between tears and poetry a little differently:

> My tongue shall bee my Penne, mine eyes shall raine
> Teares for my Inke ... (Alabaster, 1957, p. 199)

This image, like Maggie Nelson's, addresses the transformation of non-verbal tears (his "inke") into the words of poetry. The symbolic progression from tears to ink, to words, to poems parallels the psychotherapeutic process in which pain is translated into words so that something new can be "created".

"Literary artists," wrote Helmuth Plessner (1970), "are the true masters and teachers" of laughing and crying. "Our analysis has much to learn from them" (p. 11). Anne Sexton, who made art of pure agony, wrote in "The Poet of Ignorance" (Sexton, 1975) that "perhaps the moon is a frozen tear,/I do not know" (p. 29, ll. 6–7). In her words, we feel the isolation and darkness of despair, the cold distance when grief is "frozen," tears do not flow, and comfort is not forthcoming. In her poem, "The Room of My Life," she says the room has "ashtrays to cry into" (p. 9, l. 4) and we understand what I, in my psychological prose, call "smoking as a substitute for crying."

In Sexton's (1975) poem, "The Children," she juxtaposes adult and childhood pain to show us attachment and caregiving gone awry. Instead of being moved by the children's tears, the parent/adult describes them in repulsive terms like "dirty clothes" and "pus." She seems to fault the children for crying instead of speaking, "their tongues poverty." The children's tears, rather than bringing a comforting response from a caregiver, are carried away by the surf:

> The children are all crying in their pens
> and the surf carries their cries away.
> They are old men who have seen too much,
> their mouths are full of dirty clothes,
> their tongues poverty, tears like pus.
> The surf pushes their cries back.
> (p. 5, ll. 1–6)

She goes on to wish that things could be different and that connection, and therefore hope, would occur:

> … if I could listen
> to the bulldog courage of those children (p. 6, ll. 34–35)
> …
> I could melt the darkness — (p. 6, l. 38)

Identifying with another's suffering to the point of tears broadens our inner experience and our capacity for empathy. Through fiction, we share the pain of others and feel at once compassion for them and for ourselves—attachment comes full circle. Weeping, even that generated by fiction, expands our capacity to connect.

Literary artists explore the mysteries and ecstasies, the life of the soul beyond the individual self. A short story that Vladimir Nabokov (2002) wrote in his early 20s beautifully describes the sense that love is more than personal. A young man listening to his lover play the piano describes the feeling:

> And when I withdrew deep into myself the whole world seemed like that—homogeneous, congruent, bound by the laws of harmony.

I myself, you, the carnations—at that instant all became vertical chords on musical staves. I realized that everything in the world was an interplay of identical particles comprising different kinds of consonance: the trees, the water, you.... All was unified, equivalent, divine...." [Then] I realized ... that it was not you alone who were my lover but the entire Earth (pp. 14–15).

When literature embraces the next dimension—the "... unified, equivalent, divine"—the author, the character, or the reader may weep. These tears affirm a deep sense of belonging to something beyond the self rather than a longing for what is lost.

If I could have written this book as a novel, it would be the book *Like Water for Chocolate* (Esquivel, 1992). The characters in this novel reveal everything that I am trying to say about crying—they live and breathe it. (Another Latin–American novel, *Love in the Time of Cholera* by Gabriel García Márquez [1988], also demonstrates what I have been writing about but from the perspective of a male author and a weepy male protagonist.) *Like Water for Chocolate* may be surreal, but there is no question that it has much to teach about the reality of tears. We see the sensual world of the feminine—food and tears, body and soul, dream life and reality, nature and nurture—and none of these is relegated to the compartmentalized dichotomies familiar to North Americans.

We learn on the first page that the main character, Tita, is a woman destined to endure great tragedy and loss. She cried while still in her mother's womb. (Cases of this phenomenon have been documented, although none in recent medical history.) One particularly hearty intrauterine cry precipitated an early labor. Tita cried in grief as she came into the world because she already knew that she would be forbidden to marry because of her mother's insistence on an old custom: that the youngest daughter remain at home to care for her mother in old age. So great was Tita's grief at birth that she was "literally washed into this world on a great tide of tears that spilled over the edge of the table and flooded across the kitchen floor." After they dried, the cook swept up the tear residue and from it collected "enough salt to fill a 10-pound sack ..." and "it was used for cooking and lasted a long time" (Esquivel, 1992, p. 6).

When her sister was permitted not only to marry, but also to marry the object of Tita's affections, Tita understandably shed tears of grief into the wedding cake that she had baked for the wedding guests. The moment the guests took their first bite of it, "everyone was flooded with a great wave of longing ... and they began to weep.... But the weeping was just the first symptom of a strange intoxication ... that seized the guests and scattered them across the patio and the grounds and in the bathrooms, all of them wailing over lost love" (Esquivel, 1992, p. 39). The guests were seized by fits of "collective vomiting" as well as collective grief. Tita's tears of protest shed into the batter made them feel her pain, but also made their stomachs reject the celebratory cake. (Tears of protest seldom lead to pure longing or compassion.) Until Tita finally defies her mother, all of the many tears she sheds are tears of protest—"even her laughing was a form of crying" (p. 7).

After a final confrontation with her mother, Tita ends up mute and nonfunctional in the home of a caring doctor; she is devoid of any hope of attachment to anyone. She remains in that condition until a visit from her mother's cook and a visit from the ghost of the first cook who had been the only real caregiver she had ever known.

Through the caregiving of the cook and the doctor she begins to heal and then the quality of her crying changes: "She cried as she hadn't cried since she was born." These were now sad tears of despair, as opposed to the tears of angry protest that she had shed since birth. So great was her grief, however, that these tears also flowed in prodigious amounts. The doctor was "… alarmed by the stream that was running down the stairs … " which he soon realized was "… just Tita's tears." Then he blessed the cook and her soup for "… having accomplished what none of his medicines had been able to do: making Tita weep" (Esquivel, 1992, pp. 124–125).

In addition to illustrating all of the types of crying—protest and despair, as well as detached inhibited crying, the tears shed in *Like Water for Chocolate* go far beyond the personal pain of the individuals in the story. Here, we have tears as life giving (Tita was born on a tide of tears precipitated by a cry *in utero*) and life sustaining (dried tears were used to season food for years after her birth). We also see tears in the more usual sense: related to pain and loss, especially in relationship to close attachments. In this story, Tita was alienated from her mother, her sister, and her chosen lover. Finally, after a lifetime of wounds, come the tears of healing and rebirth, when Tita is at the doctor's house and is visited by the living cook and the dead cook, whose food nurtured and nourished her (seasoned as it was, however, by her own tears). In the transformative, healing stay at the doctor's house, we even have a metaphor for therapy.

Music

Music is a close relative of attachment behavior and caregiving. The *I Ching* (as cited in Edinger, 1978) describes how ancient rulers used sacred music as a way to unite individuals and "… overcome the egotism that divides men…. The sacred music and the splendor of the ceremonies aroused a strong tide of emotion that was shared by all hearts in unison, and that awakened a consciousness of the common origin of all creatures" (p. 82). The vibrations, musical tones, and rhythm of music bathe our bodies in sensual experiences that can trigger a great deal of attachment-related affect, much of it preverbal and unconscious. Music sometimes arouses joy and sometimes pain; sometimes it helps to soothe and regulate distress. Adding lyrics also opens the possibility for cognitive associations that might bring tears or soothe them.

Music is intimately connected to our earliest experiences. It is hard to call infant crying "music," but a number of people have recognized it as a precursor. The sound-making skills with which we are born and the crying out that we do to bring our protectors and loved ones are the same skills that we harness to bridge the distance between us with words and to express the beauty of it in music. Violinist Isaac Stern ("Isaac Stern loud and clear," 1990) said, "The moment a child is born, the first thing is the cry, the sound. The sound—music is the most natural of all art forms."

Peter Ostwald (1973), a psychiatrist interested in the creative arts and one of the pioneers of infant acoustical cry studies, wrote:

> Singing, too, is related to crying. The purity of a singer's voice may depend on her or his ability to duplicate certain movements that infants spontaneously make when they cry. For example, by elevating the cheeks like a baby and drawing the jaw back to raise the soft palate, it becomes possible to emit vocalic sounds resembling the pure, highly communicative cries of an infant, a technique that is practiced and taught by some opera singers (pp. 154–155).

An operatically trained speech and family therapist whom I met at a conference in the Netherlands beautifully demonstrated the acoustic, vocal, and muscular similarities between singing and crying in such a way that it was impossible to miss the parallels.

Music may be a mirror reflecting our pain or it may be a window to show us hope and healing. Crying with music depends on mood, setting, and associations. It may be about personal suffering or loss ("that was our song" or "we used to sing that song at summer camp"); universal suffering and loss ("Taps," antiwar songs, or sacred oratorios about the crucifixion of Christ); or about universal connectedness (hymns of faith, national anthems, wedding processionals and recessionals, or "Pomp and Circumstance," the weepy old graduation favorite).

A woman responding to a request for information about experiences with crying and art (Elkins, 2001) described crying so hard at a concert of Bach suites for cello that she had to leave. "I cried because (I guess) I was overcome with love. It was impossible for me to shake the sensation (mental, physical) that J. S. Bach was in the room with me, and I loved him" (p. 174).

Songs about crying are legion. Roy Orbison and Johnny Ray recorded the most famous popular songs with "Cry" in the title, but multitudes of others exist as well. I lost count after several hundred in a music index catalogued by subject. Buried in the lyrics of countless more songs, blues and otherwise, are more references to crying, much of it over the loss of love, but some with advice about crying and some in which tears are wistfully sought. Dirges and laments evoke images of crying because of their association with death and funerals. So does the sadness and longing in the third movement of Shostakovich's fifth symphony. According to his journals, this symphony was an expression of his despair after being discredited by Stalin. Apparently, his feelings resonated with some of his Russian audiences, who wept when they heard it.

Composer Jay Ungar ("Ashokan farewell," 1991), who wrote a fiddle tune that became the theme of the PBS documentary, "The Civil War," described how he wept as the composition first came to him. He leads fiddle workshops at the Ashokan Field campus of the State University of New York in the Catskills and said that this composition came out of his "post-Ashokan depression syndrome." Alone one morning, he recalled, "I started playing the fiddle, and I was really sad. I found that melody, and tears just started pouring out of my eyes" (1991, p. 28). The poignancy of the tune clearly touched many other people as well. It is a fitting expression of the suffering and loss during the United States Civil War.

Some compositions mimic crying musically. A style of singing during the 1950s and early 1960s incorporated crying into the lyrics as well as into the melody and rhythm. Gospel music historian Opal Nations calls the singing groups who performed these songs the "Weepers." Some of the performers actually shed tears as they sang, while others only made cry sounds, some stylized but others quite realistic. When Nations first played some of the records for me (he invited me to the studio when he featured 33 of them on his KPFA radio program, "Doo-Wop Delights"), I was struck by how the artists were able to incorporate crying into their singing so successfully that it left no doubt about what the sounds represented.

First performed by African–American gospel singers, the style was later taken up by some rhythm and blues groups such as Jackie Rue and the Starlites ("I Cried My Heart Out") and by crooner Johnny "the Prince of Wails" Ray ("Cry"). According to Nations, "The Bells," by Clyde McPhatter and the Dominoes, is the "classic weeper." It is a song about a disappointed lover crying at his own funeral—the bells are part of the dirge.

Stylized crying performances originally came out of gospel quartet music. Singers would perform using a sermonette style, weeping or sobbing to evoke pain, tragedy, and loss. A rhythm and blues soloist, Jackie Rue, for example, came to the microphone with a predampened hand-kerchief for his stage tears. (His secret was revealed in the liner notes of his album collection.) Johnny Ray claimed that his tears were genuine ("But who knows whether he had an onion in his pocket," quipped Nations).

Most of the songs, needless to say, are about lost (or unkind) loves. Many of the weeping singers are female but a number of men cry openly about their broken hearts as well. One of my particular Jackie Rue favorites, "They Laughed at Me," is actually a combination of laughing and crying that conveys exactly that mixture of sounds and rhythm. Such open emoting was intended to share the experience of pain and loss or, as Nations says, "to take the listener with them down the path of absolute torment," thus making the feelings mutual and communal. With music as the medium, crying was mutually (communally) evoked and mutually regulated between singer and audience.

It is perhaps the audience of which we are most likely to think when we associate weeping and music. When my younger daughter was a toddler, I would play the piano and sing to her while she sat on my lap. One song, a Czechoslovakian folk tune, made her cry every time I played it. A woman in the 1970s said she cried when Bob Dylan ended a concert at Madison Square Garden with "Blowin' in the Wind." The writer who described it said, "She cried for lots of reasons. You know them all" (Emerson, 1974).

Every year when folk singer John McCutcheon comes to the Napa Valley to do a benefit concert for hospice, he sings his composition, "Christmas in the Trenches." It is about an impromptu Christmas Eve cease-fire in Flanders during World War I. The cease-fire was initiated by some German and British soldiers who, the day before and the day after, fought each other with cannons and guns. On Christmas Eve night, though, they spontaneously left their trenches to sing Christmas carols from their respective countries, play a game of soccer, and share their rations and pictures of family. I know I am not the only one who weeps every year over this poignant juxtaposition of the human connection as it might be and the human condition when it deteriorates into war.

The next-to-last stanza of the song says "… the question haunted every heart that lived that wondrous night/'Whose family have I fixed within my sights?'" It ends with, "For the walls they'd kept between us to exact the work of war/Had been crumbled and were gone for ever more," because, as the narrator says in the last line, "on each end of the rifle we're the same." I visited the Flanders World War I museum in Belgium recently and saw letters and oral history accounts of this night. I was moved but did not cry, although I did just now as I was copying out McCutcheon's lyrics. Somehow the song manages to make me feel the pain of war and grasp the hope for peace through human connection again each time.

Opera perhaps best combines all of the tear-evoking components of music. My Jungian office partner considers going to the opera the secular equivalent of church. In a poem called "The End of the Opera," which describes the layers of relationship among opera, real life, art, transcendence, and tears, poet Howard Nemerov (1991) makes a similar point when he ends the poem with the Latin dismissal from the Catholic mass:

> Knowing that what he witnessed was only art,
> He never wept while the show was going on.
> But the curtain call could always make him cry—
> When the cast came forward hand in hand,
> Bowing and smiling to the clatter of applause,
> Tired, disheveled, sweating through the paint,
> Radiant with our happiness and theirs,
> Illuminati of the spot and flood
> Yet much the same as ordinary us.
> The diva, the soubrette, the raisonneur,
> The inadequate hero, the villain, his buffoon,
> All equaled in the great reality
> And living proof that life would follow life …
> Though back of that display ther'd always be,
> He knew, money and envy, the career,
> Tomorrow and tomorrow—it didn't seem
> At that moment as if it mattered much
> Compared with their happiness and ours
> As we wept about the role, about the real,
> And how their dissonances harmonized
> As we applauded us: *Ite, Missa est* (p. 38).

This is a poem about weeping and the opera as well as a summary of everything I have been saying about transcendent tears and music. I especially like the understated opening lines about *not* weeping during the performance because, as Nemerov wrote, it is "only art." "Only," indeed, but then he goes on to weep over precisely what art represents: "the role and the real and how their dissonances harmonize."

The Visual Arts

The visual arts also have a direct relationship to crying, in part because they appeal to the eye and because they are silent like weeping. In his book, *Pictures and Tears: A History of People Who Have Cried in Front of Paintings*, art historian James Elkins tries "to capture the frames of mind that have led people to cry" (p. x) throughout history, including those of more than 400 people who responded to his published inquiries.

As might be expected, many of these people cried for intensely personal reasons. Half of those who responded to his query, however, cried for something bigger as well. I agree with Elkins when he writes, "Any report of crying in front of a painting might really be connected to the picture itself, and not simply to the person's private life" (p. 59). When reports of crying did transcend the personal, it was for one of two reasons, which Elkins notes are "very close to each other, and yet completely opposed."

In one instance, people cry in front of paintings "because pictures seem unbearably *full* ..."; in the other, they cry "because pictures seem unbearably *empty*"(p. xi). In other words, these two apparently opposing experiences of what he later calls "absence" or "presence" represent the two complementary sides of attachment (fullness) and loss (emptiness). For an art historian, someone from a completely different academic tradition using completely different language, to come to this conclusion felt confirming of my theory, almost as if I had stumbled upon some conclusive research linking crying to attachment and loss.

I agree from an attachment viewpoint with Elkins's sense that some weeping in front of paintings is associated with a religious or spiritual state. The etymological root of the word religion, he writes, is connection (from the Latin *religere*). In describing "presence" and "absence," it makes sense, he says, to define them as a "religious feeling." Defining them in that way avoids "naming God" when talking about these experiences. Nonetheless, he says, "The final model for presence is God" and "the final model for absence is God's absence" (p. 193). In that way, to me, he links transcendent tears to transcendent attachment and loss: the presence of attachment to the divine or the absence of attachment to the divine.

At the (Mark) Rothko chapel in Houston, huge, dark canvasses surround the simple meditative space. Elkins believes that more crying has been done in front of Rothko's paintings than before any other 20th century artist, with Picasso's "Guernica" placing a "distant second" (p. 4).

In an interview in 1957, Rothko commented that "people who weep before my pictures are having the same religious experience I had when I painted them" (as cited in Elkins, 2001, p. 12). In the guest book at the chapel, Elkins found the following entries: "I can't help but leave this place with tears in my eyes"; "Was moved to tears, but feel like some change in a good direction will happen"; "Thank you for creating a place for my heart to cry"; and "Tears, a liquid embrace" (p. 11).

Elkins' analysis of the large, shades-of-black canvases in the chapel speaks to a transcendent recognition of absence and loss:

> Rothko gives us an imperfect memory of an object and its background and withholds the object itself: a deeply disappointing move because it fails, deliberately, to make human contact with the way the world is arranged. You might say he shows us, in the most profound and general senses, what loss looks like.... The paintings are like black holes.... Wherever you turn, they face you and show you nothing but blackness (p. 10).

When it comes to weeping over a sense of attachment, of presence, Elkins describes his own experience (being "choked up," although he never wept) before Giovanni Bellini's "Ecstasy of St. Francis." For him, the painting "was a kind of bible without words: it taught me how to find meaning in the smallest scrap on the forest floor, or the dullest glint from a nameless stone" (p. 84). To him, the painting represented a sense of connection with an "entire world where every twig and thorn has its measure of holiness" (p. 83).

In terms of art that depicts crying, Frida Kahlo's self-portraits illustrate how art may represent personal pain and use it to speak to universal and spiritual human suffering and connection. "The Broken Pillar" (1944), for example, shows her body pierced all over with nails in obvious reference to the crucifixion and to the traumatic physical injury that she received when impaled during a carriage accident. Her starkly rendered teardrops in that painting mirror those on weeping-Madonna paintings and sculptures found in Spanish religious art and in Mexican folk art. Another of her most frequently reproduced self-portraits shows her tearful face completely surrounded by a white lace mantilla. She looks exactly like images of the weeping Virgin Mary painted with a likeness of Frida Kahlo's face.

During a 9-month period in 1937, Pablo Picasso did a series of drawings and paintings of crying women. This period coincided with the bombing of civilians in the Spanish town of Guernica by Nazi warplanes, and with Picasso's subsequent painting of the powerful mural, "Guernica," depicting that tragedy for the Spanish pavilion at the International Exposition in

Paris. It also coincided with a tremendously painful period in Picasso's life. He was in the process of separating from his wife, Olga Koklova, ending a relationship with Maria-Theresa Walter, his mistress for almost 10 years, and beginning a new relationship with Dora Maar. Choosing the symbol of crying women to express the layers of political and personal pain fits in with the same tradition that influenced Frida Kahlo—Spanish religious paintings and sculptures of the weeping Virgin Mary.

The series that came to be known as Picasso's "Weeping Women" was collected and shown in Los Angeles and New York in 1994. While visiting with a group of my daughter's friends at dinner in New York the night after I saw the exhibit, I asked if any of them had seen it and what they thought. One young woman immediately said, "I don't think those women are weeping at all—those are screams of anguish." I agree that "Weeping Women" is a misnomer for these anguished screamers. True, their tears are clearly visible, but these women are shedding teeth-gnashing, handker-chief-wringing tears of protest rather than the quiet tears of sadness connoted by the word "weeping."

During those same months in 1937, Picasso wrote a prose poem to accompany a series of his drawings that illustrated Franco's atrocities. Judi Freeman (1994), curator of the exhibit and author of the book published to accompany it, wrote that Picasso was preoccupied with *gritos*—cries, screams, howls, and shrieks—during this period and in his poem. Picasso is screaming out against the atrocities in Spain but also reflecting on his own bitter feelings and those of the women in his life. He described Olga Koklova, the wife whom he was divorcing then, as an "evil tongue" and a "tongue of fire," which fit the images conveyed by his paintings of the so-called weeping women (p. 27).

Picasso's friend, Gertrude Stein, observed that the year 1937, when he was obsessed with the motif of crying women, represented a period of awakening for Picasso. Before that she said:

> He did not wish to allow himself to be awakened, there are moments in life when one is neither dead nor alive and for two years[1] Picasso was neither dead nor alive, it was not an agreeable period for him, but a period of rest, he, who all his life needed to empty himself and to empty himself, during two years he did not empty himself, that is to say not actively, actually he really emptied himself completely, emptied himself of many things and above all of being subjugated by a vision which was not his own vision (as cited in Freeman, 1994, p. 159).

The last comment apparently refers to ending his relationship with his wife, Olga. Stein also suggested that part of Picasso's personal awakening was triggered by his reconnection with Spain through his outrage at the events taking place there. His attachments and his losses were multiple and profound, touching him, and subsequently those who view his paintings, at that same deep level.

It is very painful to look on another's grief directly. This may explain why most paintings of sad cries of grief depict figures hunched over so that the face cannot be seen or with hands or a handkerchief covering the face. One of Van Gogh's paintings, called "Sorrow," shows a nude woman sitting on a tree stump, head resting on arms folded across her knees. Even without reading the title, one feels that she is weeping.

The most realistic examples of sad crying and grief are in photographic art. In that medium, the artist need only glimpse the subject for a moment to take a photograph and later work with the image during the process of development. A photographer has the distancing protection of a lens, whereas a painter or sculptor must stare and take in the pain for an extended period. The viewer of photographs, however, is spared nothing. I find it almost unbearable to look at some of these pictures. If I do I often find that I am moved to tears.

A book called *The Family of Woman* (Mason, 1979) contains numerous photographs of grieving women and children around the world. A picture of an older couple in Israel (Sherry Suris, p. 98) is doubly painful to look at because both are grieving deeply and because, as we see the husband looking at his wife, his face reflects her sadness as well as his own. She is gazing into space, one eye covered with a handkerchief while he, crying also, looks at her.

In her book *The Ballad of Sexual Dependency*, Nan Goldin (1986) includes a number of starkly frank and powerful photographs of women weeping. One woman is in a bar, smiling through her tears (p. 124); another is in a bathroom bathed in red light (p. 84) and another is in a bridal gown standing next to a smiling groom (p. 99). "Suzanne Crying" (p. 87) shows a close-up of a woman's downcast face with tear tracks and a tear drop on one cheek. According to Goldin, her aim is "to show exactly what my world looks like without glamorization, without glorification. This is not a bleak world but one in which there is an awareness of pain, a quality of introspection" (p. 6). Goldin says that she is not a voyeur; the camera is simply part of her, an extension of her hand. I agree that voyeurism did not seem to be the point, but "awareness of pain" understates it. To look at these criers means that we enter their world and experience pain along with them. We connect even without knowing the particulars.

Film

Films and funerals are two places where Westerners weep in public. Both are communal experiences serving a ritual function, a coming together in mutual recognition of love and loss. For both occasions the audience is seated in a receptive position, centered on a common focal point. The currents of emotion are carried throughout the assembly, thus creating affect larger than the sum of each person's individual reactions. At films, the darkness of the theater removes outside stimuli and the larger-than-life characters on the screen amplify the experience. Music cues emotional responses and rounds out the sense of ritual.

Comedian Lily Tomlin's character, Trudy, The Bag Lady, is visited by extraterrestrials who want to know about goose bumps. She takes them to a play and they get goose bumps, but from watching the audience, not from watching the stage. "Yeah," says Trudy, "to see a group of strangers sitting together in the dark, laughing and crying about the same things ... that just knocked 'em out" (Wagner, 1986, p. 212). The extraterrestrials understand instantly the ritual importance of the gathering, while we stay focused on the content of the drama.

Because putting the experience of transcendent crying into words is such a fragile affair, I was pleased to discover a brief film review that had done so successfully. It was in a brief synopsis of John Huston's film, *The Dead* (1993), which is based on a James Joyce short story. Gabriel's wife confesses to him a never-forgotten youthful love affair. The reviewer says, "You too may find your eyes filling with tears"; however, they will go beyond the obvious message about life's limitations and losses: "... they won't be simple tears of mourning. They'll be the ambiguous, 'generous tears' that Joyce says fill Gabriel's eyes, too: the tears that accompany epiphany" (p. 48). "Ambiguous" and "generous" are roomy adjectives for tears, big enough to contain "epiphany," one of the few words available in English to describe an experience of the transcendent.

Aristotle may have been right about the cathartic value in shedding tears over someone else's pain. The secret is that one must be able to make their pain one's own, but just a little bit—the pain of love lost, roads not taken, secure if sparkless marriages endured, or romances kindled and floundered. Crying over movie feelings may not be entertainment exactly. Under the right circumstances, however, it can deepen the connection we feel with the characters and in the process, with ourselves as well.

Sociologist Thomas Scheff (1979) writes that emotion, to be cathartic, must take place at the proper "aesthetic distance," where the experience of being participant and observer is properly balanced. With too much distance, no emotion is felt. With too little, the experience is too painful to be cathartic.

This was true of two memorable weeping-at-film experiences for me: *The Chosen* and a public television production of *Oranges Are Not the Only Fruit*. Both of these films are about religious conflicts between children and parents that lead to painful choices and ultimately to a rupture in the relationship, paralleling the experiences I had with my own parents.

Because *The Chosen* is about a Jewish family, my personal conflict with Christian fundamentalism was put at a comfortable aesthetic distance. I cried my way through the book, the film, and a New York stage-play version, and felt cleansed and healed by the process and by tapping into the larger dimensions of this very personal issue. *Oranges Are Not the Only Fruit*, about a Welsh girl's experiences in the culture of a fundamentalist church and family, is similar to but more extreme than my own experience. Although I cried profusely at the emotional and physical abuse the young woman endured at the hands of her mother and her church, it actually made me feel more pain instead of feeling cleansed. I could cry in protest on behalf of both of us, but for neither of us did I feel a healing comfort.

Although films are a powerful medium, I wonder whether, by allowing ourselves to be manipulated emotionally or, alternatively, by developing high-powered defenses against it, we might be mangling our emotional feedback systems. Because I did not see my first Hollywood film until I was 18 years old, I am a one-woman research subject for measuring the emotional power of films. When I made the decision to see my first film *Gone With the Wind* (the early 1960s remake), I was feeling repulsed by the emotional manipulation I had endured from the pulpit throughout my childhood and, no doubt, still retained some of the warnings about the corrupting influence of Hollywood. In that frame of mind, I was stunned by the emotional impact of the film, but I was determined *not* to cry. Over my years of movie-going, I have eventually learned to defend myself against intrusive emotion and to let myself go and cry when I feel like it.

In Robert Altman's film *The Player* about the Hollywood filmmaking industry, every plot pitched to potential producers concludes with: "And there is not a dry eye in the house!" *The Player* may be satirizing the industry, but in fact ad campaigns for films do, oddly enough, use crying as a marketing tool ("You'll laugh, you'll cry, you'll love it!" and "It's a three-hankie film!" are typical advertising slogans.)

As might be expected, we as a culture have an ambivalent relationship to crying in the movies. We use it and we enjoy it, but at the same time we are inclined to judge it as melodramatic and, of course, female. The "woman's weepie," a major film category in the 1930s and 1940s (with remakes in the 1950s), has been called the "lowliest" form of melodrama. (Male melodramas—westerns, gangster or sports movies—have the more elevated label of "adult realism.") Yet, men seem to cry at movies, too.

Entertainment Weekly (as cited in Garchick, 1995) conducted an exit poll of viewers of *Bridges of Madison County,* a sad story about lost yet enduring love. Sixty percent of the men in the audience said that they had cried. Filmmaker Steven Spielberg says that he cries at old melodramas and considers that a sign of "emotional development." He also admitted in an interview that at one point after a long dry spell when he cried over the end of a relationship, "The human being in me was pouring the tears out. But the doggone filmmaker in me ran to the other room, grabbed my Instamatic, and took my own picture. I had to have that cry on record" (Zellerbach, 1983).

Russell Baker (1982) called the film *Chariots of Fire,* a sentimental story about young men struggling to become champion runners, a "male weepie." Men in the audience, he said, like a good cry just as much as women do; however, according to him, they prefer to choke up rather than cry in "ridiculous" ways like women. The label "woman's weepie" seems to convey a demeaning attitude toward women's emotions and women's entertainment. I wonder about the social and psychological toll extracted from women and from weeping by the double standard of selling emotion and then criticizing those who buy it. Sometimes women and men may want to experience pain that is about, yet not about, their own losses. In some deep place inside the human spirit, the pull toward narrative and the pull toward attachment and closeness seem to coincide. For the same reasons that tribal cultures have storytellers who gather everyone around the fire at night, for all the simple and complicated reasons that make that feel satisfying, people sometimes cry together at films.

In "To a Skylark," Percy Bysshe Shelley calls the skylark's song "unpremeditated art." Then he writes:

> If we were things born
> Not to shed a tear,
> I know not how thy joy we ever should come near

> (as cited in Bernbaum, 1948, p. 941, ll. 92–95)

In the act of crying, we have love and loss, life and death. Crying holds the opposites: hopelessness and hope, pain and comfort, loneliness and connection. Crying is a transformative agent, a bridge between mother and child, lover and beloved, stranger and Good Samaritan, body and soul, secular and sacred.

Crying, too, is "unpremeditated art" or, as Maggie Nelson said, "poetry streaming down our cheeks" without our foreknowledge or consent. We have our infants, our bodies, our losses, and our painters, writers, and musicians to thank for keeping it from becoming a lost art. We honor and cherish it when we open our ears to its music, our eyes to its meaning, and our hearts to its bounty. We feel our pain, share it, but also transcend it and reach toward the skylark's joy.

Notes

Chapter 1

1. Tomkins' ideas anticipate neurobiological research and attachment theory on shame.

Chapter 3

1. Two residual categories of crying not related to loss will be discussed in greater detail in later chapters. The first is somatic tears that are symptomatic of physiological disorders. The second is transcendent tears triggered by a sense of union or connectedness that goes beyond personal loss to a sense of universal love or attachment.

Chapter 4

1. Vaughn and Bost (1999) summarize the theories and research on attachment and temperament.
2. See Solomon and George (1999) for a thorough description of the measurement of attachment security.

Chapter 9

1. Uncontrollable crying based on a physiological condition goes by a variety of strange sounding terms in the medical literature: emotional incontinence; pathological weeping; emotional lability; pseudobulbar affect; crocodile tears; paradoxical weeping; organic emotionalism; spasmodic crying; inappropriate crying; forced crying; and paroxysmal weeping.

Chapter 12

1. Freeman says that 2 years was an exaggeration because "it was clear that this period lasted for several months" (p. 171).

References

Ackerman, D. (1990). *A natural history of the senses.* New York: Random House.

Adams, M. (in press). My shaggy ally.

Addenda. (1994, November 25). *The Washington Post,* A 18.

Ainsworth, M. (1967). *Infancy in Uganda: Infant care and the growth of love.* Baltimore: The Johns Hopkins Press.

Ainsworth, M. D. S., Blehar, M., Waters, E., & Wall, S. (1978). *Patterns of attachment.* Hillsdale, NJ: Lawrence Erlbaum Associates.

Alabaster, W. (Ed.). (1957). *Upon the Ensignes of Christes Crucifyinge.* Baltimore: Penguin Books, 199.

American Psychiatric Association. (1994). *Diagnostic and statistical manual of mental disorders* (4th ed.). Washington, D.C.: American Psychiatric Association.

Amis, M. (1995). *The Information.* New York: Harmony Books.

The Angel Gabriel [Review of the film *The Dead].* (1992 and 1993, 12/28 and 1/4). *The New Yorker,* 48.

Aronson, T. (1995, April 30). When a mother wants her daughter to die [review of the book *Lost lullaby].* *San Francisco Sunday Examiner and Chronicle,* 7.

Ashokan farewell. (1991, March 11). *The New Yorker:* Talk of the town, 27–28.

The Atlas Peak fire. (1991, June 23). *The Napa Register,* 8.

Bader, M. J. (1996). Altruistic love in psychoanalysis: Opportunities and resistance. *Psychoanalytic Dialogues,* 6(6), 741–764.

Baker, R. (1982, October 3). The male weepies. *The New York Times,* SM 20.

Baldwin, C. (1990). *Life's companion: Journal writing as a spiritual quest.* New York: Bantam Books.

Beal, A. (2004). Seven reasons babies cry and how to soothe them. MSN family: Baby and pregnancy (On-line) Available: www.Family.msn.com

Becht, M. C., Poortinga, Y. H., & Vingerhoets, A. J. J. M. (2001). Crying across countries. In A. J. J. M. Vingerhoets & R. R. Cornelius (Eds.), *Adult crying: A biopsychosocial approach* (pp. 135–158). Philadelphia: Taylor & Francis.

Beck, A. T., Rush, A. J., Shaw, B. F., & Emory, G. (1979). *Cognitive therapy of depression.* New York: Guilford Press.

Bell, S. M. & Ainsworth, M. D. S. (1972). Crying and maternal responsiveness. *Child Development,* 43, 1171–1190.

Belsky, J. (1999). Interactional and contextual determinants of attachment security. In J. Cassidy & P. R. Shaver (Eds.), *Handbook of attachment: Theory, research, and clinical applications* (249–264). New York: The Guilford Press.

Bernal, J. (1972). Crying during the first ten days of life and maternal responses. *Developmental Medicine and Child Neurology,* 14, 362–372.

Bernbaum, E. (Ed.). (1948). *Anthology of romanticism*. New York: The Ronald Press Company, 177 & 941.

Blurton Jones, N. (1972). Comparative aspects of mother–child contact. In N. Blurton Jones (Ed.), *Ethological studies of child behavior* (pp. 305–328). London: Cambridge University Press.

Blurton Jones, N. G. & Leach, G. M. (1972). Behavior of children and their mothers at separation and greeting. In N. G. Blurton Jones (Ed.), *Ethological studies of child behavior* (pp. 217–247). London: Cambridge University Press.

Bollas, C. (1992). *Being a character*. New York: Hill and Wang.

Bombeck, E. (1980, September 25). Learning from the kids. *The Napa Register,* 7.

Borquist, A. (1906). Crying. *The American Journal of Psychology, 17,* 149–205.

Boukydis, C. F. Z. (1985). Perception of infant crying as an interpersonal event. In B. M. Lester & C. F. Z. Boukydis (Eds.), *Infant crying: Theoretical and research perspectives* (pp. 187–215). New York: Plenum Press.

Boukydis, C. F. Z. & Burgess, R. L. (1982). Adult physiological response to infant cries: Effects of temperament of infant, parental status and gender. *Child Development, 53,* 1291–1298.

Bowlby, J. (1960). Grief and mourning in infancy and early childhood. *Psychoanalytic Study of the Child, XV,* 9–52.

Bowlby, J. (1961). Processes of mourning. *The International Journal of Psychoanalysis, 42*(4–5), 317–339.

Bowlby, J. (1969). *Attachment*. New York: Basic Books.

Bowlby, J. (1973). *Separation: Anxiety and anger*. New York: Basic Books.

Bowlby, J. (1980). *Loss*. New York: Basic Books.

Brazelton, T. B. (1962). Crying in infancy. *Pediatrics, 29,* 579–588.

Brazelton, T. B. (1969). Infant development of Zenacanteco Indians of southern Mexico. *Pediatrics, 44,* 274–290.

Brazelton, T. B. (1989). *Toddlers and parents*. New York: Delacorte Press.

Breuer, J. & Freud, S. (1955). Studies on hysteria. In J. Strachey (Ed. and Trans.), *The standard edition of the complete psychological works of Sigmund Freud* (Vol. 2, pp. vii–xxxi, 1–311). London: Hogarth Press. (Original work published 1893–1895).

Brodkey, H. (1996). *This wild darkness*. New York: Henry Holt & Co. Originally published in *The New Yorker*.

Caen, H. (1996, January 11). Herb Caen. *The San Francisco Chronicle,* A-12.

Carmichael, K. (1991). *Ceremony of innocence: Tears, power and protest*. New York: St. Martin's Press.

Clinton puts his heart into farewell to Arkansas pals. (1992, December 13). *The San Francisco Examiner,* A 8.

Collins, B. (1998). *Picnic, lightning*. Pittsburgh: University of Pittsburgh Press.

Coombs, M. M., Coleman, D., & Jones, E. E. (2002). Working with feelings: the importance of emotion in both cognitive–behavioral and interpersonal therapy in the NIMH treatment of depression collaborative research program. *Psychotherapy: Theory/Research/Practice/Training, 39*(3), 233–244.

Cornelius, R. (2001). The social psychological aspects of crying. In A. J. J. M. Vingerhoets & R. R. Cornelius (Eds.), *Adult crying: A biopsychosocial approach* (pp. 159–176). Philadelphia: Taylor & Francis.

Compassionate judge. (1993, August). *New Woman,* 9.

"Dance." (1991, May 29). *The New Yorker,* 8.

Darwin, C. (1872/1965). *The expression of the emotions in man and animals*. Chicago: University of Chicago Press.

Davidson, J. R. T. (1972). Postpartum mood changes in Jamaican women: A description and discussion on its significance. *British Journal of Psychiatry, 121,* 659–663.

Donne, P. (1991, September 30). Men, women and tears. *Time,* 84.

Donovan, W. L. & Balling, J.D. (1978). Maternal physiological response to infant signals. *Psychophysiology, 15*(1), 68–74.

Donovan, W. L. & Leavitt, L. A. (1985). Physiology and behavior: Parents' response to the infant cry. In B. M. Lester & C. F. Z. Boukydis (Eds.), *Infant crying: Theoretical and research perspectives* (pp. 241–259). New York: Plenum Press.

Edinger, E. F. (1978). Psychotherapy and alchemy: III. Solutio. *Quadrant, 11*(2) (Winter), 63–85.

Ekman, P. (1973) Cross cultural studies of facial expression. In P. Ekman (Ed.), *Darwin and facial expression* (pp. 169–222). New York: The Academic Press.

Ekman, P. (1969). Pan cultural elements in facial displays of emotion. *Science, 164*(3875), 86–88.

Ekman, P. (1971). Constants across cultures in the face and emotion. *Journal of Personality and Social Psychology, 17*, 124–129.

Elkins, J. (2001). *Pictures and tears: A history of people who have cried in front of paintings.* New York: Routledge.

Emerson, G. (1974, June). A few words on crying. *Esquire, 113*, 178–179.

Ephron, N. (1983). *Heartburn.* New York: Alfred A. Knopf.

Esquivel, L. (1992). *Like water for chocolate* (Christensen, C. & Christensen, T., Trans.). New York: Doubleday.

Farber, S. K. (2000). *When the body is the target: Self-harm, pain, and traumatic attachments.* Northvale, NJ: Jason Aronson.

Feld, S. (1982). *Sound and sentiment: Birds, weeping, poetics, and song in Kaluli expression.* Philadelphia: University of Pennsylvania Press.

Field, T. & Reite, M. (1984). Children's responses to separation from mother during the birth of another child. *Child Development, 55*, 1308–1316.

Field, T., M., Gewirtz, J., Cohen, D., Garcia, R., Greenberg, R., & Collins, K. (1984a). Leave-takings and reunions of infants, toddlers, preschoolers, and their parents. *Child Development, 55*(2), 628–635.

Field, T. M., Vega-Lahr, N., & Jagadish, S. (1984b). Separation stress of nursery school infants and toddlers graduating to new classes. *Infant Behavior and Development, 7*(3), 277–284.

Fisher, C. (1987). *Postcards from the edge.* New York: Pocket Books.

Formby, D. (1967). Maternal recognition of infant's cry. *Developmental Medicine and Child Neurology, 9*, 293–298.

Fraiberg, S. (1959). *The magic years.* New York: Charles Scribner's Sons.

Freeman, J. (1994). *Picasso and the weeping women.* New York: Rizzoli International Publications. Los Angeles: Los Angeles County Museum of Art.

Freeman, L. (1973). *Your mind can stop the common cold.* New York: Peter H. Wyden, Inc.

Freud, S. (1927, December 5). Letter to Romain Rolland. In E. L. Freud (Ed.), (1975), *Letters of Sigmund Freud* (p. 388). New York: Basic Books.

Freud, S. (1961). *Civilization and its discontents* (James Strachey, Trans.). New York: W.W. Norton.

Frey, W. H. I. & Langseth, M. (1985). *Crying: The mystery of tears.* Minneapolis: Winston Press.

Frodi, A. (1985). When empathy fails: Aversive infant crying and child abuse. In B. Lester & C. F. Z. Boukydis (Eds.), *Infant crying: Theoretical and research perspectives.* New York: Plenum Press.

Frodi, A. M. & Lamb, M. E. (1980). Child abuser's response to infant smiles and cries. *Child Development, 51*, 238–241.

Frodi, A. M., Lamb, M. E., Leavitt, L. A., & Donovan, W. L. (1978). Fathers' and mothers' responses to infant smiles and cries. *Infant Behavior and Development, 1*, 187–198.

Frost, P. (1991, September 16). Off-Ramp. *The New Yorker,* 28–30.

Garchick, L. (1995, June 14). The bridges of Madison Avenue. *The San Francisco Chronicle,* E8.

Gesell, A. F. I. & Ames, L. B. (1946). *The child from five to ten.* New York: Harper and Brothers.

Gesell, A., Ilg, F. L., & Ames, L. B. (1956). *Youth: The years from ten to sixteen.* New York: Harper and Row.

Gimbutas, M. (1989). *The language of the goddess.* New York: Harper and Row.

Glick, I. O., Weiss, R. S., & Parkes, M. C. (1974). *The first year of bereavement.* New York: John Wiley and Sons.

Goldin, N. (1986). *The ballad of sexual dependency.* New York: The Arperture Foundation.

Gordon, R. E., Gordon, K. K., Gordon-Hardy, L., Hursch, C. J., & Reed, K. G. (1986). Predicting postnatal emotional adjustment with psychosocial and hormonal measures in early pregnancy. *American Journal of Obstetrics Gynecology, 155*(1), 80–82.

Gorer, G. (1965). *Death, grief, and mourning in contemporary Britain.* London: The Cresset Press.

Green, R., McAllister, T., & Bernat, J. (1987). A study of crying in medically and surgically hospitalized patients. *American Journal of Psychiatry, 144*(4), 442–447.

Greenacre, P. (1945a). Pathological weeping. *Psychiatric Quarterly, 15*, 62–75.

Greenacre, P. (1945b). Urination and weeping. *American Journal of Orthopsychiatry, 15*, 81–88.

Greenacre, P. (1965). On the development and function of tears. *The Psychoanalytic Study of the Child*, *XX*, 209–219.

Gustafson, G. E. & Green, J. A. (1994). Robustness of individual identity in the cries of human infants. *Developmental Psychobiology*, *27*(1), 1–9.

Habenstein, R. & Lamers, W. (1963). *Funeral customs the world over*. Milwaukee: Bulfin Printers, Inc.

Hargrove, J. T. & Abraham, G. E. (1982). The incidence of premenstrual tension in a gynecologic clinic. *The Journal of Reproductive Medicine*, *27*(12), 721–724.

Harris, B. (1981). "Maternity blues" in East African clinic attenders. *Archives of General Psychiatry*, *38*, 1293–1295.

Hartman, H. (1958). *Ego psychology and the problem of adaptation*. New York: International University Press, Inc.

Hastrup, J. L. & Baker, J. G. (1986). Crying and depression among older adults. *Gerontologist*, *26*(1), 91–96.

Hastrup, J. L., Kraemer, D. L., & Bornstein, R. F. (1985). Crying frequency of 1- to 12-year-old boys and girls. Paper presented at the meeting of the North Eastern Psychological Association, Boston, MA.

Hazan, C., & Shaver, P. (1987). Romantic love conceptualized as an attachment process. *Journal of Personality and Social Psychology*, *52*, 511–524.

Heilbrun, G. (1955). On weeping. *Psychoanalytic Quarterly*, *24*, 245–255.

Herbert, G. (1633). The collar. In *Columbia Grangers* (On-line). Available: www.columbiagrangers.org

Hesse, E. (1999). The Adult Attachment Interview. In J. Cassidy & P. R. Shaver (Eds.), *Handbook of attachment* (pp. 395–433). New York: The Guilford Press.

Hitchens, C. (1996, March 31). Cry, baby: cheap weeps at the Academy Awards. *The Washington Post*, G1 & G7.

Hoover-Dempsey, K. V., Plas, J., & Wallston, B. S. (1986). Tears and weeping among professional women: In search of new understanding. *Psychology of Women Quarterly*, *10*(1), 19–34.

Howes, C. & Eldredge, R. (1985). Responses of abused, neglected, and nonmaltreated children to the behaviors of their peers. *Journal of Applied Developmental Psychology*, *6*(2–3), 261–270.

Howes, C. & Farver, J. (1987). Toddlers' responses to the distress of their peers. *Journal of Applied Developmental Psychology*, *8*(4), 441–452.

Hunziker, U. A. & Barr, R. G. (1986). Increased carrying reduces infant crying: A randomized control trial. *Pediatrics*, *77*, 641–648.

Isaac Stern loud and clear. (1990, September 23). *San Francisco Chronicle Datebook*, 7.

Johnson, B. (1988). *Lady of the beasts*. San Francisco: Harper and Row.

Kalish, R. A. & Reynolds D. K. (1976). *Death and ethnicity: A psychocultural study*. Los Angeles: University of Southern California Press.

Kalsched, D. (1996). *The inner world of trauma: Archetypal defenses of the personal spirit*. New York: Brunner-Routledge.

Kavanaugh, D. (Ed.). (1978). *Listen to us: The children's express report*. New York: Workman.

Kepecs, J., Rabin, A., & Robin, M. (1951a). Atopic dermatitis. *Psychosomatic Medicine*, *13*(January–February), 1–9.

Kepecs, J. G., Robin, M., & Brunner, M. J. (1951b). Relationship between certain emotional states and exudation into the skin. *Psychosomatic Medicine*, *13*(January–February), 10–17.

Kincaid, J. (1990, June 25). Cold heart. *The New Yorker*, pp. 28–40.

Kirkland, J., Deane, F., & Brennan, M. (1983). About CrySOS, a clinic for people with crying babies. *Family Relations: Journal of Applied Family and Child Studies*, *32*(4), 537–543.

Kitzinger, S. (1989). *The crying baby*. New York: Viking Penguin Inc.

Klinkenborg, V. (1992, February 17) Family stories [Review of the book *Come from away: Memory, war and the search for a family's past*]. *The New Yorker*, 89–92.

Koestler, A. (1964). *The act of creation*. New York: MacMillan.

Kohut, H. (1971). *The analysis of the self*. New York: International Universities Press.

Konner, M. J. (1972). Aspects of the developmental ethology of a foraging people. In N. Blurton Jones (Ed.), *Ethological studies of child behavior*. London: Cambridge University Press.

Kottler, J. (2001). Theories of crying. In A. Vingerhoets & R. Cornelius (Eds.), *Adult crying: A biopsychosocial approach* (pp. 1–17). Philadelphia: Taylor & Francis.

Kottler, J. A. (1996). *The language of tears*. San Francisco: Jossey-Bass.

Kracke, W. (1981). Kagwahiv mourning. *Ethos*, *9*(4), 258–275.

Kracke, W. (1988). Kagwahiv mourning II. *Ethos, 16*(2), 209–222.

Kraemer, D. L. & Hastrup, J. L. (1986). Crying in natural settings: Global estimates, self-monitored frequencies, depression and sex differences in an undergraduate population. *Behavior Research and Therapy, 24* (3), 371–373.

Kraemer, D. L., Hastrup, J. L., Sobota, M., & Bornstein, R. F. (1985). Adolescent crying: norms and self-control. Paper presented at the meeting of the Eastern Psychological Association, Boston, MA.

Krauser, P. (1989). Tears. *Journal of the American Medical Association, 261* (June 23/30), 3612.

Labott, S. (2001). Crying in psychotherapy. In A. J. J. M. Vingerhoets & R. R. Cornelius (Eds.), *Adult crying: A biopsychosocial approach* (pp. 213–226). Philadelphia: Taylor & Francis.

Labott, S., Ahleman, S., Wolever, M., & Martin, R. (1990). The physiological and psychological effects of the expression and inhibition of emotion. *Behavioral Medicine, 16*(4), 182–189.

Labott, S. & Martin, R. (1987). The stress-moderating effects of weeping and humor. *Journal of Human Stress, 13*(4), 159–164.

Landreth, C. (1940). Consistency of four methods of measuring one type of sporadic emotional behavior (crying) in nursery school children. *Journal of Genetic Psychology, 57,* 101–118.

Lee, S. (1991, June 23). Five for five: The films of Spike Lee (excerpts). *Image: The San Francisco Examiner,* 24–28.

Lester, B. & Boukydis, C. F. Z. (Eds.). (1985). *Infant crying: Theoretical and research perspectives.* New York: Plenum Press.

Lester, B. M. & Zeskind, P. S. (1979). The organization and assessment of crying in the infant at risk. In T. M. Field, A. M. Sostek, S. Goldberg, & H. H. Shuman (Eds.), *Infants born at risk* (pp. 121–144). New York: Spectrum.

Löfgren, L. B. (1965). On weeping. *International Journal of Psychoanlysis, 47,* 375–383.

Lorberbaum, J., Newman, J. D., Horwitz, A. R., Dubno, J. R., Lydiard, R. B., Hamner, M. B., Bohning, D. E., & George, M. S. (2002). A potential role for thalamocingulate circuitry in human maternal behavior. *Biological Psychiatry, 51,* 431–445.

Main, M. & Solomon, J. (1990). Procedures for identifying infants as disorganized/disoriented during the Ainsworth Strange Situation. In M. T. Greenberg, D. Cicchetti, & E. M. Cummings (Eds.), *Attachment in the preschool years* (pp. 121–160). Chicago: University of Chicago Press.

Márquez, G. G. (1988). *Love in the time of cholera* (Edith Grossman, Trans.). New York: Penguin Books.

Mason, J. (Ed.). (1979). *The family of woman.* New York: Ridge Press.

Maudsley, H. (1996). *Matrix, 3*(10), 3.

Maynard, O. (1982). *Judith Jamison.* New York: Doubleday and Co.

McEntire, S. J. (1991). *The doctrine of compunction in Medieval England: Holy tears.* Lewiston, New York: The Edwin Mellen Press.

McGrath, C. (1979, October 22). Husbands. *The New Yorker,* 40–46.

McGreevy, A. & Heukelem, J. V. (1976). Crying, the neglected dimension. *Canadian Nurse, 72*(1), 18–21.

McPhee, J. (1993, 12/20). Irons in the fire. *The New Yorker,* 94–113.

Miller, A. (1983). *For your own good* (Hildegarde and Hunter Hannum, Trans.). New York: Farrar, Straus, Giroux.

Montague, S. (Ed.). (1486/1970). *Malleus Maleficarum.* New York: Benjamin Blom, Inc.

Morsbach, G. (1980). Maternal recognition of neonates' cries in Japan. *Psychologia, 23,* 63–69.

Morsbach, G. & Bunting, C. (1979). Maternal recognition of their neonates' cries. *Developmental Medicine and Child Neurology, 21,* 178–185.

Nabokov, V. (2002). "Sounds," In: *The Stories of Vladimir Nabokov.* New York: Vintage International, pp. 14–24. (First published in *The New Yorker*).

Nelson, J. K. (1979) An ego psychological and object relations study of crying. (Dissertation, California Institute for Clinical Social Work).

Nelson, J. K. (1998). The meaning of crying based on attachment theory. *Clinical Social Work Journal, 26*(1) (Spring, 1998), 9–22.

Nelson, J. K. (2000). Clinical assessment of crying and crying inhibition based on attachment theory. *Bulletin of the Menninger Clinic, 64*(2) (Fall 2000), 509–529.

Nelson, M. and Nelson, C. (1996). New Year's Day. *Not sisters.* New York: Soft Skull Press, 15.

Nemerov, H. (1991, June 24). The end of the opera. *The New Yorker,* 38.

Nevius, C. W. (2003, May 11). Director gets a birds'-eye view of flight [Review of the film *Winged migration*]. *San Francisco Chronicle*, D4.

Newsham, B. (2000, May 22). Somebody's mother. *San Francisco Chronicle*, D8.

Novick, K. K. (1986). Talking with toddlers. *Psychoanalytic Study of the Child, 41*, 277–286.

Ostwald, P. (1973). *The semiotics of human sound*. The Hague: Mouton.

Ostwald, P. & Peltzman, P. (1974). The cry of the human infant. *Scientific American, 230*, 84–90.

Peterson, J. (1968). *The Littles take a trip*. New York: Scholastic Book Services.

Pizer, S. A. (1996). Negotiating potential space: Illusion, play, metaphor, and the subjunctive. *Psychoanalytic Dialogues, 6*(5), 689–712.

Pizer, S.A. (1998). *Building bridges: The negotiation of paradox in psychoanalysis*. Hillsdale, NJ: The Analytic Press.

Plessner, H. (1970). *Laughing and crying: A study of the limits of human behavior* (Churchill, James S., Trans.). Evanston: Northwestern University Press.

Pynoos, R. S., Nader, K., Frederick, C., Gonda, L., & Stuber, M. (1987). Grief reactions in school age children following a sniper attack at school. *Israel Journal of Psychiatry and Related Science, 24*(1), 53–63.

Radcliffe-Brown, A. R. (1922). *The Andaman Islanders*. Cambridge: The University Press.

Rebelsky, F. R. B. (1972). Crying in infancy. *The Journal of Genetic Psychology, 121*, 49–57.

Rottenberg, J., Gross, J. J., Wilhelm, F. H., Najmi, S., & Gotlib, I. H. (2002). Crying threshold and intensity in major depressive disorder. *Journal of Abnormal Psychology, 111*(2), 302–312.

Ruddick, B. (1963). Colds and respiratory introjection. *International Journal of Psychoanalysis, 44*, 2.

Saber, A. & Mazlish, E. (1980). *How to talk so kids will listen and listen so kids will talk*. New York: Rawson, Wade.

Sagan, C. (1977). *Dragons of Eden: Speculations on the evolution of human intelligence*. New York: Random House.

Schafer, R. (1976). *A new language for psychoanalysis*. New Haven and London: Yale University Press.

Scheff, T. J. (1979). *Catharsis in healing, ritual, and drama*. Berkeley: University of California Press.

Scheirs, J. & Sijtsma, K. (2001). The study of crying: Some methodological considerations and a comparison of methods for analyzing questionnaires. In A. Vingerhoets & R. Cornelius (Eds.), *Adult crying: A biopsychosocial approach* (pp. 277–298). Philadelphia: Taylor & Francis.

Scheper-Hughes, N. (1992). *Death without weeping*. Berkeley: University of California Press.

Schoch, R. (1992, April). A conversation with Scheper-Hughes. *California Monthly*, pp. 18–23.

Schore, A. (1994). *Affect regulation and the origin of the self*. Hillsdale, NJ: Lawrence Erlbaum.

Schore, A. N. (2003). *Affect dysregulation and disorders of the self*. New York: W.W. Norton.

Searl, M. N. (1963). The psychology of screaming. *International Journal of Psychoanalysis, 44*, 193–205.

Seifritz, E., Esposito, F., Neuhoff, J. G., Lü-thi, A., Mustovic, H., Dammann, G., von Bardeleben, U., Radue, E. W., Cirillo, S., Tedeschi, G., & Salle, F. D. (2003). Differential sex-independent amygdala response to infant crying and laughing in parents versus nonparents. *Biological Psychiatry, 54*, 1367–1375.

Sexton, A. (1975). *The awful rowing toward God*. Boston: Houghton Mifflin.

Simos, B. G. (1979). *A time to grieve: Loss as universal human experience*. New York: Family Service Association of America.

Smith, J. (1989, December 28). Stories behind male tears. *San Francisco Chronicle*, B4.

Smith, P. (1974). Social and situational determinants of fear in the playgroup. In M. Lewis & L. Rosenblum (Eds.), *The origins of fear* (pp. 107–129). New York: John Wiley & Sons.

Spitz, E. H. (1999). *Inside picture books*. New Haven: Yale University Press.

Spitz, R. A. (1965). *The first year of life*. New York: International Universities Press.

St. James-Roberts, I. (1989). Persistent crying in infancy. *Journal of Child Psychology and Psychiatry and Allied Disciplines, 30*(2), 189–195.

Steer, R., Beck, A., Brown, G., & Berchick, R. (1987). Self-reported depressive symptoms that differentiate recurrent-episode major depression from dysthymic disorders. *Journal of Clinical Psychology, 43*(2), 246–250.

Stendhal, R. (1994). *Gertrude Stein in words and pictures*. Chapel Hill: Algonquin Books.

Stephens, B. (1991). A cry in the wilderness: Shekhinah as psychological healer. *Journal of Psychology and Judaism, 15*(1), 29–42.

Tennyson, A. L. (1847). The princess: A medley. In: *Columbia Grangers* (On-line). Available: www.columbiagrangers.org

Tetrick, Andrea. (1996) F-Train. *Wordwrights*, Summer, 14.

Tomkins, S. S. (1963). *Affect, imagery, consciousness: The negative affects.* New York: Springer.

Urban, G. (1988). Ritual wailing in Amerindian Brazil. *American Anthropologist, 90,* 385–400.

Van Buren, A. (1980, January 28). Dear Abby. *The San Francisco Chronicle,* 14.

van Haeringen, N. J. (2001). The (neuro)anatomy of the lacrimal system and the biological aspects of crying. In A. J. J. M. Vingerhoets & R. R. Cornelius (Eds.), *Adult crying: A biopsychosocial approach* (pp. 19–36). Philadelphia: Taylor & Francis.

Vingerhoets, A. (2001). Appendix. In A. Vingerhoets & R. Cornelius (Eds.), *Adult crying: A biopsychosocial approach* (pp. 303–316). Philadelphia: Taylor & Francis.

Vingerhoets, A. J. J. M., Assies, J., & Poppelaars, K. (1992). Prolactin and weeping. *International Journal of Psychosomatics, 39,* 81–82.

Viorst, J. (1986). *Necessary losses.* New York: Ballantine Books.

Voices of the rainforest: A day in the life of the Kaluli people (1991). [CD recorded by Steven Feld] Rykodisc/Mickey Hart Series.

Wagner, J. (1986). *The search for signs of intelligent life in the universe.* New York: Harper and Row.

Wallerstein, R. (1967). Reconstruction and mastery in the transference psychosis. *Journal of the American Psychoanalytic Association, 15,* 555–583.

Warner, M. (1976). *Alone of all her sex: The myth and the cult of the Virgin Mary.* New York: Alfred A. Knopf.

Wasz-Höckert, O., Lind, J., Vuorenkoski, V., Partanen, T., & Valanne, E. (1968). *The infant cry: Spectrographic and auditory analysis.* Philadelphia: Lippincott.

Wasz-Höckert, O., Michelsson, K., & Lind, J. (1985). Twenty-five years of Scandinavian cry research. In B. M. Lester & C. F. Z. Boukydis (Eds.), *Infant crying: Theoretical and research perspectives* (pp. 83–104). New York: Plenum Press.

Weinstein, F. (1987). Letter. *American Journal of Psychiatry, 144*(4), 529.

Weston, J. (1968). The pathology of child abuse. In R. Helfer & C. Kempe (Eds.), *The battered child.* Chicago: The University of Chicago Press.

Wills, G. (1992, October 12). From the campaign trail: Clinton's hell-raiser. *The New Yorker,* 92–101.

Wilson, K. (1987, October 6). A few tears don't make Schroeder anyone's Patsy. *The Los Angeles Times,* 7.

Wolff, P. H. (1969). The natural history of crying and other vocalizations in infancy. In B. M. Foss (Ed.), *Determinants of infant behavior IV* (pp. 81–109). London: Methuen.

Wolkstein, D. & Kramer, S. (1983). *Inanna queen of heaven and earth.* New York: Harper and Row.

Wood, E. & Wood, C. (1984). Tearfulness: A psychoanalytic interpretation. *Journal of American Psychoanalytic Association, 32*(1), 117–136.

Yazmajian, R. (1966). Pathological urination and weeping. *Psychoanalytic Quarterly, 35,* 40–46.

Zahn-Waxler, C. Radke-Yarrow, M., & King, R. A. (1979). Child rearing and children's proscocial initiations toward victims of distress. *Child Development, 50,* 319–330.

Zellerbach, M. (1983, April 13). What men say about crying. *The San Francisco Chronicle,* 37.

Zisook, S., DeVaul, R., & Click, M. J. (1982). Measuring symptoms of grief and bereavement. *American Journal of Psychiatry, 139*(12), 1590–1593.

Permissions

Grateful acknowledgement is given to the following for their permission to reprint materials that appear in this book:

Excerpts from *The Awful Rowing Toward God* by Anne Sexton. Copyright © 1975 by Loring Conant, Jr., executor of the estate of Anne Sexton. Reprinted by permission of Houghton Mifflin Company. All rights reserved.

Lines from "Shoveling Snow with Buddha" from *Picnic, Lightning* by Billy Collins, © 1998. Reprinted by permission of the University of Pittsburg Press.

Excerpt used as stand-alone quote from *The Search for Signs of Intelligent Life in the Universe* by Jane Wagner. Copyright © 1986 by Jane Wagner Inc. Reprinted by permission of HarperCollins Publishers, Inc.

Lines from "Cold Heart" by Jamaica Kincaid. Copyright © 1990 by Jamaica Kincaid. Reprinted with the permission of the Wylie Agency Inc.

Lines from "New Years Day" by Maggie Nelson, from *Not Sisters*. Reprinted with permission.

Lines from *Like Water for Chocolate* by Laura Esquivel, published by Doubleday. Reprinted with permission.

Excerpts from *Pictures and Tears* by James Elkins. Reproduced by permission of Routledge/Taylor & Francis Books, Inc.

Lines from "F-Train" by Andrea Tetrick, first published in *Wordwrights, #7*, Summer 1996 edition. Reprinted with permission.

Lines from "Christmas in the Trenches" by John McCutcheon. Reprinted with permission.

Lines from "Off-Ramp" by Polly Frost, first published in *The New Yorker*. Reprinted with permission.

Material from *Beck Depression Inventory, Second Edition*, by Aaron T. Beck. Copyright © 1996 by Aaron T. Beck. Reproduced by permission of the publisher, Harcourt Assessment, Inc. All rights reserved.

Lines from "Husbands" by Charles McGrath, first published in *The New Yorker*. Reprinted with permission.

Lines from "The End of the Opera" by Howard Nemerov, first published in *The New Yorker*. Reprinted with permission.

Index

A

Abraham, G., 139
Ackerman, Diane, 197
Adams, Maureen, 24
Adult Cry Inventory, 32
Adults
    abuse of children by, 53–55, 66,
      159–160
    attachment styles, 23–27,
      102–104
    caregiving of children by,
      20–23, 70–75
    crying in the absence of clear or
      appropriate stimulus,
      122–124
    depression in, 126–128,
      140–141
    dramatic crying with shallow
      emotion in, 128
    gender and crying by, 3–6, 7,
      8–9, 15–16, 91–94, 137–140
    healthy crying in, 104, 109–111
    infantile crying by, 121–122
    inhibited crying in, 40–41,
      77–79, 113–114, 128–132
    prolonged or frequent crying
      in, 124–125, 140–141
    spiritual weeping by, 195–218
    substance abuse by, 131–132
Affect, Imagery, Consciousness:
    The Negative Affects, 9
Affect regulation, 165–170
Ahleman, S., 136, 152
Ailey, Alvin, 201
Ainsworth, Mary, 44, 46, 48, 57, 58,
    102, 120
Alabaster, W., 203
Alacrima, 142
Alcoholism, 131–132
Alecson, Deborah Golden, 105
Allan-Lee, Jeff, 67
Altman, Robert, 216
American Journal of Psychology, 197
American Psychiatric Association,
    128
Ames, L. B., 69, 138
Amis, Martin, 29
Anxious-ambivalent attachment
    style, 103, 120
Appropriate crying, social
    discomfort with, 125–126
Aristotle, 215
Aronson, T., 105
Assessment, *105–109.*

DATE DUE